...IEVAL & RENEWAL
ssourcement
IN CATHOLIC THOUGHT

The middle years of the twentieth century marked a particularly intense time of crisis and change in European society. During this period (1930-1950), a broad intellectual and spiritual movement arose within the European Catholic community, largely in response to the secularism that lay at the core of the crisis. The movement drew inspiration from earlier theologians and philosophers such as Möhler, Newman, Gardeil, Rousselot, and Blondel, as well as from men of letters like Charles Péguy and Paul Claudel.

The group of academic theologians included in the movement extended into Belgium and Germany, in the work of men like Emile Mersch, Dom Odo Casel, Romano Guardini, and Karl Adam. But above all the theological activity during this period centered in France. Led principally by the Jesuits at Fourvière and the Dominicans at Le Saulchoir, the French revival included many of the greatest names in twentieth-century Catholic thought: Henri de Lubac, Jean Daniélou, Yves Congar, Marie-Dominique Chenu, Louis Bouyer, and, in association, Hans Urs von Balthasar.

It is not true — as subsequent folklore has it — that those theologians represented any sort of self-conscious "school": indeed, the differences among them, for example, between Fourvière and Saulchoir, were important. At the same time, most of them were united in the double conviction that theology had to speak to the present situation, and that the condition for doing so faithfully lay in a recovery of the Church's past. In other words, they saw clearly that the first step in what later came to be known as *aggiornamento* had to be *ressourcement* — a rediscovery of the riches of the whole of the Church's two-thousand-year tradition. According to de Lubac, for example, all of his own works as well as the entire *Sources chrétiennes* collection are based on the presupposition that "the renewal of Christian vitality is linked at least partially to a renewed exploration of the periods and of the works where the Christian tradition is expressed with particular intensity."

In sum, for the *ressourcement* theologians theology involved a "return to the sources" of Christian faith, for the purpose of drawing out the meaning and significance of these sources for the critical questions of our time. What these theologians sought was a spiritual and intellectual communion with Christianity in its most vital moments as transmitted to us in its classic texts, a communion that would nourish, invigorate, and rejuvenate twentieth-century Catholicism.

The *ressourcement* movement bore great fruit in the documents of the Second Vatican Council and deeply influenced the work of Pope John Paul II.

The present series is rooted in this renewal of theology. The series thus understands *ressourcement* as revitalization: a return to the sources, for the purpose of developing a theology that will truly meet the challenges of our time. Some of the features of the series, then, are a return to classical (patristic-medieval) sources and a dialogue with contemporary Western culture, particularly in terms of problems associated with the Enlightenment, modernity, and liberalism.

The series publishes out-of-print or as yet untranslated studies by earlier authors associated with the *ressourcement* movement. The series also publishes works by contemporary authors sharing in the aim and spirit of this earlier movement. This will include any works in theology, philosophy, history, literature, and the arts that give renewed expression to Catholic sensibility.

The editor of the Ressourcement series, David L. Schindler, is Gagnon Professor of Fundamental Theology and dean at the John Paul II Institute in Washington, D.C., and editor of the North American edition of *Communio: International Catholic Review,* a federation of journals in thirteen countries founded in Europe in 1972 by Hans Urs von Balthasar, Jean Daniélou, Henri de Lubac, Joseph Ratzinger, and others.

RETRIEVAL & RENEWAL
Ressourcement
IN CATHOLIC THOUGHT

volumes published

Mysterium Paschale
Hans Urs von Balthasar

Essays in Communio, volume 1: The Church in the Modern World
Pope Benedict XVI

The Heroic Face of Innocence: Three Stories
Georges Bernanos

The Letter on Apologetics and *History and Dogma*
Maurice Blondel

Prayer: The Mission of the Church
Jean Daniélou

On Pilgrimage
Dorothy Day

We, the Ordinary People of the Streets
Madeleine Delbrêl

The Discovery of God
Henri de Lubac

Medieval Exegesis, volumes 1-3:
The Four Senses of Scripture
Henri de Lubac

Letters from Lake Como:
Explorations in Technology and the Human Race
Romano Guardini

The Epiphany of Love:
Toward a Theological Understanding of Christian Action
Livio Melina

Divine Likeness: Toward a Trinitarian Anthropology of the Family
Marc Cardinal Ouellet

The Portal of the Mystery of Hope
Charles Péguy

In the Beginning:
A Catholic Understanding of the Story of Creation and the Fall
Joseph Cardinal Ratzinger

In the Fire of the Burning Bush:
An Initiation to the Spiritual Life
Marko Ivan Rupnik

Love Alone Is Credible:
Hans Urs von Balthasar as Interpreter
of the Catholic Tradition, volume 1
David L. Schindler, ed.

Hans Urs von Balthasar: A Theological Style
Angelo Scola

The Nuptial Mystery
Angelo Scola

The Epiphany of Love

Toward a Theological Understanding
of Christian Action

Livio Melina

William B. Eerdmans Publishing Company
Grand Rapids, Michigan / Cambridge, U.K.

Published 2010 by
Wm. B. Eerdmans Publishing Co.
2140 Oak Industrial Drive N.E., Grand Rapids, Michigan 49505 /
P.O. Box 163, Cambridge CB3 9PU U.K.
www.eerdmans.com

Printed in the United States of America

15 14 13 12 11 10   7 6 5 4 3 2 1

Library of Congress Cataloging-in-Publication Data

Melina, Livio.
The epiphany of love: toward a theological understanding of Christian action /
Livio Melina.
p.   cm.   — (Ressourcement)
Includes bibliographical references.
ISBN 978-0-8028-6536-6 (pbk.: alk. paper)
1. Love — Religious aspects — Christianity.   I. Title.

BV4639.M417   2010
241′.4 — dc22

2010013890

The translation of *The Epiphany of Love: Toward a Theological Understanding of Christian Ethics* was prepared from an Italian manuscript by Susan Dawson Vasquez and revised by Stephan Kampowski.

The introduction first appeared as "The Fullness of Christian Action: Beyond Moralism and Antimoralism," in *Logos: A Journal of Catholic Thought and Culture* 8, no. 3 (summer 2005): 123-40. Reprinted by permission.

The concluding chapter first appeared as "Action, the Epiphany of an Ever-Greater Love," in *Communio* 35 (2008): 255-72. Reprinted by permission.

I understood that Love alone
stirred the members of the Church to act.

ST. THÉRÈSE OF LISIEUX

Contents

Contents

Contents

Abbreviations of Magisterial Documents

DV   *Dei Verbum*
Vatican Council II, Dogmatic Constitution, 18 November 1965

FR   *Fides et Ratio*
John Paul II, Encyclical Letter, 14 September 1998

GS   *Gaudium et Spes*
Vatican Council II, Pastoral Constitution, 7 December 1965

LG   *Lumen Gentium*
Vatican Council II, Dogmatic Constitution, 21 November 1964

VS   *Veritatis Splendor*
John Paul II, Encyclical Letter, 6 August 1993

Introduction

A Light for the Renewal of Morality

> There are no problems more insoluble than those that do not exist. Would that be the case with the problem of action, and would not the surest means of resolving it, the only one, be to suppress it? To unburden consciences and to give life back its grace, its buoyancy and cheerfulness, wouldn't it be good to unload human acts of their incomprehensible seriousness and their mysterious reality? The question of our destiny is terrifying, even painful, when we have the naïveté of believing in it, of looking for an answer to it, whatever it may be, Epicurean, Buddhist or Christian. We should not raise it at all.[1]

These are the provocative words with which one of the major contemporary thinkers, Maurice Blondel, begins his masterpiece dedicated to the mystery of human action. These words, uttered at the end of the nineteenth century, seek to denounce the project of diluting the problem of morality to the point of rendering it nonexistent.

Certainly today we are more aware than ever of the gravity of the problem of morality for humankind. The attempt to avoid the central question has led to the multiplication of particular problems, which seem to be ever more devoid of any solution. Consequently, we may

---

1. Maurice Blondel, *Action (1893): Essay on a Critique of Life and a Science of Practice,* trans. Oliva Blanchette (Notre Dame: University of Notre Dame Press, 1984), p. 16.

grasp the fundamental paradox of our time: "Our culture, which is characterized by the eclipse of morality, is tormented by problems of ethics."[2] The torment referred to is not easily grasped in an explicit form, but it can be perceived and is disseminated in the form of a pessimism that will only get worse and lead to the progressive demoralization of society. It is this spiritual situation that Charles Taylor calls "the unease of modernity."[3] The more action lacks a reference to an ultimate meaning and the less morality is understood as the way to perfection, the more a moralism of rules becomes oppressive.

A substantial number of moral disputes — which have so proliferated in the media — have contributed to this confused situation. The artificiality of their arguments and the disconcerting pluralism of the positions taken foster a deep-seated conviction that the domain of morality is constituted by a series of opinions from among which each individual may choose according to taste and point of view. The result calls to mind the image of the Tower of Babel on which everyone works busily but without anyone understanding anyone else. Something similar was described in the chaotic panorama presented by Alasdair MacIntyre in *After Virtue* when he spoke of "a disquieting suggestion."[4]

Catholic moral thought was no stranger to this state of affairs. After the Second Vatican Council and the bitter polemics surrounding the encyclical *Humanae Vitae,* Catholic thought focused, in a unilateral and reductive way, on questions of normative morality. Certain authors, in search of a more "open" interpretation of moral norms, introduced ways of arguing based on proportionalism into the debate,[5] with the result that the permanent and universal character of the precepts taught by the magisterium was called into question. The intent was to liberate human beings from the restrictions of an impersonal law by offering in its stead methods for solving problems — that is, criteria for arriving at particular normative judgments — whether by means of carefully evaluating the consequences of an action, considered teleologically, or by af-

2. Georges Cottier, "Racines philosophiques de la crise contemporaine," *Seminarium* 39 (1988): 331.

3. Charles Taylor, *The Ethics of Authenticity* (Cambridge, MA: Harvard University Press, 1992), p. 10.

4. Alasdair MacIntyre, *After Virtue: A Study on Moral Theory* (London: Duckworth, 1985), pp. 1-5.

5. See Bernard Hoose, *Proportionalism: The American Debate and Its European Roots* (Washington, DC: Georgetown University Press, 1987).

firming the primacy of the subjective conscience, understood as a creatively autonomous tribunal. The incapacity of these proposals to shed light on the true moral problem has subsequently led some authors, who also form part of this intellectual current, to affirm the necessity of a "new casuistry," in order to assist in the discovery of answers adequate to the pressing problems of contemporary life.[6]

In the face of this situation, the challenge for Catholic moral theology is radical. It is no longer a matter of responding to specific questions about particular matters (as does old and new casuistry) or of elaborating some method for the formulation of norms (as normative ethics attempts to do). Rather, it is a matter of *comprehending the mystery of human action* in its proper dynamism. This is precisely the challenge that this volume wants to take on, guiding the reader on a path that seeks to recover the integrality of moral experience and its place in Christian existence. This path aims at rediscovering in moral action an *epiphany of love* and attempts to help us recognize a profound synergy between human and divine action.

Now, the full acceptance of the moral experience contained in our actions urges us above all to a *fundamental change of perspective*. Morality can no longer be understood as a simple list of principles directing our choices and helping us to come to correct moral judgments. It is necessary to grasp the meaning of action and the way it implicates the acting subject. Thus, the very object of morality, now conceived within a larger and more comprehensive horizon, is redefined. It is no longer only a question of "what should I do?" as Kant had it, but rather of "who am I called to be?"

Above and beyond its specific doctrinal points, John Paul II's encyclical *Veritatis Splendor* has identified two deep-seated roots that led to the global and systematic questioning of the moral patrimony of Catholic morality: the rupture of the connections between freedom and truth and between faith and morality (VS 4). The first of the two takes place at the philosophical level and reflects the crisis of postmodernity, which denies reason the possibility of access to any universal and permanent truth and thus abandons freedom to a subjectivistic choice. In this way, the only remedy for public ethics becomes contractualist proceduralism. The second, whose origin is theological, goes even deeper and

---

6. See James F. Keenan and Thomas A. Shannon, eds., *The Context of Casuistry* (Washington, DC: Georgetown University Press, 1995).

can also be seen as the fundamental cause of the first rupture. By sever-
ing the interior unity and totality of the act of faith, the breach between
faith and morality legitimizes a pluralism of ethical references compatible with one's ecclesial belonging. The consequence of these two rup-
tures is precisely the loss of the intrinsic meaning of the human act and
its relation to God.

In this sense, the crisis of post-conciliar moral theology can be interpreted as the crisis of post-Tridentine manualist moral theology and its
methodology. The two principal deficiencies of the old and new
manualist moral theology are connected to the divisive factors mentioned above and can be described as "legalism" and "extrinsicism."[7] On
the philosophical level, the law is seen not as an expression of a truth
about the good but as a principle of mere obligation derived from the will
of a legislator. On the theological plane, the moral dimension is thought
to be autonomous and extrinsic with respect to faith and grace. In order
to remedy these deficiencies, it will be necessary to explore perspectives
and find philosophical and theological categories that — by overcoming
the theoretical framework of manualistic theology, proportionalism, and
autonomous ethics — permit the constitutive relations between freedom
and truth and between faith and morality to be reestablished.

One can express the task that to my mind *Veritatis Splendor* has entrusted to moral theology for its authentic renewal in these terms: What
is at stake is not so much the search for principles by which we can develop argumentative systems that help us judge our actions with preci-
sion. Rather, what we are looking for is a new light cast upon our actions
that illuminates their fullness in the mystery of Christ.[8] We may want to
think of one fundamental ray of light shed upon the mystery of Christian action, a ray that can be dispersed into three rays corresponding to
the three primary colors, which in their unity constitute the full spec-
trum of light. Each of these rays gives rise to a deepening of Christian
action, and all three together lead to a new moral perspective.

In the first place, it seems to me that the question of the *originality of
moral truth* is decisive. "He who does what is true comes to the light" (Jn

7. For a critical description of legalism one can refer to Germain Grisez, "Legalism,
Moral Truth, and Pastoral Practice," in T. J. Herron, ed., *The Catholic Priest as Moral
Teacher and Guide* (San Francisco: Ignatius Press, 1990), pp. 107-30; on extrinsicism see
Angelo Scola, *Questioni di antropologia teologica,* 2nd ed. (Roma: PUL-Mursia, 1997).
8. See Livio Melina, José Noriega, and Juan José Pérez-Soba, *La plenitud del obrar
cristiano: Dinámica de la acción y perspectiva teológica de la moral* (Madrid: Palabra, 2001).

3:21).[9] This means overcoming the darkness that engulfs a person who has lost the connection between freedom and truth, and it implies understanding morality as a path toward integral human fulfillment. The light we are seeking belongs to human reason and is rooted in the truth of moral experience. In fact, the truth referred to here is not just any truth whatsoever — it is the truth about the very meaning of life. For this reason, freedom is neither indifferent nor extraneous to this truth but is always involved in its perception. As Blondel has shown, moral evidence is mediated by the practical experience of freedom. The perception of the truth about the good has as its necessary price the risking of oneself in effective action.

A consequence of this dramatic nature of human action is that the method of moral knowledge cannot be merely deductive. Although morality has its basis in metaphysics and anthropology, it differentiates itself epistemologically from them. This is what is meant by the originality of practical truth — a truth that is not found in a judgment or in conformity to some norm but in the realization of an excellent action and that is recognized connaturally: Only the one who loves knows the authentic good. Placing "oneself *in the perspective of the acting person*" (VS 78), as *Veritatis Splendor* calls for, means looking at action from within, seeing it as the building up of the person who, in acting, grows toward complete fulfillment. Such an excellence in action is impossible without the presence of a stable disposition in the person, which allows the fullness hidden within the action itself to be grasped. Here the cognitive and dynamic role of the virtues comes into play.

A rational reflection on the practical dynamism of the virtues and on the way in which the different "goods for the person" are ordered to the "good of the person" allows us to establish the existence of intrinsically evil acts, which under no circumstances and for no motives can ever be carried out ethically.[10] Negative moral norms, which prohibit these acts, are valid always and without exception *(semper et pro semper):* they are "moral absolutes." The indispensable normative dimension, however, does not constitute the original element of morality. Rather, this dimension presents a path for the discernment of the truth about the good, having a pedagogical function that allows us to accom-

---

9. Scripture citations are taken from the RSV or NRSV.

10. See Livio Melina, *Sharing in Christ's Virtues,* trans. William E. May (Washington, DC: Catholic University of America Press, 2001), pp. 81-83.

plish the truth in our actions even when we are not yet virtuous and to enter already at this stage on a way of perfection that is a response to Christ's calling.

Second, it is *the light of Christ* that must illuminate the mystery of human action. It is in these terms that *Veritatis Splendor* directs us to the question about the good, citing the Psalms:

> "There are many who say, 'O that we might see some good! Let the light of your face shine on us, O Lord!'" (Ps 4:6) The light of God's faces shines in all its beauty on the countenance of Jesus Christ, "image of the invisible God" (Col 1:15), "the reflection of God's glory" (Heb 1:3). (VS 2)

Thus, in Christ the light of human fullness is revealed to us. It is a matter of that full revelation of "man to man himself" and of the manifestation of "his supreme calling" (GS 22), to which *Gaudium et Spes* calls our attention. And it is precisely through the mediation of Christ's action that we fulfill our mission received from the Father. For this reason, when speaking of the fullness of Christian action, we refer to *filial action,* which does not terminate in itself but has its origin and end in the Father's love that continues in the mission of the Spirit. Christian action is a participation in Christ's action in a living union with him. This is possible to the degree that, through the dynamic of his self-donation, the Holy Spirit, the Uncreated Gift, introduces himself into the dynamism of our action. Through the gifts and the virtues, he spurs on our action interiorly and transforms it so as to give it a new significance, which is marked by the primacy of grace and friendship with Christ.[11]

The fullness of Christian action can be included, then, under the category of "the fruits of the Spirit," a category that is at the summit of Thomistic ethics, in line with the traditional interpretation of Galatians 5:16-25.[12] The fruits are the perfect expression of the synergy between God and the spiritual person who lives in charity. The human perfec-

---

11. See José Noriega, "Movidos por el Espíritu," in Melina, Noriega, Pérez-Soba, *La plenitud del obrar cristiano,* pp. 183-200. The complete development of this theme can be found in José Noriega, *"Guidados por el Espíritu": El Espíritu Santo y el conocimiento moral en Tomás de Aquino* (Rome: PUL-Mursia, 2000).

12. See Thomas Aquinas, *Summa theologiae* I-II, q. 70, a. 1. In regards to this see Michel Ledrus, *I frutti dello Spirito: Saggi di "etica evangelica,"* ed. A. Tulumello (Cinisello Balsamo: Edizioni San Paolo, 1998), pp. 15-36.

tion of the virtues manifests itself visibly and publicly in fruits that contain the testimony of the Spirit, the new principle of action.

The beginning of this new dynamism is connected to an explicit human act: faith. Faith, precisely insofar as it is a supreme expression of freedom, is the acceptance of Christ's action in us, thus opening up a new horizon of life. Christian life cannot be understood as the mere application of the principles of faith to actions that are in themselves purely human. Rather, it must be understood as the development of that fundamental choice for Christ[13] that is possible only in communion with the Church and that has the kingdom of God as its end. It is necessary to root ourselves in such depths in order to overcome the dramatic separation of faith and life that is described in *Veritatis Splendor* (VS 88).

At this point, this sort of elucidation of action contributes to the solution of two unavoidable problems. The first concerns the disproportion that exists between human action and the end that it is called to achieve. Even with the infusion of divine grace, the Christian is only able to live this condition through hope in the gift, nurtured continually by the Eucharist, the bread for our journey. Moreover, the universality of this path also necessarily includes (although secondarily) a normative reference, which, however, is not only formal but also is strictly connected to Christ's mission, a mission that is historically prolonged through the Spirit in the Church.

And so we come to the third and last of the lights that illuminate action — that which derives from *love*. Once Christ appeared, the light was made concrete and was converted into the light of a gaze, the gaze of love. "And Jesus, looking at him, loved him" (Mk 10:21). The intertwining of gazes presented to us by the gospel story of the rich young man leads to the development of a new dimension, one essential to the full comprehension of the mystery of human action: *interpersonality*. It is a term often invoked but not sufficiently integrated in its moral dimension. In love, the dynamic unity of the objective communication of the good appears in the context of an intersubjective polarity. Through

---

13. See *Veritatis Splendor*, n. 66. Regarding faith as the fundamental choice of the Christian, see also Joseph Ratzinger, "Faith as Conversion-Metanoia" and "Faith as Knowledge and Praxis — The Fundamental Option of the Christian Credo," in *Principles of Catholic Theology: Building Stones for a Fundamental Theology* (San Francisco: Ignatius Press, 1987), pp. 57-78; Juan José Pérez-Soba, "La fe como elección fundamental," in Melina, Noriega, Pérez-Soba, *La plenitud del obrar cristiano,* pp. 201-15.

the moral good, the light of love clarifies for us the problem of the relationship between the person and nature.[14]

We have drawn near to the ray of light. The three fundamental colors — the truth of action, its theological dimension, and the interpersonal element of love — are the primary colors that, in their mixture in the immense variety of life situations, give us the fascinating colors of life, a life that is itself full of light. These three colors and these three rays of light do not present themselves to us in the form of clear and distinct ideas, but rather in the unity of a new perspective, one focused on the acting person. Certainly, we cannot see the light directly but perceive it only through its reflections, as in a mirror (see 1 Cor 13:12). This reflective light, which has its source in Christ, illumines the life of his Church. We can recognize it in the lives of the saints, for whom — Blondel notwithstanding — "action is no longer the expression of a lack or a need that desires its satisfaction. For them, rather, action is the initial fruit of the fullness of love, which tends to grow by communicating itself so as to embrace everyone in the dynamism of divine action, which in turn anticipates, sustains, and guides human action."[15]

As I am bringing this introduction to a close, I would like to express my sincere gratitude to Mrs. Susan Dawson Vasquez, who has translated the parts of the book that did not yet exist in English. Furthermore, I am very grateful to Professor Stephan Kampowski, whose helpful suggestions and whose generosity and intelligence in editing the volume have been decisive for the realization of this project.

---

14. See Juan José Pérez-Soba, "Il bene e la persona: Chiavi per un colloquio morale," *La Scuola Cattolica* 129 (2001): 801-20.

15. Livio Melina, *Cristo e il dinamismo dell'agire: Linee di rinnovamento della teologia morale fondamentale* (Rome: PUL-Mursia, 2001), p. 35.

PART ONE

Love: The Origin of Action

Love, Desire, Action

"Why do you ask me about the good? There is only One who is good" (Mt 19:17). This is Jesus' response to the rich young man who approaches him with the moral question: "Teacher, what good must I do to gain eternal life?" For Jesus, the ethical questioning inevitably has a theological depth. What then is the relationship between the question regarding the good and the question regarding God, between the ethical demand and the religious sense?[1] This chapter will explore the question from the perspective of the dynamism of practice, which is at the heart of human action. Following the suggestions found in *Veritatis Splendor,* which offers the invitation to "place oneself in the perspective of the acting person" (VS 78), I will examine the relationship between the moral good and God from the point of view of action in order to grasp the specifically moral dimension of human action.

In action, Maurice Blondel identified the philosophical place in which the meaning of life is decided. "It is into action that we shall have to transport the center of philosophy, because there is also to be found the center of life."[2] In acting, humans are revealed as persons and it is precisely through their actions that they establish themselves. Karol Wojtyla affirms: The person "experiences an action as acting, as doing, of which he is the subjective agent and which is also a profound image

1. On this see the proceedings of the first colloquium organized by the International Area of Research on the Status of Moral Theology: Livio Melina and José Noriega, eds., *Domanda sul bene e domanda su Dio* (Rome: PUL-Mursia, 1999).

2. Maurice Blondel, *Action (1893): Essay on a Critique of Life and a Science of Practice,* trans. Oliva Blanchette (Notre Dame: University of Notre Dame Press, 1984), p. 13.

and manifestation of what his ego is composed of (what it actually is)." Our action, therefore, is not merely an expression of the human spiritual faculties *(actus humanus);* it is also the fulfillment of the unique and unrepeatable person *(actus personae).*[3] In action, the entire person is involved in aspiring to the good.

However, we are not only interested in a philosophical point of view but also in a theological one, and thus we must also ask ourselves: How is God involved in a person's actions? The believer knows that God is at work in us "both to will and to work" (Phil 2:13). God is always at work (see Jn 5:17). And further, how is Jesus, who said to his disciples "without me you can do nothing" (Jn 15:5), involved in human action? Here, the question that Hans Urs von Balthasar poses at the beginning of his *Theo-Drama* appears in all its force: "Who acts, who can act, if God is on stage?"[4] If God, by his very essence, must be "all in all" (Sir 43:28) in order truly to be God, then where is the space for a human person to act?

For there to be true action, there will also have to be a space for the dramatic risk of human freedom. *"Initium ut esset creatus est homo, ante quem nullus fuit"*: the human person was created with the power of beginning something new, according to the thought-provoking expression of St. Augustine, which inspired Hannah Arendt's action theory.[5] Freedom is the power to introduce novelty into the cyclical time of history, breaking the preestablished schemes of physical laws and natural instincts. If an act is the expression of the person, then acting in the theo-drama will be the interacting of divine and human persons without confusion or division *(inconfuse et indivise).* What then could be the principle for understanding this synergy?

---

3. Karol Wojtyla, *The Acting Person,* trans. A. Potocki (New York: Springer, 2000), p. 48.

4. Hans Urs von Balthasar, *Theo-Drama: Theological Dramatic Theory,* vol. 2: *The Dramatis Personae: Man in God,* trans. G. Harrison (San Francisco: Ignatius Press, 1990), p. 17.

5. Augustine, *De civitate Dei,* XII, 20.4. For a study of Hannah Arendt's action theory in the light of her work *Der Liebesbegriff bei Augustin* (Berlin: Springer, 1929), see the doctoral dissertation by Stephan Kampowski, *Arendt, Augustine, and the New Beginning: The Action Theory and Moral Thought of Hannah Arendt in the Light of Her Dissertation on St. Augustine* (Grand Rapids: Eerdmans, 2008), written under my direction at the Pontifical John Paul II Institute for Studies on Marriage and Family in Rome.

1. The Drama of Desire

We will begin with a question: What is at the origin of human action? What provokes its incessant tending toward a fulfillment that is always sought and never exhaustively reached?

A lack seems to lie at the origin of our action and thus a desire. We feel the need for something, feel that we are lacking something, and we are seeking fulfillment. There is something missing, but what? We are full of desire, of restlessness, of plans, and of proposals. At the heart of our movement toward something and someone we run into our needs; at least that is what it seems like. Desire, according to Augustine's well-known expression, is the "soul's thirst": "For everyone who desires to obtain something is burning with desire. Desire itself is the thirst of the soul. And see what desires stir in human hearts."[6]

But do we really know what we want? Do we really understand what we desire and what we are always reaching for in our actions? Blondel observed that "our desires often hide from us our true desires."[7] Indeed, our desires are often confused, enigmatic, disproportional, unbalanced, even to the point that we must say that we want something of which we really have no idea. The actual goal of our desire remains dark and mysterious to us. The will, unlike desire, knows the object of its striving and thus, by means of its particular choices, confirms desire's immediate and "instinctive" motion. Nevertheless, the will experiences a structural disproportion within itself. It is in the will that desire is expressed and made concrete. In fact, according to Aquinas, "desire is an inclination of the will to the gaining of some good."[8] In turn, however, the will discovers that it is preceded by a desire that dwells in it and the depth of which it does not know.

Here we run into the structural excess that Blondel pointed out as an insurmountable disproportion between the willing will (*volonté voulante*) and the willed will (*volonté voulue*).[9] What becomes the object

---

6. Augustine, *Enarrationes in Psalmos*, 62.5: "Omnis qui sibi vult aliquid praestari, in ardore est desiderii: ipsum desiderium sitis est animae. Et videte quanta desideria sint in cordibus hominum . . ."

7. Blondel, *Action (1893)*, p. 167. On this, see César Izquierdo, "Dinamismo della volontà e crisi del desiderio," *Rivista Teologica di Lugano* 3 (1998): 291-305.

8. Thomas Aquinas, *Summa contra gentiles*, 3.26.8: "Desiderium est inclinatio voluntatis in aliquod bonum consequendum."

9. Blondel, *Action (1893)*, p. 134.

of the deliberate will never exhausts the original openness of the movement of the will. Persons discover that their clear and determinate will is always preceded by a more radical and indeterminate willing, which is open to the infinite. They discover that their desires are nothing but the ever partial and inexorably unsatisfied expression of a more fundamental desire, the object of which escapes them.

Already the ancients associated the term "desire" with *sidera,* the stars.[10] But what does desire have to do with the stars? Its original semantic sphere seems to be the sacred language of the oracles, of anxiously searching the stars for some sign of assurance that the heart's hopes will be fulfilled. With respect to the verb *considerare,* which has the same root, desire would therefore be a moment of disappointment, casting down a gaze that was originally turned toward the stars. In this way the characteristic ambiguity of desire may be appreciated. On the one hand there results a deflection of our original yearning for the heavens (the infinite), a restless wandering among earthly objects without being able to find in them either an adequate satisfaction of our aspirations or a sure sign that the hope inscribed in our heart will come true (this wandering has rightly been called the "nomadic character of desire").[11] On the other hand, it can be observed that desire, although versed toward the finite, continues to bear within itself the memory of and the nostalgia for the infinite. In every one of our desires this *Sehnsucht* for the heavens remains as a secret yearning, never attained in the finite.

The category of desire, therefore, shows itself to be anthropologically revelatory of the creaturely indigence constitutive of the human being. We are beings thrown into the world with the original promise that our thirst for the infinite will be quenched, but we inevitably run up against disappointment. If the reality that we encounter awakens the promise, it also painfully denies it, such that in the face of desire we are obliged to make a fundamental choice of attitude. We must either affirm and confirm the heart's inherent promise — notwithstanding disap-

10. See Alfred Ernout and Antoine Meillet, *Dictionnaire étymologique de la langue latine: Histoire des mots* (Paris: C. Klincksieck, 1932), p. 897; *Thesaurus linguae latinae,* vol. V, pars I, D (Leipzig: B. G. Teubner, 1909-34), pp. 697-710. The original meaning deduced from the etymology is: "amissum vel absentem requirere," "libido absentem videndi."

11. Francesco Botturi, *Desiderio e verità: Per un'antropologia cristiana nell'età secolarizzata* (Milan: Massimo, 1985), pp. 124-26.

pointments, maintaining an openness to the possibility of fulfillment (which is not within the reach of any human "doing") — or we must renounce the promise of the infinite and adapt to the finite.

The reasonableness of the first attitude is evident in the fact that it does not entail a rejection or negation — as the second attitude does — of any element of human experience. Above all it does not require censure of the most interesting and decisive element of the heart: the promise.[12] If, on the one hand, faithfulness to that promise requires affirming the existence of a suitable answer to our desire and if, on the other hand, realism excludes that such an answer can be situated within the horizon of human doing, then it follows that the answer can only be given in the form of a gift from an Other. The fulfillment of desire can only be believed and awaited, not projected or constructed as some task to be done.[13]

In unrivaled verse, the great poet Dante expressed desire's original yearning as well as its temptation to turn in upon itself:

> Everyone confusedly apprehends a good in which the mind may be at rest and desires it, so that each strives to reach it, and if the love is sluggish that draws you to see it or gain it, this terrace, after due repentance, torments you for that. Other good there is which does not make men happy; it is not happiness, it is not the good Essence, the fruit and root of every good.[14]

---

12. These anthropological perspectives are evocatively outlined by Luigi Giussani in his writings, particularly in *Morality: Memory and Desire,* trans. K. D. Whitehead (San Francisco: Ignatius Press, 1986), and in *The Religious Sense,* trans. J. Zucchi (San Francisco: Ignatius Press, 1990).

13. See Giuseppe Angelini, "Il senso orientato al sapere: L'etica come questione teologica," in G. Colombo, ed., *L'evidenza e la fede* (Milan: Glossa, 1988), p. 416.

14. Dante Alighieri, *The Divine Comedy, Purgatorio,* canto XVII, 127-35: "Ciascun confusamente un bene apprende / nel qual si queti l'animo, e disira: / per che di giugner lui ciascun contende. / Se lento amore in lui veder vi tira, / o a lui acquistar, questa cornice, / dopo giusto penter, ve ne martira. / Altro ben è che non fa l'uom felice; / non è felicità, non è la buona / essenza, d'ogne ben frutto e radice." The English translation given here and throughout this chapter is that by John D. Sinclair (New York: Oxford University Press, 1961). I owe the suggestion of this citation to Luigi Giussani's *Si può vivere così? Uno strano approccio all'esistenza cristiana* (Milan: Rizzoli, 1994), p. 67, where it appears in the context of a particularly interesting meditation on freedom (62-79). For a study on *disìo* in Dante's work, see Massimo Camisasca, *Riflessioni de medio corso* (Forlì: Nuova Compagnia, 1994), pp. 19-33.

The aspiration for complete fulfillment dwells, confusedly, within the human heart's restless searching. Ours is a heart that desires in every thing loved the final end that alone grants happiness. The ascent from purgatory is essentially the purification of desire because, freed from bonds of limited and apparent satisfaction ("pure and ready to mount to the stars"),[15] it can be assumed into the same movement by which God moves the universe; so, finally, it can there find its peace, contemplating "the Love that moves the sun and the other stars."[16]

Certainly, also the rich young man's question recounted in Matthew's Gospel testifies to this restless seeking. Christ's answer directs the man's gaze toward God: "Why do you ask me about the good? There is only One who is good" (Mt 19:17). *Veritatis Splendor* comments:

> To ask about the good, in fact, ultimately means to turn toward God, the fullness of goodness. Jesus shows that the young man's question is really a religious question, and that the goodness that attracts and at the same time obliges man has its source in God, and indeed is God himself. God alone is worthy of being loved "with all one's heart, and with all one's soul, and with all one's mind" (Mt 22:37). (VS 9)

But how can we desire God? How can our actions have God as their goal? In one of his poems, Goethe reminds us: "The stars we never long to clasp; We revel in their light."[17] God enters into the perspective of our praxis as the reference point of human action. The desire that dwells in us is that of *knowing* God and of *enjoying* communion with him.[18] The

---

15. *Purgatorio,* canto XXXIII, 145: "Puro e disposto a salire a le stelle."

16. *Paradiso,* canto XXXIII, 143-45: "Ma già volgeva il mio disio e 'l velle, / sì come rota ch'igualmente è mossa, / l'amor che move il sole e l'altre stelle" (but now my desire and will, like a wheel that spins with even motion, were revolved by the Love that moves the sun and the other stars).

17. Johann Wolfgang Goethe, "Comfort in Tears," in *The Poems of Goethe,* trans. E. A. Bowring (New York: Hurst & Co., 1881): *Trost in Tränen:* "Die Sterne, die begehrt man nicht, man freut sich ihrer Pracht."

18. Aquinas proposes the difference between the end for which *(finis cuius)* and the end by which *(finis quo):* "Finis dupliciter dicitur: scilicet ipsa res quam adipisci desideramus; et usus, seu adeptio aut possessio illius rei" *(Summa theologiae,* I-II, q. 2, a. 7); "Dicendum est quod finis est duplex, scilicet cuius et quo, ut Philosophus dicit" *(Summa theologiae,* I, q. 26, a. 3, ad 2). See Wolfhart Pannenberg, *Grundlagen der Ethik: Philosophisch-theologische Perspektiven* (Göttingen: Vandenhoeck & Ruprecht, 1996), pp. 68-69. Recall that Friedrich Schleiermacher, in his *Introduction to Christian Ethics,*

perfect beatitude that human desire yearns for cannot be a thing or a person but only a practical good, that is, an action. Human desire has an activity as its goal. Also all other creatures, also the animals, have God as their end — but this is the topic of a speculative, not a practical reflection. It is only for human persons, from our original perspective of praxis, that knowing God is the Supreme Good, the one for whom our desire yearns and in whom our aspirations of happiness are fulfilled.

Nevertheless, it is at precisely this point that a great risk for every ethical conception of Aristotelian pedigree seems to emerge, a risk to which Wolfhart Pannenberg calls attention, echoing Augustinian themes: the risk of a radical "perversion of the topic of ethics" by which the subjective and selfish element of aspiring to happiness becomes the decisive criterion for affirming that God is the Supreme Good.[19] God, therefore, would no longer be the Supreme Good. Instead, the satisfaction of the human desire for happiness would take over that role.

Even from other points of view, the problem of desire seems to lend itself to misunderstandings and ambiguities that highlight its constitutive drama. It is the singular reality we encounter that arouses desire, provoking its thirst for fulfillment, while always leaving it unsatisfied. In fact, the singular reality provoking desire does so only "as a sign of the infinite, which is the true driving force of desire."[20] What the singular reality can immediately offer is pleasure, of brief duration, while the true goal of the aspiration — joy — is not always readily accessible. The dramatic structure of desire thus emerges, which Angelo Scola expresses in these terms: "Although human beings are capable of the infinite, their finiteness prevents them from disposing of it. In this sense, joy ultimately depends on opening ourselves to the face of the Infinite."[21] Here also the root of desire's dramatic nature is announced: the final goal of our aspirations is a relationship with a free person, not with

---

trans. J. C. Shelley (Nashville: Abingdon, 1989), uses this distinction, although not as decisively.

19. Pannenberg, *Grundlagen der Ethik,* pp. 34-40. See the discussion regarding this matter with Martin Rhonheimer, "Ethik als Aufklärung über die Frage nach dem Gutem und die aristotelische 'Perversion des ethischen Themas': Anmerkungen zu W. Pannenbergs Aristoteleskritik," *Anthropotes* 13 (1997): 211-23; Wolfhart Pannenberg, "Eine Antwort," *Anthropotes* 13 (1997): 485-92.

20. See Angelo Scola, "Differenza sessuale e procreazione," in Angelo Scola, ed., *Quale vita? La bioetica in questione* (Milan: Mondadori, 1998), pp. 143-68 (here p. 155).

21. Scola, "Differenza sessuale," p. 156.

a thing. Otherness always establishes an insurmountable difference. The other, toward whom my desire tends, escapes my definitive grasp; this implies the painful experience of missing something.

It is precisely in relation to the otherness of its point of reference that the need to moderate our desire becomes known. Left to its spontaneous dynamic, it renders us slaves to our immediate impulses, obstructing the necessary detachment that leaves space for listening to the other.[22] The purpose of the law is exactly that of putting a limit to deaf and blind desire, allowing for the respect of the other. In this sense, the Apostle Paul brings the entire law back to the single precept of "you shall not covet" (Rom 7:7). The suppression of any reference to an object of the prohibition (see the ancient commandment reported in Ex 20:17 and Deut 5:21: coveting of another man's wife, goods, etc.) gives the prohibition a new meaning. It is the very act of desiring that is forbidden.[23] Every type of desire is condemned here as contrary to God's holy law.

Intense and excessive, disordered and imperious, desire inevitably seems wrapped up in itself, in concupiscence, and seems to condemn human persons to the impossibility of loving God and neighbor.[24] Is precisely desire, which gives birth to the movement of action, therefore the greatest obstacle to achieving the fulfillment that our action hopes for?[25]

2. The Priority of Love over Desire

We now find ourselves faced with something new and unexpected that changes the direction of our reflection. If, instead of pressing forward

22. On this see the suggestive observations regarding temperance made by Giuseppe Angelini, *Le virtù e la fede* (Milan: Glossa, 1994), pp. 65-121.

23. See Jean-Baptiste Édart, "De la nécessité d'un sauveur: Rhétorique et théologie de Rm 7:7-25," *Revue Biblique* 105 (1998): 359-96.

24. For the Pauline vision of ἐπιθυμία see Ceslas Spicq, *Théologie morale du Nouveau Testament,* I (Paris: Gabalda et C., 1970), pp. 184-89. More in general, F. Büchsel, ἐπιθυμία, in G. Kittel and G. Friedrich, eds., *Grande Lessico del Nuovo Testamento,* vol. IV (Brescia: Paideia, 1968), pp. 593-604. On concupiscence interpreted as the desire that makes us incapable of love on a horizontal as well as vertical level, see Maurizio Flick and Zoltán Alszeghy, *Il peccato originale,* 2nd ed. (Brescia: Queriniana, 1974), pp. 279-93.

25. An essential panorama of the tendencies in theology on the theme of desire in its orientation to salvation can be found in Elmar Salmann, "Felicità o salvezza? Riflessioni su un binomio difficile," in R. Battocchio and A. Toniolo, eds., *Desiderio di felicità e dono della salvezza* (Padua: Messaggero, 1998), pp. 79-98.

and following the dynamic of desire, we turn back, going upstream to reach the sources, then new light is shed on the mystery of action. Desire is preceded by something, by a more original reality: "Love precedes desire,"[26] Thomas affirms in the context of a question on the order of the human passions. Following Aquinas's lead, we will continue our reflection on the relationship between love and desire and on the mystery of human action.

Before action, therefore, there is a passion. The motion of our action originates from an attraction that comes from an external reality, influencing us and arousing our desire. Every acting person, regardless of who he or she may be, "does every action from love of some kind."[27] Indeed, in order to desire, it is necessary to love. We desire because we love: *"desiderium . . . ex amore."*[28] Love has an ontological priority over desire and every other passion, such that love is the primary and common root of every action.[29]

What is this original love? In what does it consist?[30] We are not speaking here of natural love, which is the metaphysical principle of the movement of all creatures toward the perfect Good, which they spontaneously love more than themselves.[31] Rather, it is a love that is the principle of every affective movement toward union. As Juan José Pérez-Sobas's thorough work on the Thomistic conception of love shows, Aquinas significantly innovates on the natural dynamic of love as the desire of the good that Aristotle described. In fact, Aquinas takes the perspective of love as a "uniting and binding force" — found in Pseudo-Dionysius[32] —

26. Aquinas, *Summa theologiae,* I-II, q. 25, a. 2: "Amor praecedit desiderium."

27. Aquinas, *Summa theologiae,* I-II, q. 28, a. 6: "Omne agens, quodcumque sit, agit quamcumque actionem ex aliquo amore."

28. Aquinas, *Summa contra gentiles,* 4.54.5.

29. Thomas Aquinas, *In De divinis nominibus,* IV, 9, 401: "Est autem amor prima et communis radix omnium appetitivarum operationum; quod patet inspicienti per singula: nihil enim desideratur nisi quod est amatum; neque aliquis gaudet de re habita, nisi quia amat eam; nec aliquis tristatur de aliquo, nisi quia est contrarium amato."

30. On this subject I refer to the well-documented study by Juan José Pérez-Soba, *Amor es nombre de persona. Estudio de la interpersonalidad en el amor en Santo Tomas de Aquino* (Rome: PUL-Mursia, 2001), which is a doctoral thesis written under my direction.

31. Aquinas, *Summa theologiae,* I, q. 60, a. 5: "Sequitur quod [omnis creatura . . .] naturali dilectione etiam Angelus et homo plus et principalius diligat Deum quam seipsum.

32. Aquinas, *Summa theologiae,* I-II, q. 25, a. 2, arg. 2: "Vis unitiva et concretiva." Pseudo-Dionysius, *De divinis nominibus,* 4.12 (Patrologia graeca 3.709).

to its extreme consequences. This implies a constitutive and irreducible polarity between lover and beloved that is only comprehensible in an interpersonal context.

Out of all the spiritual operations, love is distinguished by a particular characteristic. Its act does not refer only to one but to two objects.[33] From this comes the clear and profound definition that Thomas privileges: *"In hoc enim praecipue consistit amor, quod amans amato bonum velit"* — love consists specifically in this, in wanting the good for the beloved.[34] The act of love is thus addressed to both the beloved and to his or her good. The affective level of the person is assumed and overcome on the elective level of an act that wants the good within the dynamic of a relationship between two persons.

It is the good that moves desire and provokes action, and this good exercises its causality within the dynamic of love between two persons. In order to be attractive, the good must be known and somehow be anticipated in the experience of a correspondence. Now the good of love, the good that love seeks, is precisely union with the beloved: *"Amor est vis unitiva et concretiva."* Therefore, there must be a union that precedes and provokes the desire for union: "Union precedes the movement of desire."[35]

If union is the goal toward which love tends, how can it also be its beginning? Here Aquinas proposes a fundamental distinction between *real* union, which consists in the actual conjunction between beloved and lover, and *affective* union, which instead is that first, intentional union experienced as an original promise of fulfillment that precedes and provokes every movement tending toward achieving a true union with the beloved.[36] The other person is intimately present to the lover as an interior form of his or her being, even before the lover is effectively joined to that person.

Before action, therefore, there is an initial promise of fulfillment in

---

33. Aquinas, *Summa theologiae,* I-II, q. 26, a. 4; *Summa contra gentiles,* 1.91.

34. Aquinas, *Summa contra gentiles,* 3.90.6. Although this is of Aristotelian origin (see *Rhetorica,* 2.4, 1380b 35-36), in Aquinas it finds an exceptional and constant development in light of the new perspective offered by Pseudo-Dionysius.

35. Aquinas, *Summa theologiae,* I-II, q. 26, a. 2: "Unio praecedit motum desiderii."

36. See Aquinas, *Summa theologiae,* I-II, q. 26, a. 2. On the dynamism of love, see Angelo Scola, *Identidad y diferencia: La relación hombre y mujer* (Madrid: Encuentro, 1989); and Paul J. Wadell, *The Primacy of Love: An Introduction to the Ethics of Thomas Aquinas* (Mahwah, NJ: Paulist Press, 1992).

the communion of love with the other. Before being a desire, bent on its satisfaction, love is a gift, or even more, the original gift. Inscribed in our acts and our attitudes, impressed upon the very dynamism that moves us to act, there lies a promise of union that stands before our deliberate intentions. As the promise of communion, love precedes our desire and guides it. In recognizing this gracious anticipation, we find the sure norm of action, a norm that is older and greater than our will.[37] To act is to assent to this original promise. It suffices to think of the ties of friendship and affection that unite us with other persons. Bonds of friendship are never born of a decision but rather are a gift that we welcome with wonder and gratitude. They are an event that precedes freedom and gives it meaning. Decision, in which human action takes shape, is a *con-sensus* that gives credit to the promise of good sensed in the presence of the other and that adheres to it.

The discovery of love's original character and of its constitutive interpersonal reference also allows us to clarify the question of the desire of the good, freeing it from every eudaemonistic ambiguity. In love there is always the reference to another person, and the good is always willed within the perspective of love for the person of the other. The original experience of love, with its irreducible polarity of two subjects, is thus the hermeneutic locus that definitively clarifies the moral relevance of the desire of the good.[38] What desire seeks through action is finally revealed in the love of friendship. It does not only seek its satisfaction, it seeks the person of the other with whom to be united and to whom to give oneself in the memory of the original gift, completely directed toward the realization of perfect communion.[39] It does not only seek pleasure, it seeks *gaudium* — joy — in the encounter with the other. Desire has an ecstatic character: It is the vocation to love.

The reference to the subject in his or her irreducible dimension of identity and difference with the other allows us to overcome the circularity of the definition of good with which Aristotle begins his *Nicomachean Ethics:* "The good has rightly been declared to be that at which all things aim"[40] — along with the consequent danger of a eudaemonism that locks action up in itself in the search for a subjective

37. See Angelini, *Le virtù e la fede,* pp. 79-94.
38. Juan José Pérez-Soba, "La irreductibilidad de la relación interpersonal: Su estudio en Santo Tomás," *Anthropotes* 13 (1997): 175-200.
39. See Scola, "Differenza sessuale e procreazione," 155.
40. Aristotle, *Ethica Nicomachea,* 1094a 3.

and self-referential fulfillment of one's desire. The good is not measured by desire. Rather, it is the good that measures desire and this good has its hermeneutic criteria in the love of friendship. The beatitude that each person seeks and that provokes action[41] is the consequence of a just relationship of love with the other: *ordo amoris*. Love is desire's salvation in the sense that desire can be saved from its ambiguity when it comes to recognize the precedence of the gift and entrusts itself to the hope of communion that love discloses.

In their very physicality, which through their spontaneous inclinations gives birth to desire, human persons discover the pledge of a fulfillment that becomes clear in love. It is precisely in the dynamic of love that the immediate impulses and passions, illuminated and moderated by the truth about the good, become virtues.[42] They become operational energies that allow a personal integration and the appropriate expression of action according to all the complex dimensions of the human being, *anima et corpore unus*.[43]

To act, therefore, is to have faith. As Blondel affirms, "in every act, there is an act of faith."[44] It is assenting to the promise implicit in the original gift that is made in being itself and in the relationships that contextualize existence,[45] and tending toward fulfillment. This can be better understood by looking at that radical vice and supreme temptation that the spiritual, patristic, and monastic tradition called sloth, and that Aquinas describes as the paralysis of action, a "weariness of work."[46] It is born of the sadness felt with regard to the final end — that is, the spiritual good of friendship with God and neighbor — which no longer seems within reach and thus no longer attracts the person but rather causes a distaste of everything. Sloth thus destroys hope and, with hope, the very energy to act. Action dies when love grows cold,

41. Augustine, *De moribus Ecclesiae catholicae*, 1.3.4: CSEL 90.6 (*Patrologia Latina* 32.1312): "Beate certe omnes vivere volumus; neque quisquam est in hominum genere, qui non huic sententiae, antequam plene sit emissa, consentiat."

42. See Wadell, *Primacy of Love*, p. 90: He calls the virtues "strategies of love."

43. *Gaudium et Spes*, n. 14: "Though made of body and soul, man is one."

44. Blondel, *Action (1893)*, p. 4.

45. See Angelini, *Le virtù e la fede*, p. 82.

46. See Aquinas, *Summa theologiae*, II-II, q. 35, a. 1: "taedium operandi." On the subject of sloth in Aquinas in relationship to a text on hope, which will be treated here shortly (Aquinas, *Summa contra gentiles*, 4.54), see the study by Jean-Charles Nault, *Le saveur de Dieu. L'acédie dans le dynamisme de l'agir* (Rome: Lateran University Press, 2002), written under my direction.

when the desire for the true good is extinguished and the will no longer reaches out to achieve it.

3. The Encounter That Awakens Love and Makes It Possible

The drama of desire, restless and unsatisfied by anything finite, is clarified by the hermeneutic that love offers it. Love is the original gift that precedes desire and makes it possible, directing it toward fulfillment in the communion of persons. But now a new and more serious problem for action seems to arise — is love truly possible? And how is it possible? How can human action ever achieve it if it is the height of the good toward which it tends and which, in faith, we know to be communion with God, who is the Supreme Good, and with human persons, who bear his image? How can its original tension avoid being wrapped up in itself, exhausting itself in the desperation that paralyzes action? Blondel speaks of something *necessary* for action that is also, at the same time, *impracticable* for human persons.[47] Here, then, we must move to a level of reflection that is different from the preceding one, passing on to speak about salvation history, which is proper to theology, applying and bringing to fruition what we have previously gathered from the hermeneutics of human action.

As we have seen, at its root love has a moment of passivity, in which the influence of another person is felt. Love is awakened in an encounter, that is, in a unique personal event wherein the promise of fulfillment is realized in a presence that offers itself as accompaniment along the journey and as assistance in achieving the goal. In paragraphs 7-9 of *Veritatis Splendor,* the question concerning the good is placed within the existential context of the rich young man's encounter with Jesus. It is in his dialogue with Christ that the ethical problem comes to be defined as a "question . . . about the full meaning of life" (VS 7) to which only God can be the answer because "there is only One who is good" (Mt 19:17). Ultimately it is an "echo of a call from God who is the origin and goal of man's life" (VS 7). It is the fascination of the person of Jesus that has reawakened these questions. It is dialogue with him that has clarified them, placing a radical and unforeseen choice before our freedom, the possibility of a new history in following a particular person.

47. Blondel, *Action (1893),* p. 297.

In Book IV of the *Summa contra gentiles,* Aquinas offers a surprising illumination on the connection between the moral dynamics and the Christological event, illustrating the reasons why the incarnation of the Son of God was fitting.[48] The incarnation is seen as the most efficient aid in tending toward beatitude. In fact, the immense distance that separates human nature from divine nature would inevitably throw human persons into despair of ever reaching the beatitude which they desire and which consists in the direct vision of God.[49] Now, the assumption of human nature on the part of the Son of God allows persons to elevate their hope toward such beatitude, finally made possible, and permits them to move toward it fervently. Regarding this matter, the Angelic Doctor recounts the passage of John's Gospel: "I came so that they might have life and have it in abundance" (Jn 10:10), thus demonstrating that his conception of our ultimate goal as a *visio Dei* is not at all intellectualistic. Supreme beatitude consists in the act of love with which persons know the Father and, in Christ and through the Holy Spirit, give themselves to him: "This is eternal life, that they should know you, the only true God, and the one whom you sent" (Jn 17:3).[50]

We can thus affirm that Christ, revealing the goal that attracts us and showing us that beatitude consists in communion with God, anticipates this goal in the encounter with him and makes it possible. In this way, Jesus becomes the one who, in freeing us from desperation, allows us to act. Joining the human and the divine in himself, he freely allows us access to what is necessary so that our actions might reasonably aim for their goal.[51]

For those who receive him, the encounter with Christ develops in friendship with him. The Holy Spirit makes Christ contemporary to persons of all times in the Church, thus granting even to us, in a mysteriously more profound way, the experience of his company that was given to his first disciples.[52] Moreover, the work of the Holy Spirit makes the

---

48. Aquinas, *Summa contra gentiles,* 4.54.

49. For a panorama of the essential points of the debate on the complex question of the desire to see God, I refer the reader to Giuseppe Colombo, *Del soprannaturale* (Milan: Glossa, 1996), pp. 249-331.

50. As shown in Ghislain Lafont, *Structures et méthode dans la Somme Théologique de saint Thomas d'Aquin* (Bruges: Desclée de Brouwer, 1961), p. 53, beatitude in the *Summa* indicates the fullness of the intimacy of personal communion with God.

51. See Martin Rhonheimer, *La prospettiva della morale: Fondamenti dell'etica filosofica* (Rome: Armando, 1994), pp. 62-73.

52. See Jean Laffitte, "Contemporanéité du Christ à l'homme de tous les temps dans

human person an "other Christ," rendering him or her a participant in the same love that moved Christ to act: the love of charity that is the fruit of the Holy Spirit.

Christ's presence to us thus takes on an absolutely personal form: "Christ is our wisest and greatest friend," Aquinas affirms, illustrating the specific way of regulating action in the context of the new law.[53] He principally guides us by his counsel, as one would do with a friend, rather than by precepts as one would do with servants (see Jn 15:15). In the dynamism of friendship, the beloved becomes the rule of the lover. Through affective union, what our friend wants will begin to appear fitting and connatural to us.[54]

By virtue of its intrinsic beauty, friendship with Christ informs and penetrates the entire human structure of action, its dynamics and impulses, causing it to participate in the ideal of communion with God. Love of charity thus becomes the "form of the virtues" because it orients the human virtues toward a higher goal, which they could never reach by themselves, i.e., it allows them to reach God and joins us to him in everyday activity.

Jesus Christ thus reveals himself to theological reflection as the ultimate basis of action, as the one who guarantees the good of action, being also its definitive substance. He is at the same time the end and the origin of action, the alpha and the omega. As its end, Christ reveals the destiny of action as communion with God, which is fully realized in the kingdom. In proposing to human freedom the ultimately appropriate object of its aspiration, Christ saves desire, allowing it to be fixed on the true good.[55] This salvation will have the aspect of the redemption of desire

---

le premier chapitre de l'Encyclique 'Veritatis Splendor'," in Graziano Borgonovo, ed., *Gesù Cristo, legge vivente e personale della santa Chiesa: Atti del IX Colloquio Internazionale di Teologia di Lugano (15-17 June 1995)* (Casale M.: Piemme, 1996), pp. 211-23.

53. Aquinas, *Summa theologiae*, I-II, q. 108, a. 4: "Christus maxime est sapiens et amicus."

54. See Thomas Aquinas, *Scriptum super Sententiis*, III, d. 27, q. 1, a. 3, ad 2: I owe this reference — just as some other intuitions on the way that the gift of wisdom works as a friendship making us connatural to the friend — to the doctoral research conducted by José Noriega, *"Guidados por el Espíritu": El Espíritu Santo y el conocimiento moral en Tomás de Aquino* (Rome: PUL-Mursia, 2000), which was written under my direction.

55. See *The Divine Office: Liturgy of the Hours*, vol. 4, prayer for the 21st Sunday in Ordinary Time: "O God, you who make us one in mind and heart, grant your people to love what you command and desire what you promise so that, among the things of this world, our hearts might be fixed on your word, wherein lies true joy."

through the cross. In order to rediscover its original fullness and to open itself to the dynamism of love, desire will have to be cleansed of the concupiscence of the flesh (Rom 7:4-5). The fulfillment of freedom's aspiration will necessarily take on the aspect of mortification. Participating in Christ's paschal mystery, Christians, who possess the Spirit of God, will become capable of following the desires of the Spirit (see Gal 5:17), "crucif[ying] their flesh with its passions and desires" (Gal 5:24) and letting themselves be led by the Spirit (see Gal 5:25). The promised beatitude will be a participation, given in the communion with Jesus, in the Son's perfect act of knowledge and love toward the Father in the Spirit.

Christ is at the origin of human action in that he is the efficient cause of love. As Creator and Redeemer, Christ is the source of action without, however, substituting free human causality. Grace does not exclude but rather includes the freedom of human action. It does not replace human responsibility, nor is it extrinsically juxtaposed to it. Rather, grace precedes human freedom, provoking and enabling it to give its irreplaceable consensus.

4. Human Action and Divine Love

Human action finds its purest source in the love that God gives human persons in Christ. This gift of love, however, in no way suppresses the human element of action. It transforms it, sustaining it, since love does not suppress anything of the beloved. It follows that persons, in their friendship with Christ, must "be intelligent."[56] Love uses the virtue of prudence in order to find actions that truly express and achieve that which it loves most.[57]

Asserting that God's love is at the origin of human action means asserting that it is God himself who moves persons to communion with him. It is God who calls human persons to be joined to him. This is why the fullness of Christian prudence consists in docility to the Spirit, who attracts us precisely through the beauty of human action, in which the communion among persons is announced.

56. See Ceslas Spicq, *Connaissance et moral dans la Bible* (Fribourg-Paris: Cerf, 1985), pp. 141-55.

57. Augustine, *De moribus Ecclesiae catholicae,* 1.14.25: "Prudentia, amor ea, quibus adjuvatur, ab eis, quibus impeditur, sagaciter seligens."

But how can persons unite themselves to God in their daily lives, so full of trifles and difficulties? Can all our daily acts perhaps ultimately be directed toward God? Would our neighbor then be just a pretext for loving God? "The friends of my friends are my friends" — God's friends become my friends because I love them with a new love, with the love with which God himself loves them and which allows me to participate in the gift of his Spirit. By virtue of this love, the desire that orients me toward my neighbors is transformed, since what I now desire for them is their true destiny, communion with God. My action, in establishing communion, will allow both of us to be in communion with God. Friendship with Christ thus finds its fulfillment in the Church: "Where two or three are gathered together in my name, there am I in the midst of them" (Mt 18:20).

Nevertheless, the action that is born of friendship with Christ and that leads us to communion struggles with a certain incapacity to draw upon its ultimate perfection. There is something that we continue to experience as imperfection: we wish that our actions were truly capable of building the kingdom of God, of making it present in all its salvific strength. A structural and painful inadequacy still remains, which however has the function of opening action up to a further fullness in the hope of its complete fulfillment.

5. The "Thread" That Binds Action to Future Fulfillment

The encounter with Jesus Christ does not obstruct desire or stop action (see 2 Thess 3:10). However, the disciple's action unfolds in a new context — the constitutive tension toward fulfillment is oriented toward a future that is well defined as goal and that, in some way, is already anticipated in the present. The future is determined in the promise and rescues action from insignificance, while its mysterious anticipation in the present gives action its driving force.

After the encounter with Jesus, the dynamism of action is directed toward the coming of God's kingdom: there all the promises and expectations of the human heart will find their superabundant fulfillment beyond all desire. This is why the liturgy, in the prayer for Sunday of the 20th Week in Ordinary Time, connects love, promise, and desire: "O God, you who have prepared every good beyond imagination for those who love you, infuse in us the sweetness of your love so that, loving you in everything and above everything, we might obtain the good you have promised, which surpasses our every desire."[58] The possibility of attaining the goods that surpass all desire is bound to the exercise of a love that is infused in us.

Desire, rescued by love, becomes hope, the object of which is the possibility of reaching, with God's help, that arduous future good that is eternal life, the enjoyment of God himself.[59] Hope is the soul of action and of the moral dynamism: "Every one who thus hopes in him purifies himself as he is pure" (1 Jn 3:3).

In Hebrew, the word "hope" is tied to that of "thread" (*tiqwah* from *qwh, qaw,* rope; see Josh 2:18-21: Rahab's scarlet cord).[60] Even in everyday language we say "a thread of hope." Hope, therefore, is a thread that connects our present action with its future destiny. To hope means to tether the future promised to the present. The paleo-Christian and medieval symbol of hope was the anchor, recalling Hebrews 6:18-20. Hope is a sure and firm anchor for our lives. In fact, it allows human action to lean on the hidden and real presence of Jesus, who entered into the innermost shrine.

But where is this thread that rescues action? And how is it connected to our present? If for Aristotle, "happiness . . . comes as a result of virtue,"[61] for Christians, who recognize perfect happiness to consist in communion with God, there exists an insurmountable discrepancy between their actions and this promised goal. As Aquinas authoritatively asserts in direct opposition to Aristotle: "Human deeds, since they are not required for happiness, as the efficient cause thereof, can be required only as dispositions thereto."[62] In fact, neither human persons

58. *Liturgy of the Hours,* vol. 4, Prayer for the 20th Sunday in Ordinary Time.

59. Aquinas, *Summa theologiae,* II-II, q. 17, aa. 1, 2. This is how the *Catechism of the Catholic Church* speaks of hope: "Hope is the theological virtue by which we desire the kingdom of heaven and eternal life as our happiness, placing our trust in Christ's promises and relying not on our own strength, but on the help of the grace of the Holy Spirit" (1817).

60. Gianfranco Ravasi, "L'attesa di Abramo e la speranza del popolo ebraico: Il Cristo sperato," *Communio* (Italian edition) 148 (1996): 13-23.

61. Aristotle, *Ethica Nicomachea,* 1.9, 1099b 16.

62. Aquinas, *Summa theologiae,* I-II, q. 5, a. 7: "Opera hominis, cum non requirantur ad beatitudinem eius sicut causa efficiens, ut dictum est, non possunt requiri ad eam nisi sicut dispositiones."

nor any other creatures can achieve beatitude on their own natural re-sources.[63]

In the dynamism of action, the thread of hope is expressed through the doctrine of merit in which the excellence of action and the synergy of the human and the divine are made real. It is the dimension of human ac-tion by which an act cooperates as the secondary cause of beatitude, which God gives us and of which he himself is the principal cause. In the Christological context of the Third Part of the *Summa theologiae,* Aquinas observes that what is obtained also on one's own merit is possessed in a more noble way than what is received as pure gift. In fact, those who ob-tain something through their own merit savor it and appreciate it more, because they have it through their own agency and thanks to their own ef-forts.[64] In this way, God wants the beatitude to which he has gratuitously called us to be our own and, in Christ, gives us the grace to merit it.

The infinite transcendence of divine causality is exalted precisely by including the contribution of human action, which works as a meritori-ous secondary cause in the acquisition of the supernatural gift — beati-tude — which Christ alone can merit for us because Christ's redemp-tive action, as *gratia capitis* (the grace of the head), is the cause of human persons' merit. Acting as head of the body, which is the Church, he has merited for us too and continues to merit for us in our every action. If, in Christ, God is the principal cause of merit, then this causality flows back ecclesially to Christians and sustains the necessary human contri-bution of their action. A fully human action, then, is also a most pro-foundly divine action in us.

In this way, the paradox of action — which consists in the fact that persons are created capable of God and with the natural desire of union with him but incapable of achieving this desire through their own ef-forts — is resolved through the gift of friendship with Christ. "God did give us free-will, with which we can turn to God, that he may make us happy."[65] Indeed, as Aquinas explains resorting to the Aristotelian the-ory of friendship: "what we do by means of our friends, is done, in a sense, by ourselves."[66] Human freedom is fulfilled in adherence to God

63. Aquinas, *Summa theologiae,* I-II, q. 5, a. 5.

64. Aquinas, *Summa theologiae,* III, q. 19, a. 3.

65. Aquinas, *Summa theologiae,* I-II, q. 5, a. 5, ad 1: "Sed dedit ei liberum arbitrium, quo possit converti ad Deum, qui eum faceret beatum." This theme is the object of an il-luminating reflection in the research of José Noriega cited above.

66. Aquinas, *Summa theologiae,* I-II, q. 5, a. 5, ad 1.

as the one who, in Christ, makes us his friends in order to elevate our actions to the goal that our desire yearns for: seeing God. In this way, in actions accomplished in Christ and at the origin of the human dynamism there is God himself, who gives persons the capacity of being at the height of this vocation that surpasses every desire.

Merit is the dimension of human action through which persons united to Christ dispose and prepare themselves for the perfect happiness of communion with God.[67] Acting in Christ through charity from now on realizes an anticipation of eternal beatitude, an anticipation at once mysterious and real, on which hope — and thus also action — can be built. In fact, charity already actualizes a *communicatio beatitudinis*[68] in the present.

Starting from these premises, the original Thomistic doctrine of the beatitudes emerges. The beatitudes are excellent acts in which an initial beginning of the eternal beatitude *(inchoatio beatitudinis)*[69] is foreshadowed in an imperfect but real way. In the patristic tradition, the beatitudes have always represented an important chapter for Christian morality, beginning with Augustine's commentary on the Sermon on the Mount.[70] The great bishop of Hippo sees the beatitudes as Jesus' response to the question of happiness, which moves persons to act. Saint Thomas inserts the beatitudes into the new dynamism of action, which is prompted by the virtues and the gifts of the Spirit, interpreting them as a sure anticipation of the final end of the eternal beatitude in the excellent actions that persons accomplish. They thus feed hope,[71] which is

67. Aquinas, *Summa theologiae,* I-II, q. 69, a. 2: "Spes futurae beatitudinis potest esse in nobis . . . propter aliquam praeparationem vel dispositionem ad futuram beatitudinem, quod est per modum meriti."

68. Aquinas, *Summa theologiae,* II-II, q. 25, a. 3; see Pérez-Soba, *Amor es nombre de persona,* 119.

69. *Summa theologiae,* I-II, q. 69, a. 2: on this theme, see also the doctoral thesis by Olivier Bonnewijn, *La béatitude et les béatitudes: Une approche thomiste de l'éthique* (Rome: PUL, 2001), written under my direction.

70. Augustine, *De sermone Domini in monte.* I acknowledge Servais Pinckaers, *The Sources of Christian Ethics,* trans. M. T. Noble (Washington, DC: Catholic University of America Press, 1995), pp. 134-67, for having drawn my attention to this tradition, which "modern" manualistic morality focused on norms has forgotten.

71. Aquinas, *Summa theologiae,* I-II, q. 69, a. 1: "Beatitudo est ultimus finis humanae vitae. Dicitur autem aliquis iam finem habere, propter spem finis obtinendi, unde et philosophus dicit, in I Ethic., quod *pueri dicuntur beati propter spem;* et apostolus dicit, Rom. VIII, *spe salvi facti sumus.* Spes autem de fine consequendo insurgit ex hoc quod

nourished in this life by the first fruits *(primordia fructuum)* that begin to appear and that are like the beginning of the reward awaiting us in eternity.

Certainly, the beatitudes maintain a paradoxical character because the happiness of which they give us a taste is hidden under the veil of a seeming defeat.[72] In the action of the disciple who follows Jesus, the kingdom begins as a seed buried in the earth or as a well-hidden treasure. It begins amid tears and persecution. Only the action of those who follow the Lord without reserve, sharing in the destiny of the Messiah rejected and crucified, reveals a mysterious participation in the beatitude of Jesus, who rejoices in the Father's love.[73]

6. Conclusion

The questions with which we began, "How is God involved in human action?" and, "How can human persons remain the protagonists of their action if 'God is at work in us, both to will and to work' (Phil 2:13)?" have in the course of this reflection found clues for an answer. Desire has been revealed to us as a first call to communion, since it is always love that precedes it and provokes it in the dynamism of action. Human action shows its proper dimensions within the drama of the interaction of personal freedom, both human and divine. It is precisely through friendship that the mysterious synergy of God and human persons in action is brought about.

In his commentary on Romans, Aquinas explains Paul's expression: "All who are moved by the Spirit of God are sons of God" (Rom 8:14), by resorting to a threefold distinction.[74] In the first place, referring to

---

aliquis convenienter movetur ad finem, et appropinquat ad ipsum, quod quidem fit per aliquam actionem."

72. Hans Urs von Balthasar thus concludes his work on the drama of human action within God's pathos with a chapter entitled "Slain and Victorious," *Theo-Drama: Theological Dramatic Theory,* vol. 4: *The Action,* trans. G. Harrison (San Francisco: Ignatius Press, 1994), pp. 471-503.

73. In *Veritatis Splendor,* the beatitudes are presented as "a sort of self-portrait of Christ, and for this very reason . . . [as] invitations to discipleship and to communion of life with Christ" (VS 16). In the same sense, see Joseph Ratzinger, *To Look on Christ: Exercises in Faith, Hope, and Love* (New York: Crossroad, 1991), pp. 57-62.

74. Thomas Aquinas, *Super Epistolam ad Romanos lectura,* 8.3.635.

animals that lack reason, he observes that we say, "they are acted upon or moved and do not act *(aguntur et non agunt)*" because they are moved by nature and not by a principle proper to action. This is the level of blind desire that compels creatures to seek satisfaction. Human persons, on the contrary — and this is the second level — act *(agunt)*, in that they perform voluntary actions. They know their goal, and, in acting, move toward it by an interior principle, motivated by the known end.[75] By the voluntary character of their acts, human beings reflect the image of God in freedom, which gives them dominion over their own actions. Their desire is thus moderated by the judgment of reason, which allows them to grasp the truth about the good. It is reason, open to the infinite, that creates the space for freedom in their actions. Moreover, freedom is true to its nature if it accepts its vocation to love, recognizing the person of the other and giving itself to the other.

The perfection of the movement of freedom, however, is found on a third level that, strangely, seems to lead us back to the first. Spiritual human beings who, through grace, have become children of God are again *aguntur,* that is, acted upon or moved. In fact, they are moved by a new instinct that the Spirit creates in them and that stirs them to act. And yet the Spirit's action does not destroy the natural perfection of a person's voluntary acts. Spiritual human beings are moved by the Spirit *(Spiritu Dei aguntur)* and, at the same time, act *(agunt)*. Their freedom, moved by the Spirit, assents to the suggestions of their friend, interiorly urging them to carry out "the good works that God has prepared in advance, that we should walk in them" (Eph 2:10). For the saints, therefore, "action is no longer the expression of a lack or a need that desires its satisfaction. For them, rather, action is the initial fruit of the fullness of love, which tends to grow by communicating itself so as to embrace everyone in the dynamism of divine action, which in turn anticipates, sustains, and guides human action."[76]

---

75. These are the three factors that define the *voluntarium* in the *Summa theologiae,* I-II, q. 6, a. 1.

76. Livio Melina, *Cristo e il dinamismo dell'agire: Linee di rinnovamento della teologia morale fondamentale* (Rome: PUL-Mursia, 2001), p. 35.

Acting for the Good of Communion

"Freedom then is rooted in the truth about man, and it is ultimately directed towards communion" (VS 86). With this assertion, *Veritatis Splendor* establishes the context of the meaning of free human action — its origin, its condition of possibility, and its finality. Communion is indicated as the intrinsic goal that gives meaning to freedom, the good that prompts us to act. In effect, the moral adventure begins when we permit the encounter with another person to reach us and to call us to go out of ourselves in order to establish a communion rooted in truth.

But how is the good of communion related to the dynamism of action? This theoretical question has two sides to it. First, we must determine what is the essential content of intentionality and verify whether this content can be interpreted in interpersonal terms. Second, we must think of the relationship — which is intrinsic to the intentionality from which action arises — between this interpersonal element (*communion* as the relationship of love between two persons) and the objective element (the *good* as the content that specifies an act of the will).

This does not mean imposing an extrinsic rule on action or conducting a metaphysical reflection from which to draw normative consequences, but rather going to the very heart of the moral dynamism in order to grasp there the intrinsic presence of communion as (1) an *end,* as (2) an original *gift* and *promise* of fulfillment, and thus also as (3) a *normative truth.* This is the methodological perspective that we will follow: the definition of interpersonal communion must emerge from an inquiry into practical reason — reason, that is, insofar as it is open to be informed by the attraction of the good. The criterion of truth, therefore, is not so much the correspondence of our discourse with what is the case, but the correspondence with what can fully satisfy the rational desire stirred up by the good of communion.[1]

1. Acting *for* Communion: Communion as the Intrinsic *End* of the Dynamism of Action

In classical Thomist analysis, the dynamism of action is characterized by structural elements, among which stand out the fundamental aspiration to happiness, the will's natural inclination to the good, intention, and choice. Every act of the will is structurally directed toward a good. Nevertheless, since the will is a *rational* appetite, it is necessary that it aims at a good precisely by reason of its goodness, that is, as a good in and for itself. The good that agrees with human persons *secundum rationem* is what Aquinas calls the "honest good" *(bonum honestum)* defined as the good that "draws us by its virtue and attracts us by its excellence."[2] This definition describes the original experience of persons' transcendence in regard to the sphere of their subjective desires. This is the experience of the encounter with a reality that deserves our respect because of its intrinsic dignity, not because of whatever particular benefit we could draw from it. What encounter and what reality are we speaking of here? Practical reason shows us that only a person can be the ultimate end of the intention that animates human action because only persons deserve to be loved for themselves, as an end and never just as a means.

1. See Thomas Aquinas, *Sententia libri Ethicorum,* 6.2.104-8: "Bonum practici intellectus non est veritas absoluta, sed veritas *confesse se habens,* idest concorditer ad appetitum rectum, sicut ostensum est, quod sic virtutes morales concordant." On this see Livio Melina, *La conoscenza morale: Linee di riflessione sul Commento di san Tommaso all'Etica Nicomachea* (Rome: Città Nuova, 1987), pp. 114-19; Martin Rhonheimer, *Praktische Vernunft und Vernünftigkeit der Praxis: Handlungstheorie bei Thomas von Aquin in ihrer Entstehung aus dem Problemkontext der aristotelischen Ethik* (Berlin: Akademie Verlag, 1994), pp. 81-116.

2. Aquinas, *Sententia libri Ethicorum,* 10.9.86-91: "Quod sua vi nos trahit et sua dignitate nos allicit." The definition is dealt with by Marcus Tullius Cicero, *De inventione* 2.52.157. See Melina, *La conoscenza morale,* pp. 58-59.

a. Communion as the Fulfillment of Love

We are brought to this conclusion mainly by the analysis of what, for Aquinas, is the fundamental passion and motive of every action: love. "Every agent, whatever it be, does every action from love of some kind."[3] We act to obtain an end, the desired and beloved good. This is why "every act [that] proceeds from any passion, proceeds also from love as from a first cause."[4] This highlights two decisive elements: first of all, there is the responsive character of action, which is moved by an external reality seen as desirable; then, there is also the dimension of the constitutive indigence of the human person, who is incomplete and in need of an other to be perfect. Action is born of the subject's tension toward completion in the union with this element that is other than the self. Action is pervaded by the desire to reach a good that is given to persons as an initial gift and that, at the same time, contains the promise of a unique fullness which can only be achieved in action.

A moment of passivity lies at the origin of desire, in which the person receives the gift of an initial union. A certain correspondence to and inclination toward the reality that first struck and attracted the person is felt.[5] This gift is love, the first union that occurs within the person's interiority, and that thus, by nature, is intentional and affective *(unio affectus)*. In virtue of its dynamic, it orients persons toward achieving full possession, that is, real union *(unio realis)* with the good that gave birth to the movement of desire.[6] Free initiative is situated exactly between this moment of passivity, which occurs gratuitously, and its fulfillment in the *unio realis*, in its effective conjunction with the reality itself. In fact, according to a definition given by Pseudo-Dionysius, love is "a uniting and binding force" *(vis unitiva et concretiva)*,[7] which implies a polarity between lover and beloved that can only be achieved in an interpersonal context. In particular, as has been convincingly demonstrated,

---

3. Thomas Aquinas, *Summa theologiae,* I-II, q. 28, a. 6: "Omne agens, quodcumque sit, agit quamcumque actionem ex aliquo amore."

4. Aquinas, *Summa theologiae,* I-II, q. 28, a. 6, ad 2: "Unde omnis actio quae procedit ex quacumque passione, procedit etiam ex amore, sicut ex prima causa."

5. An analysis of some of Aquinas's texts on affectivity is found in Angelo Scola, *The Nuptial Mystery,* trans. M. Borras et al. (Grand Rapids: Eerdmans, 2005), pp. 59-64.

6. See Aquinas, *Summa theologiae,* I-II, q. 25, a. 2.

7. Pseudo-Dionysius, *De divinis nominibus,* 4.12 *(Patrologia graeca* 3.709d): καὶ ἥστι τοῦτο δυνάμεως ἑνοποιοῦ καὶ . . . συγκρατικῆς; see Aquinas, *Summa theologiae,* I-II, q. 25, a. 2.

the term *concretivus* indicates a manner of union that respects the difference between lover and beloved in all its concreteness: it thus signifies a relationship of an interpersonal nature, characterized by unity and difference, in which otherness is not eliminated in an indistinct fusion but becomes the basis of communion.[8] In this sense, the notion of good is definitively clarified only in the context of love and of interpersonal love. We can thus conclude this first analysis of the dynamism of action by affirming that the good to which action aspires is effective communion with the beloved.

b. Communion as Act

Interpersonal communion, as the goal of action, is itself essentially an act, not a state or a mode of being. It is, therefore, a "communicating of oneself" in the active and dynamic sense of the term. It is the convergence of at least two acts by different subjects who reciprocally correspond to one another on an intentional level. According to Maurice Nédoncelle's precise definition, "Communion is the co-penetration of two acts that, through the concurrence of their intentionality, each grow in their original character."[9]

The fact that the communion of persons is an act and that it is brought about through the intentional convergence of two acts can be fully understood only if one considers the personalist dignity of the act as an *actus personae.* Karol Wojtyla's reflection in his main work, *The Acting Person,* has shown how the act that is truly free is the reality through which persons realize themselves, communicating themselves to others.[10] Since persons give themselves through their acts, the acts

8. On this, see Angelo Scola, *Identidad y diferencia: La relación hombre y mujer* (Madrid: Encuentro, 1989). For the Thomistic interpretation of the Dionysian text see Juan José Pérez-Soba, *Amor es nombre de persona: Estudio de la interpersonalidad en el amor en Santo Tomás de Aquino* (Rome: PUL-Mursia, 2001).

9. Maurice Nédoncelle, *La réciprocité des consciences: Essai sur la nature de la personne* (Paris: Aubier-Montaigne, 1942), p. 43: "La communion est la pénétration de deux actes qui accroissent chacun leur caractère original, par la coïncidence de leur intentionnalité."

10. See Karol Wojtyla, *The Acting Person,* trans. A. Potocki (New York: Springer, 2000), pp. 96-101. In fact, here we are dealing with the person and the act not as two distinct realities each in themselves but as a single, profoundly united reality.

of communion between persons are what define them as acting persons. For their acts to bring about communion, persons must be entirely present in their acts, identifying themselves with them. "Communion" means the actualization of a community in which the individual person is not only safeguarded and respected in his or her irreducible originality but where the person definitively realizes him- or herself in the freedom of the gift of self and the acceptance of the other.[11]

The moment of freedom in action determines the constitution of the end that is willed "for itself." This end is the beloved, toward whom action is directed in order to bring about communion. The judgment that guides choice becomes rational only when it is based upon the absolute of the person toward whom it is tending, a person who deserves to be loved for him- or herself. In fact, the proper goal of an act of love is always and only a person, understood as *ultimum dilectum,* the ultimate goal of the affective dynamism.[12] Only a person can correspond to this ultimate dimension of love and benevolence. In the concise words of Fr. Marie-Dominique Philippe, O.P.: "A person's proper goal can be nothing other than the other person who loves him, whether another human person or God."[13] This is why the love of friendship, which has a person as its goal, is love in the proper and principal sense of the term *(simpliciter),* while love of concupiscence is love in a secondary and derived sense *(secundum quid),* because what one loves here is desired in view of another.[14]

---

11. For this definition of communion, see Karol Wojtyla, *Sources of Renewal: The Implementation of the Second Vatican Council* (San Francisco: HarperCollins, 1980).

12. Thomas Aquinas, *Scriptum super Sententiis,* IV, d. 49, q. 1, a. 2, qc. 1, ad 3: "Sed illud quod diligitur amore benevolentiae, potest esse ultimum dilectum." Thomas's context regards the personal finality of the divine creative act.

13. Marie-Dominique Philippe, "Personne et interpersonnalité: Être et esprit," in *L'anthropologie de saint Thomas,* ed. Norbert M. Luyten (Fribourg: Editions Universitaires Fribourg, 1974), pp. 124-60, here 133.

14. Aquinas, *Summa theologiae,* I-II, q. 26, a. 4: "Haec autem divisio [amoris in amorem amicitiae et concupiscentiae] est secundum prius et posterius. Nam id quod amatur amore amicitiae, simpliciter et per se amatur: quod autem amatur amore concupiscentiae, non simpliciter et secundum se amatur, sed amatur alteri. . . . Et per consequens amor quo amatur aliquid ut ei sit bonum, est amor simpliciter, amor autem quo amatur aliquid ut sit bonum alterius, est amor secundum quid."

c. The Intentionality of Action and Communion

Every action is thus born within this fundamental intentionality of love and is mainly characterized by it. It tends to bring about this finality through the choice of actions that constitute *goods for the person* to whom it is directed. Modern moral reflection has mostly concentrated on this moment of choice, studying it from the point of view of freedom, that is, as an autonomous decision. The limitation of this perspective is that it grasps single actions in isolation and from without, abstracting from the subject who performs them and the temporal conditions in which they are carried out. In this way, the intentional and interior dynamic is lost from view, starting with what constitutes the action itself as an expression of the person and which determines its specifically moral form.[15]

Now, the intention that is directed toward the person of the other is not given by nature, although nature itself does imply a structural formality that favors it. The moment of freedom *(electio)* is essential to the dynamic of love as the love of benevolence. In fact, it implies desire's subordination to the truth about the good of the other as other, in contrast to a mere affective spontaneity, intent on self-fulfillment as the satisfaction of one's proper lack. Such an act of choice requires the affirmation of the other in his or her otherness, so that the intention may truly find its end in that other. Moreover, by its very structure, such an intentional affirmation of the other also demands the affirmation of all those goods that promote otherness.

Hence the fact that the first act of freedom is the determination of one's own fundamental intentionality in the person of the beloved, which is why the choice of the friend is necessary.[16] The act through which we choose our friends, recognizing them for their "absolute" personal worth, as an end in themselves and never just as a means,[17] thus

15. On this see, above all, the contribution made by Servais Pinckaers, "Le rôle de la fin dans l'action morale selon saint Thomas," in Servais Pinckaers, *Le renouveau de la morale: Études pour une morale fidèle à ses sources et à sa mission présente* (Paris: Téqui, 1979), pp. 114-43; as well as that of Martin Rhonheimer, *La prospettiva della morale: Fondamenti dell'etica filosofica* (Rome: Armando, 1994).

16. Paul J. Wadell, *Friendship and the Moral Life* (Notre Dame: University of Notre Dame Press, 1989), indicates how the first and fundamental moral choice is that of living in friendship, opening oneself to the other, accepting him or her so as to walk together toward the fullness of love.

17. This is Kant's second, personalist formulation of the categorical imperative: "The

carries a particular weight. It establishes the fundamental orientation of intentionality, qualifying the goodness of the acting person's will. We can say, as does Cornelio Fabro, that the fundamental morality of human action, on the basis of which the human will can be called good or bad, is decided in the determination of one's concrete ultimate personal end.[18] This existential basic choice always has a personal content. It is thanks to the absolute of the person, perceived through his or her action, that freedom determines itself, surpassing the original indetermination of the natural will.

While the *good of the person* as a person can only be achieved through the exercise of freedom,[19] this good is possible in the first place because intentionality is oriented toward the good of communion. In fact, the perfection of the agent is not an ideal of self-realization or self-sufficiency, enclosing the person into him- or herself, but an action that allows communion among persons.

d. Communion with God: The Final End of Action

A person, therefore, is the ultimate goal of our love. As totalities of meaning that do not admit of any reference beyond themselves within the same order of reality, persons deserve to be loved for themselves. We can thus say that the human person, as an object of love, is an "absolute." But he or she is only a "relative" final end. Let us try to understand this paradox that leads us to the heart of one of the main problems in interpreting Christian morality: the relationship between the love of God and love of neighbor.

In effect, as the entire great tradition of Christian theology, starting

---

rational being . . . is, therefore, never to be employed merely as means, but as itself also, concurrently, an end," Immanuel Kant, *Critique of Practical Reason,* trans. T. K. Abbott (New York: Prometheus Books, 1996), p. 109. On this, see Karol Wojtyla, *Love and Responsibility,* trans. H. T. Willetts (San Francisco: Ignatius Press, 1981), pp. 27-28.

18. Cornelio Fabro, "Orizzontalità e verticalità nella dialettica della libertà," in *Riflessioni sulla libertà* (Rimini: Maggioli, 1983), pp. 44-46.

19. This is that good which depends only on the person's free self-determination and which is not conditioned in any manner by factors extraneous to the person's freedom. This was clearly asserted in Carlo Caffarra, "'*Primum quod cadit in apprehensione practicae rationis*' (I-II, q. 94, a. 2): Variazioni su un tema tomista," in *Attualità della Teologia Morale: Punti fermi — problemi aperti, Studies in Honor of Rev. P. J. Visser, CSSR,* Studia Urbaniana 31 (Rome: Urbaniana University Press, 1987), pp. 143-64.

with Augustine,[20] has sustained, in confronting the choice of the final end, freedom is confronted with the radical alternative between the love of God above any other love and the love of self pushed to the point of contempt for God. Properly speaking, our neighbor, that is, another human person, can never constitute the final end that moves our freedom. He or she can be the occasion for determining our fundamental intentionality but not the final end in which it rests. In effect, divine causality — the ultimate source of the good of the person of the other perceived as a gift, which precedes the very freedoms of the subjects — is necessarily present in every interpersonal relationship.[21] The recognition, perhaps implicit and unreflected, of God the Creator's mysterious presence in interpersonal relationships is the indispensable condition of the authentic love of the person of the other as other. Only in the, at least implicit, perspective of God's presence is love of the other authentic, such as to guarantee that it does not fall back into itself. In this sense Robert Spaemann recalled that, basically, only a religious argument can be given against murder. Only where the incommensurability of the other is recognized as something *sacred,* as something of divine origin, is there a reason not to treat the other as a thing to be arbitrarily possessed or destroyed.[22]

Communion with God in action is not only the implicit presupposition that guarantees the possibility of authentic communion among persons. It is also and above all the explicit end that alone can quench the desire that gives birth to action and that is elicited by the encounter with the personal presence of Jesus Christ. In the light of revelation, theology knows that the communion we are called to, as our ultimate and supreme good, is with the Persons of the Most Holy Trinity, beyond anything that we could think or imagine. And in this way, theologians can understand better what is sought and mysteriously anticipated in every human communion, even if it is never fully known or given. In the *Summa theologiae,* Aquinas uses the term "beatitude" — communion in action with God — to express the final good that moves human action.

20. Augustine, *De civitate Dei,* 14.28; *Enarrationes in Psalmos,* 64.2.26; *De Genesi ad litteram,* 11.15.20.

21. On this theme, see Juan José Pérez-Soba, "Dall'incontro alla comunione: Amore del prossimo e amore di Dio," in Livio Melina and José Noriega, eds., *Domanda sul bene e domanda su Dio* (Rome: PUL-Mursia, 1999), pp. 109-30.

22. Robert Spaemann, *Happiness and Benevolence,* trans. J. Alberg (Notre Dame: Notre Dame University Press, 2000).

In effect, beatitude is not different from love of charity, that is, from that special form of friendship with God, but it is the activity of *caritas* perfectly fulfilled. Love of charity, which fixes human intentionality upon God, is based on the communication of eternal beatitude, which is thus not just a future goal but also a good already given in intimacy with God.[23]

In summary, friendship with God is our happiness precisely because it is the action in which our intentionality is perfectly preceded and embraced by the intentionality of God's love, whose very life is the communion of perfect love among the divine Persons.[24] In Aquinas's work, beatitude is also what designates God's fully actual essence. Every true communion in our state of life is a real participation in and not just an image of this supreme good to which the heart aspires in action.

2. Action *Beginning from* Communion: Communion as the Original *Gift* and the *Promise* of Fulfillment

a. The Experience of a Disproportion

Intent on communion, the dynamism of action is confronted with a structural and historical disproportion regarding the end toward which it tends. In fact, no human reciprocity can satisfy our aspiration to a communion whose real unity respects otherness without leaving it simply exterior to ourselves. In the limitation and sinfulness of the human situation, the other's irreducible difference inevitably arises as an obstacle to full communion, and the attempt to overcome it can only lead to eliminating the richness that derives from reciprocity.[25]

Our historical situation, marked by original sin and its consequences, impedes benevolence toward a friend of such a kind that does not somehow seek to turn the intention back to ourselves. The rupture

---

23. Aquinas, *Summa theologiae,* II-II, q. 25, a. 3: "Fundatur super communicatione beatitudinis aeternae."

24. See Roger Guindon, *Béatitude et théologie morale chez St. Thomas d'Aquin* (Ottawa: Éditions de l'Université d'Ottawa, 1956), p. 256.

25. An analysis of the drama deriving from the asymmetry of the I-thou relationship, with particular but not exclusive reference to the man-woman relationship, can be found in Scola, *Nuptial Mystery,* pp. 116-21.

of the original bond of charity with God deprives the dynamism of action of its ultimate point of reference and thus of its impetus. At the same time, it also prejudices the truth of an authentic love of benevolence for other persons, smothering the breath of gratuity that only the perspective of the infinite in love for the other's destiny can give. In the moral experience, then, the reciprocity of wills in communion is only a fragmentary moment of grace, a possible hope that is often unavoidably frustrated. Human freedom, oriented toward communion, needs to be freed, that is, needs to rediscover its original capacity for the gift of self and the acceptance of the other.

Such a disproportion, dramatically experienced as the obstruction of the goal of communion that action tends toward, risks provoking a paralysis of action.[26] The insurmountable distance that separates the actual human situation from the communion we aspire to with others and with God bears with it the temptation of desperation and consequent inaction. Given the delusion and the failure of action, which seems to fall short of the original promise, the supreme temptation is to shun the risk of the gift of self in the actions we accomplish, that is, to attempt to save ourselves without giving ourselves to the other.[27] This retreat can also manifest itself in formalism, for which action no longer expresses the person, who remains separate from it. However, the attempt to save one's life without risking it in the gift of self means exactly condemning oneself to turning in on oneself and to being sterile (see Mk 8:35).

b. The Encounter with Christ and the Liberation of Freedom

It is only through the gratuitous event of an encounter that the hope of achieving communion, and thus also the energy to act, can be reawakened. Certainly, every true human encounter with other persons made in the image of God, in the measure that we let ourselves be touched by

---

26. Maurice Blondel, *Action (1893): Essay on a Critique of Life and a Science of Practice,* trans. Oliva Blanchette (Notre Dame: University of Notre Dame Press, 1984), pp. 332-44. Here he speaks of a death of action as the first possible option in the face of the structural disproportion between the infiniteness of the willing will and the finitude of the objects effectively willed.

27. See Giuseppe Angelini, *Teologia morale fondamentale: Tradizione, Scrittura e teoria* (Milan: Glossa, 1999), pp. 586-88.

it, has the character of an e-vent, that is literally, a "coming-out," and re-calls the gift of an original communion that is not the fruit of human action but rather the gratuitously given basis of all action. Nevertheless, it is only the encounter with Christ, the perfect image of the Father, that can liberate freedom and once again bring forth the energy of the gift. As we have already seen in the previous chapter, the connection between the dynamism of action and the Christ event is illuminated in Book IV of the *Summa contra gentiles,* where Aquinas illustrates the reasons for the fittingness of the incarnation of the Son of God. Only God's new and extraordinary closeness to human nature accomplished in the incarnation allows us to hope for the happiness promised in communion with God, thus allowing us to fervently reach for it, overcoming the supreme temptation of despair, which paralyzes action. The unity between the human and the divine nature that came about in the incarnation of the Word is the new principle for action.

In Christ's human existence, freedom shows itself capable of the gift of self that creates communion. Living in radical unity with the Father, Jesus can give himself in complete filial trust, without reserve and without fear of losing himself. He lives his death on the cross as the supreme act of his filial freedom. He knows that he has to die in order to fulfill the Father's will and gather those who are scattered into unity (Jn 11:45-54).[28] The Eucharistic offering of his body to the Father to bring us unity manifests the extraordinary fruitfulness of love and its capacity to generate communion beyond the limits of space and time. Truly, love is stronger than death (see Song 8:6); it allows a life of action!

c. The Original Gift of the Eucharist in the Church

Jesus' acceptance of his Eucharistic self-offering is the basis for communion among persons as well as the place from which Christian action springs forth as Eucharistic action ("Do this in memory of me," Lk 22:19). In this sense, the Eucharist is the original gift. The *communio sanctorum,* as Henri de Lubac has shown, originally meant a common liturgical participation in the "holy things," which then — through the free concurrence of those who take part in it — is called to bear fruit by

28. On this, see Damiano Marzotto, *L'unità degli uomini nel vangelo di Giovanni* (Brescia: Paideia, 1977), pp. 131-40.

becoming an interpersonal communion among the saints.[29] This is the communion, the ultimate reality *(res)*, in view of which the sacrament *(res sacramenti)* exists. The Eucharist's fruitfulness can be seen in the effective achievement of ecclesial communion only if human freedom lets itself be involved and transformed by the divine gift.[30] It is this implication of our freedom in history that justifies the repetition of Eucharistic liturgical celebrations in time, making us contemporaries with Christ who is the fullness of time.

Only Christ's action upon the cross, which is perennially present in the Eucharist, achieves the communion to which the dynamism of human action aspires. Human action is not excluded by Christ's Eucharistic action but is included in it. In the Eucharist, the source of Christian action, the faithful are given the very action of Christ, his charity, which in his gift of self through his sacrifice on the cross generates communion among human beings and between human beings and God. The primacy of divine doing provokes human persons' free and active "letting it be done."[31] In order to achieve the communion it aspires to, human action must take on the form of a free consent to Jesus' Eucharistic action, participating in it intimately and allowing itself to be permeated and informed by it. In this sense, Mary's "yes" to the Son's Eucharistic sacrifice is the prototype and the model for the action of the Church and of the Christian.

Thus the constitutive ecclesial dimension of action emerges. It is born of the communion of the Church, the dwelling place of morality,[32] and extends to build the community itself "for the life of the world." Action, therefore, has a precise historical residence, identifiable in space and time, which does not, however, imply a denial of universality.[33] The

29. See Henri de Lubac, "Credo sanctorum communionem," *Communio* 1 (1972): 22-31.

30. On this, see Carlo Caffarra, *Living in Christ: Fundamental Principles of Catholic Moral Teaching* (San Francisco: Ignatius Press, 1987), pp. 18-20.

31. Hans Urs von Balthasar, *Theo-Drama: Theological Dramatic Theory,* vol. 4: *The Action,* trans. G. Harrison (San Francisco: Ignatius Press, 1994), pp. 361-88.

32. Allow me to recall my own article, Livio Melina, "Ecclesialità e teologia morale: Spunti per un 'ridimensionamento' teologico della morale," *Anthropotes* 5 (1989): 7-27.

33. The opposing demands of a concrete reference to a historical community and universality have been debated in the comparison between "communitarians" and "liberals": A. Ferrara, ed., *Comunitarismo e liberalismo* (Rome: Editori Riuniti, 1992); G. dalle Fratte, ed., *Concezioni del bene e teoria della giustizia: Il dibattito tra liberali e comunitari in prospettiva pedagogica* (Rome: Armando, 1995).

Church is not a cult that promotes its own, particular moral truths; but she is "catholic," holding within her communion the historical prophecy of the unity of all persons in the kingdom of heaven. Insofar as she is "Christ's relevance [Latin: *'simultas temporum'* = 'contemporaneity'] for people of all times" (VS 25), the Church is not only the sphere within which Christian moral action, in its dynamic tension toward communion, is made possible. She is also, according to Augustine's definition, *"Ecclesia morum regula,"*[34] the rule of its actualization in history through her life, her Tradition of doctrine and holiness, and her magisterium.

3. Acting *in* Communion: Communion as the *Truth* and the *Rule* of Action

Up to this point we have seen how communion enters into the dynamism of action as its intrinsic finality that pervades the person's intentionality and as the original gift that provokes and sustains our freedom seeking to achieve the promise. Now we must focus on the second aspect of the theoretical question proposed at the beginning of this chapter: What is the relationship between the interpersonal element of communion and the objective element of the good that specifies the will that chooses? This is a truly crucial point in our reflection because it precisely regards the criteria of the truth of action. How is the movement of normative rationality inherent to the intentionality of communion without losing its objective character?

a. Recognizing the Truth about the Good: The Condition for Communion

The human act finds its fundamental criteria of moral goodness in being an act of true love that promotes and realizes communion with the other, desiring the other's true good. Here we are dealing with what, according to Aquinas, is the specific characteristic of the movement of love, which distinguishes it from all other movements of the soul.[35] Love does not tend to one but to two objects at the same time: to the other person with

---

34. Augustine, *De moribus Ecclesiae catholicae,* 1.30.62.
35. Aquinas, *Summa theologiae,* I-II, q. 26, a. 4.

whom it desires to enter into communion and to the good that is willed for that person and which constitutes the necessary mediation of the effective expression of love in action. "To love is to will the good for someone."[36] If our ultimate and formal intentionality is directed to the person of the other, it passes through the choice of what is truly good for that person. The good of a particular action, which our will chooses from the perspective of communion, has an objective weight, independent of the subject, which must be verified by reason as to its capacity to effectively promote the good of the person of the other. The guarantee that this is an authentic love of friendship, in which the acting person's intention does not turn in on itself but goes out of itself (ecstasy) and remains focused on the friend who is loved for him- or herself,[37] is given by the will's submission to the truth about good, which creates communion. The good's objectivity, recognized in an original way by reason, is the condition of authenticity for the communion that is sought after and that is dependent on what precedes the intention.

The desired communion thus becomes the immanent rule of action through the consideration of the truth about the good of the beloved. Action truly aims at communion if it tends toward the good of the person, accepting to respect and promote those "goods for the person" that are the object of one's choices.

b. Moral Virtues at the Service of the Truth about the Good and Communion

The moral virtues ensure the rationality of our choices, relating the two objects of love, the person and the good. Consequently, they also ensure the unity between our fundamental intentionality and our concrete choices. In fact, insofar as they are the person's stable operative dispositions toward the good, the moral virtues bring about the integration of affectivity in the judgment of what is truly good for the other thanks to a connatural knowledge of the action's end, that is, of the person loved for him- or herself.[38]

36. Aristotle, *Rhetoric*, 2.4: "Amare est velle alicui bonum."

37. Aquinas, *Summa theologiae*, I-II, q. 28, a. 3; Pseudo-Dionysius the Areopagite, *De divinis nominibus*, IV, l. 10.

38. In Thomistic thought, the original dimension of connaturality proper to moral knowledge was rediscovered by Jacques Maritain, "De la connaissance par connatura-

At the heart of the virtues lies prudence, the perfection of practical reason, as the measure of the good of the person. The virtues make us love what is truly worthy of love, the true good. This saves the discourse of the virtues from the danger of the subjectivism of arbitrary tastes and from the historical relativism of the various cultures and social contexts. The defining characteristic of the virtues, that is, what distinguishes them from spontaneous inclinations, conventional dispositions, and culturally acquired habits, is prudence, "right reason applied to action."[39] In fact, there is no moral virtue without prudence, which determines the rational measure of action that is rooted in the universal principles about the good.

Nevertheless, true moral knowledge of the concrete particular cannot come about without the moral virtues. There is no prudence without the moral virtues.[40] In Aquinas's mature synthesis in the *Summa theologiae,* there is a well-articulated theory of practical reason that begins from universal principles that are specified by the virtues as expressions of the truth about the good of the person. However, in concrete action practical reason can draw light from these universal principles only in synergy with the virtues, on the strength of a connaturality with the good of the entire moral subject.[41] The rationality of the virtues is not rationalism.

The perspective of the rationality intrinsic to the virtues also shows us that it is the concrete subject who knows and not his or her faculties considered abstractly.[42] The concrete person knows from within his or

---

lité," *Nova et vetera* 55 (1980): 181-87; and Rafael Caldera, *Le jugement par inclination chez saint Thomas d'Aquin* (Paris: Vrin, 1980). New perspectives on the value of connaturality are also offered, from a literary perspective, by Martha Nussbaum, *Poetic Justice: The Literary Imagination and Public Life* (Boston: Beacon Press, 1995), chapter 3; and by Jean-Luc Marion, *L'intentionnalité de l'amour: En hommage à E. Lévinas* (Paris: Vrin, 1986), pp. 111ff., who asserts that only love allows us to discover the irreplaceable uniqueness of the other, the other's *haecceitas.*

39. Aquinas, *Summa theologiae,* II-II, q. 47, a. 2: "Recta ratio agibilum."

40. See Melina, *La conoscenza morale,* pp. 191-202.

41. For a presentation of Aquinas's conception of practical reason, besides my text previously mentioned above and the work of Martin Rhonheimer, see the studies by Giuseppe Abbà, in particular *Felicità, vita buona e virtù: Saggio di filosofia morale* (Rome: LAS, 1989), pp. 144-50. Also, Daniel Westberg, *Right Practical Reason: Aristotle, Action, and Prudence in Aquinas* (Oxford: Clarendon Press, 1994).

42. Cornelio Fabro, "La dialettica d'intelligenza e volontà nella costituzione esistenziale dell'atto libero," in *Riflessioni sulla libertà* (Rimini: Maggioli, 1983), pp. 57-85.

her commitment to action, that is, within the dynamic of love. Practical knowledge of the good does not refer to a detached reason but to a historically situated, concrete person with a complex identity: "Hic homo singularis intelligit,"[43] and we can add: vult, eligit, amat . . . This allows us to overcome the moral intellectualism that separates the moment of judgment from the moment of effective praxis and considers moral knowledge as a phase prior to action, independent from the quality of life, from personal dispositions, and from the person's effective praxis.[44]

Although in their singularity they are directed to specific goods for the person, the virtues are expressions of a single love[45] and can even be defined as "strategies of love."[46] The apprehension of the good, which appears on the horizon of love, implies perceiving a unity with the other person. In the love of friendship, the good of the beloved is seen as the good of an other self.[47] The goods for the person are perceived within the intentionality of love, which first of all gives importance to the person of the other.

In their very ontological structure, the virtues thus have a communal character. The intentionality of virtue's dynamism is rooted in the gift of an initial communion and moves toward its effective and complete achievement. Ethical reflection based on the virtues offers to the ethics of love a rationality that saves it from emotionalism and decisionism, guaranteeing the place of the true good within communion. This becomes evident if we consider the twofold connection of virtue: on the one hand to love and on the other to practical reason, which understands and establishes the ends of action.

Love of charity — which regards the final intention directed to the

43. Thomas Aquinas, *De unitate intellectus contra Averroistas,* III.

44. In this sense I refer to the pertinent observations of Blondelian inspiration made by Angelini, *Teologia morale fondamentale,* pp. 555-67, which denounce the intellectualistic trend prevalent in both Scholastic tradition and the most recent proposals advanced in moral theology.

45. Augustine's expressions by which he leads the four cardinal virtues back to love are well known: "Itaque illas quatuor virtutes . . . sic etiam definire non dubitem, ut temperantia sit amor integrum se praebens ei quod amatur; fortitudo, amor facile tolerans omnia propter quod amatur; iustitia, amor soli amato serviens, et propterea recte dominans; prudentia, amor ea quibus adiuvatur ab eis quibus impeditur, sagaciter seligens" (Augustine, *De moribus Ecclesiae catholicae,* 1.15.25).

46. Paul J. Wadell, *The Primacy of Love: An Introduction to the Ethics of Thomas Aquinas* (Mahwah, NJ: Paulist Press, 1992), p. 90.

47. See Aquinas, *Summa theologiae,* I-II, q. 28, a. 1.

good of the person in communion with God and neighbor — is revealed in the virtuous choices that refer to the proximate ends of action. Such choices of particular acts are not simply means that are extrinsically or technically related to the end,[48] but they are first realizations of the end, which is anticipated in them. The communion that is hoped for is thus prepared and anticipated in the action that is chosen. Reason, which opens itself to the truth about the good of the person and regulates the will's choice of goods for the person, is thus the intrinsic criterion of love's intentionality, which seeks to build communion.

c. Natural Law from the Perspective of Communion

In the perspective of communion, the traditional doctrine of natural law is placed in a new light.[49] This doctrine emphasizes the fact that action has elements that do not depend on a choice. On the one hand, it is not possible to will the good of the person unless the objective mediation of goods for the person has been accepted. This submission of the will to the truth corresponds to obedience to natural law and demonstrates the recognition of the presence of God the Creator in the communion among persons. The exterior character of natural law highlights the fact that the ultimate criteria of truth in the choices we make are not at our arbitrary disposal. They do not depend on the will and are the condition of the goodness of our choices.[50] It also marks God's otherness as an ever implicit polarity in moral choices.

On the other hand, the goods for the person have no moral relevance if not within love's teleological perspective, that is, within the affirmation of the person willed for him- or herself. The good that is willed, the object of the choice, is considered by reason in view of the

48. This is utilitarianism's fundamental error, which is primarily an error at the level of the theory of action. See Melina, *La conoscenza morale,* pp. 49-53.

49. On this theme see the observations made by Alasdair MacIntyre, *Three Rival Versions of Moral Enquiry: Encyclopaedia, Genealogy, and Tradition* (London: Duckworth, 1990), pp. 134-40, which place the Thomistic theme of natural law within the comprehensive context of the morality of the good life and the virtues, as well as chapter 8 of his preceding study, *Whose Justice? Which Rationality?* (Notre Dame: Notre Dame University Press, 1988), which offers a reinterpretation of natural law in terms of friendship.

50. See Giuseppe Abbà, *Lex et virtus: Studi sull'evoluzione della dottrina morale di San Tommaso d'Aquino* (Rome: LAS, 1983), p. 230.

friend's will.[51] The act of choosing is thus situated within an interpersonal context. The ultimate moral rationale, the criteria of our choices, is their capacity to establish communion in obedience to the truth about the good of our friend, which is established by divine law. In fact, it is only in obedience to this truth that the wills of friends can be united.

The moral quality of an action is thus verified by communion with God the Creator and brought about through respecting the truth about the good of the person. Natural law reveals itself as the "code of the Covenant between creative Wisdom and the human person, a covenant inscribed in man's very reason."[52] In communion with God the Creator one can also establish communion with the other person in action.

In Christ, the incarnate eternal Wisdom and the "Beginning" of creation, the indications of the natural law are seen in a definitive light because he has taken on human nature and "illumines it in its constitutive elements and in its dynamism of charity towards God and neighbor" (VS 53). The covenant, therefore, also takes on a new face, that of Christ who makes himself present to us in an entirely personal way. As we have mentioned in the previous chapter, Aquinas points out that "Christ is our wisest and greatest friend."[53] Christ's gift of action, through charity, the virtues, and the gifts of the Holy Spirit, is found at the heart of human action as the energy that makes communion among persons possible. The very action of the Christian becomes the place of communion with Christ where two subjects, divine and human, meet, and in their unity promote communion among human beings.

4. Concluding Reflections

To conclude I would like to propose two reflections related to the Christological dimension of the approach outlined here and its fruitfulness for the sphere of sexual and conjugal morality.

---

51. On this topic see Aquinas, *Summa theologiae,* III, q. 18, a. 5, ad 2, where Thomas, in the context of the study on Christ's human will, asserts that: "Conformitas voluntatis humanae ad voluntatem divinam attenditur secundum voluntatem rationis, secundum quam etiam voluntates amicorum concordant, inquantum scilicet ratio considerat aliquod volitum in ordine ad voluntatem amici."

52. Caffarra, *Living in Christ,* p. 102.

53. Aquinas, *Summa theologiae,* I-II, q. 108, a. 4: "Christus maxime est sapiens et amicus."

a. For a Christ-Centered Morality

I believe within this perspective one can outline an authentic Christocentric morality, which is not only focused on Christ's *being,* understood as the basis of human action, but also on the participation of the Christian's action, through the Spirit, in Christ's Eucharistic *action.* The first Christocentric model, developed from a dogmatic perspective, considers the relevance of the Christological foundation *sub ratione entis.* Not understanding the specificity of the practical perspective it either risks being pointless — as, after a very suggestive anthropological treatment, it ends up entrusting the concrete mediation of action to subjective conscience — or it simply repeats legalistic patterns that are extrinsic to action.

The second model, in contrast, taking into account the specific intentional dimension of the dynamism of action, allows us to think of a more intimate Christological reference to action. For example, in St. Bonaventure's moral theology the idea of "participating in Christ's virtues" was central.[54] St. Thomas, in his moral thought, developed more the idea of participating in Christ's excellent action through the beatitudes.[55]

b. Perspectives for Sexual and Conjugal Morality

We can also catch a glimpse of the fruitfulness of such a renewed approach for sexual and conjugal morality. In fact, in this way the dimension of marriage and the family can be understood from its specific intentionality, which is directed to the communion of persons. The norms, therefore, do not remain exterior or opposed to passion and desire. Conjugal chastity is not a "repression of instinct" as it is in the Stoic and Kantian approach that has influenced Catholic tradition but which

54. Bonaventure, *Collationes in Hexaëmeron,* 6.10; Aquinas, *Scriptum super Sententiis,* III, d. 34, q. 1, a. 1. On Bonaventure's morality see, among others, Ambrogio Nguyen Van Si, *Seguire e imitare: Cristo secondo san Bonaventura* (Milan: Ed. Bibl. Francescana, 1995). Some developments along these lines can also be found in my *Sharing in Christ's Virtues: For a Renewal of Moral Theology in Light of Veritatis Splendor,* trans. William E. May (Washington, DC: Catholic University of America Press, 2001).

55. In this sense, see the study by Olivier Bonnewijn, *La béatitude et les béatitudes: Une approche thomiste de l'éthique* (Rome: PUL, 2001).

John Paul II has overcome in his Wednesday Catecheses on human love in the divine plan. From the theological point of view, it is possible to think of conjugal love as participation in the love of Christ the Bridegroom for the Church his Bride. It is a participation in Christ's own Eucharistic dedication, made possible through the virtue of charity.

The perspective of the virtues also permits us to appreciate the unique character of married and family life as an authentic personal vocation that informs an entire life, giving concrete shape to an ideal of holiness and entrusting persons with an ecclesial mission.[56] Since the circumstances of life are very particular, it is not possible to establish rules and norms for all cases. Only if the moral subjectivity of the spouses is truly integrated by the virtues and directed toward interpersonal communion can they discover the concrete forms of that excellent action which will help them achieve communion in the difficulties of everyday life.[57]

Chaste spouses possess a unique knowledge of their partner. It is an affective knowledge, thanks to which they can discover the singularity and absoluteness of their beloved. It is a knowledge that is given through an emotional reaction in the face of every practicable good in which they discover the possibility of communion. It is virtue that allows for the truth of its fulfillment. From this unique knowledge of the person they love, spouses can direct their action toward one another. In this way, the virtue of chastity makes possible the gaze upon the beloved — in his or her unique preciousness and irreducible singularity — and allows the spouses to grasp the body's nuptial meaning. As John Paul II affirmed, the gift of piety enhances this gaze, which discovers in the other spouse the divine mystery of the "temple of the Holy Spirit."[58]

---

56. On this topic, see Jean Laffitte and Livio Melina, *Amor conyugal y vocación a la santidad* (Santiago de Chile: Ed. Universidad Católica de Chile, 1996).

57. Aquinas, *Sententia libri Ethicorum,* VII, 10, 74-91: "Et in hoc plurimum differt studiosus [virtuosus] ab aliis, quod in singulis operabilibus videt quid vere sit bonum, quasi existens regula et mensura omnium operabilium."

58. John Paul II, *Man and Woman He Created Them: A Theology of the Body,* trans. Michael Waldstein (Boston: Pauline Books & Media, 2006), pp. 352-53: "If purity disposes man to 'keep his own body with holiness and reverence,' as we read in 1 Thessalonians 4:3-5, piety as a gift of the Holy Spirit seems to serve purity in a particular way by making the human subject sensitive to the dignity that belongs to the human body in virtue of the mystery of creation and of redemption. Thanks to the gift of piety, Paul's words 'Or do you not know that your body is a temple of the Holy Spirit within you . . . and that you do not belong to yourselves?' (1 Cor 6:19) take on the convincing power of an experience and be-

*   *   *

The redefinition of happiness in terms of communion allows the concept of happiness — as that which action aims at as its ultimate goal — to carry a renewed value in the moral life, freeing it from suspicions of eudaemonistic individualism.[59] If, as *Veritatis Splendor* affirms, the goal of freedom is communion and if this dynamic can only be achieved in fidelity to the truth about the human person, then, thanks to the perspective opened by this rereading of the concept of happiness in terms of communion, the human act is seen in the context of a practical morality that shapes the whole life in the perspective of communion. Such unity is the fruit of the gift of an original communion, which freedom has the task of making fruitful, so that human life may reflect the glory that characterizes the life of communion of the Most Holy Trinity.

---

come a living and lived truth in actions. They also open fuller access to the experience of the spousal meaning of the body and of the freedom of the gift connected with it, in which the deep face of purity and its organic link with love reveals itself."

59. On this, see Servais Pinckaers, *The Sources of Christian Ethics,* trans. M. T. Noble (Washington, DC: Catholic University of America Press, 1995).

· III ·

The Practical Dimension
of a Believing Reason

The Church's magisterium has affirmed the original vigor of faith as the "new and original criterion for thinking and acting in personal, family, and social life" against the "serious and destructive dichotomy that separates faith from morality" (VS 88). Such a practical dimension of Christian belief is rooted in the very nature of the faith, which in proposing a truth for living implies "a decision involving one's whole existence" (VS 88). This decision, however, passes through reason. We are not speaking of a blind fideism that sacrifices conscience to obedience and thus condemns the will to heteronomy. The magisterium itself asserts that without a "universal truth about the good" (VS 32) that is recognizable by human reason and that can guide our choices in practical life, there is no true freedom.[1] Rational mediation is intrinsic to the practical relevance of the faith, which clothes and transforms the believer's existence, fully respecting its dynamisms and elevating its potentialities.

In this chapter I intend to explore the connections between faith, reason, and praxis, demonstrating, on the one hand, the existence of a practical dimension of belief and, on the other, the original character of the rational mediation related to moral action. Between truth and freedom there is not a mechanical and extrinsic deduction from the latter to the first but a circularity and reciprocal co-implication.[2] Illustrating these connections demands a critical confrontation not only with the

1. John Paul II, *Fides et Ratio,* n. 98.
2. John Paul II, *Fides et Ratio,* n. 90.

46

question of autonomy, which has occupied the debate in moral theology in these last decades, but also with the problem of intellectualism, which more deeply and widely characterizes the modern discussion.

1. The Question of the Believer's Moral Autonomy and the Magisterium's Response

The claim of the believer's moral autonomy originates in the criticism of the presumed "legalism" of the post-Tridentine Catholic manualist tradition.[3] The term "legalism" identifies the tendency to base the law's obligatory nature simply upon the authority of a divine or human legislator, side-stepping the mediation of reason or subjective conscience. According to the criticism, the result is a heteronomous morality that is incapable of respecting individual freedom or of guaranteeing that persons of diverse religious conviction can live together sociably. The demand that morality be rational is joined to the need for a universal dialogue on the *humanum* that begins from foundations common to every person of good will, including nonbelievers. The argument further maintains that if faith were assumed as the directly regulatory principle of the moral life, faith would threaten the person's free self-determination and obstruct dialogue in the current pluralistic context.

In this way the insistence on autonomy, proper to the Enlightenment and especially to Kant, is taken up again. According to this approach, for human persons the moral law cannot be other than what they give themselves. Besides, it is observed that the practical norms of Christian and human morality, insofar as they are determined by right reason, are materially or categorically identical to one another.[4] In this way, some would like to establish that right reason and not faith is the medium for the knowledge of practical moral norms. For them, the influence of faith is merely one of transcendental inspiration, while it is

3. See Sergio Bastianel, *Autonomia morale del credente: Senso e motivazioni di un'attuale tendenza teologica* (Brescia: Morcelliana, 1980), which offers a panorama of the most important authors. The programmatic text of this current of thought is Alfons Auer, *Autonome Moral und christlicher Glaube* (Düsseldorf: Patmos, 1971). Very influential, especially in the Italian context, is Josef Fuchs, *Responsabilità personale e norma morale* (Bologna: Dehoniane, 1978).

4. Josef Fuchs, "Esiste una morale propriamente cristiana?" *Sussidi 1980* (Rome: PUG, 1980), pp. 203-24.

excluded from the operations whereby reason formulates the concrete rules of action. This is the sense in which reason would then be "autonomous." On this view, faith exercises merely a parenetic function with respect to action, exhorting the person to follow what reason has autonomously recognized as good but without intervening in the determination of what is good or offering any instruction in its regard.

For moral theology the consequences of this approach, which tends to separate faith from morality, are very grave. In the first place, the properly theological sources of knowing (revelation, tradition, and the magisterium) would have to be rigorously excluded from the workings of ethics, which is conceived of mainly as normative ethics. In fact, any reference to authority of whatever type is, on principle, in opposition to the inescapable autonomous character of the decisions of conscience.

In the second place, faith, although acknowledged as the fundamental option of human freedom, is then paradoxically considered irrelevant for concrete actions. These, in turn, are then evaluated according to an empirical and materialistic criterion, foreign to the quality of the person's intention. Faith, separated from its contents, becomes formalistic, and concrete actions, separated from faith, lose every symbolic transparency.[5]

Moreover, whatever the effective intentions of these authors may be, autonomous reason as it is defined here in its nature and its task inevitably tends to deteriorate into a self-contradictory, fragmentary relativism the moment it begins formulating concrete moral judgments.[6] The adoption of normative ethical theories such as consequentialism and proportionalism,[7] frequent among these authors, leads to the negation of moral absolutes, which have always been affirmed in the Catholic tradition.[8] While the core of the moral experience escapes attention,

5. On this theme, see the sharp critique conducted by Giuseppe Angelini, "Il senso orientato al sapere: L'etica come questione teologica," in G. Colombo, ed., *L'evidenza e la fede* (Milan: Glossa, 1988), pp. 387-443, here pp. 425-30.

6. See Maurizio Chiodi, "La coscienza, l'agire, la fede: Oltre il dibattito sull'autonomia della morale," in G. Angelini and M. Vergottini, eds., *Invito alla teologia II — Teologia morale e spirituale* (Milan: Glossa, 1999), pp. 51-78.

7. See Bernard Hoose, *Proportionalism: The American Debate and Its European Roots* (Washington, DC: Georgetown University Press, 1987).

8. See William E. May, *Moral Absolutes: Catholic Tradition, Current Trends, and the Truth* (Milwaukee: Marquette University Press, 1989); John Finnis, *Moral Absolutes: Tradition, Revision, and Truth* (Washington, DC: Catholic University of America Press, 1991).

what takes center stage is the technical calculation of advantages and disadvantages that derive from the adoption of a certain course of action, considered as an external event that changes the state of affairs in the world.

The papal magisterium warned against these consequences, which are opposed to "healthy doctrine," reaffirming "the intrinsic and unbreakable bond between faith and morality" (VS 4)[9] and thus also reasserting the consequent authority held by revelation, tradition, and the magisterium in the determination of moral norms as well as the universal and immutable value of the moral commandments, particularly those that always and without exception forbid intrinsically evil acts (see VS 115). As we have already mentioned in a preliminary way, this reaffirmation is not fideistic but based on the "rational determination of the morality of human acting" established by the "doctrine of the object as a source of morality" (VS 82). In order to understand this moral object, it is necessary to situate oneself within the perspective of the acting person (see VS 78).

In this way, the encyclical *Veritatis Splendor* does not only denounce the consequences of the theological tendencies that support autonomy — consequences that are incompatible with Catholic morality — but it also identifies the direction to be taken for surpassing insufficient presuppositions on the theoretical level. In fact, the fundamental limitations of these theological tendencies are found on the level of epistemology and action theory. It is precisely here, however, that also the speculative insufficiency of the manualist tradition is found. In effect, autonomous ethics and normative morality share the same problem: posing the problem of the rules of just action, they take on the exterior perspective of a third person (a judge or confessor) called upon to judge the act. This is the point of view of modern ethics inaugurated by Thomas Hobbes and Francisco Suárez, which has lost the classical perspective, and in particular that of Saint Thomas, which is one of the "first person." Such a "first person ethics," developed from the perspective of the acting subject, understands the subject within his or her tension toward the good, seeing action as free praxis that is more or less compatible with the perfection of a life that is truly good and worthy of

9. For a critical panorama of the theological debate surrounding the encyclical, see Alberto Bonandi, *"Veritatis Splendor": Trent'anni di teologia morale* (Milan: Glossa, 1996), in particular, pp. 45-61.

the person.[10] An appropriate theory of moral action thus places itself within the person's existential and practical dynamism, which, through free action, is called to fulfillment in a human good worthy of the person's nature.

2. The Practical Dimension of Reason and the Inevitability of "Believing" in Order to Access the Truth about the Good

In the perspective of moral praxis that I have just outlined there is an unavoidable circularity between truth and freedom. In effect, the truth we are talking about here regards the good, that is, the "good of the person" as such. It is a truth that pertains to that praxis through which persons are fulfilled as persons. In a properly moral sense, the good of the person does not regard the acquisition of advantages or disadvantages obtained through a change in the exterior state of affairs but rather consists in the perfecting of human nature, which is constitutively incomplete, through freedom. It is the good that depends only upon the person's free self-determination; it is a "practical" good. As Carlo Caffarra affirms: "The final perfection of persons is an act of the person: the act through which persons — and no one else in their place — fulfill and actualize themselves."[11] This is the perfection of personal *being* as such, which is very different from the perfection of *having*. This is the good that is immanent to *acting* itself, which is distinct from the external result of *making*. The moral good is the good of the person freely realized in action. This is the level at which we can understand the incommensurability of the good of the person *ut persona* in respect to all other goods. "What will it profit a man, if he gains the whole world and forfeits his life?" (Mt 16:26).

In this sense, the cognitive element that aims at truth is situated within the tension of the whole person toward his or her good as a per-

10. Regarding this, see Giuseppe Abbà, *Felicità, vita buona e virtù: Saggio di filosofia morale* (Rome: LAS, 1989), pp. 97-104; and in the same sense, Martin Rhonheimer, *La prospettiva della morale: Fondamenti dell'etica filosofica* (Rome: Armando, 1994).

11. Carlo Caffarra, "'Primum quod cadit in apprehensione practicae rationis' (I-II, q. 94, a. 2): Variazioni su un tema tomista," in *Attualità della Teologia Morale: Punti fermi — problemi aperti, Studies in Honor of Rev. P. J. Visser, CSSR,* Studia Urbaniana 31 (Rome: Urbaniana University Press, 1987), pp. 143-64.

son. The truth referred to here is not any truth whatsoever but the truth about the very meaning of life. This is why freedom is neither indifferent nor foreign to it but is, from the beginning, involved in its perception. Moral evidence is mediated by the experience of freedom. In fact, the necessary price of perceiving the truth about the good is always risking oneself in real action.[12] "He who does the truth comes to the light" (Jn 3:21).

Aquinas's mature reflection, developed in *questio* 6 of *De Malo,* also serves to illuminate the mutual co-implication of the good and the true. He writes that formal causality, which specifies the act, belongs to the intelligence, whereas final causality, which commands free action, belongs to the will. In the apprehension of the good, we perceive the truth about its goodness, while in turn we grasp this perception of the truth about the good as a particular good, insofar namely as it is an end of the intellect. The *bonum,* the object of the will, and the *verum,* the object of reason, are reciprocally clarified and implied.[13]

Knowledge of the truth about that good which concerns the person as such demands its free determination and the practical risk of action. The entire person is involved in a unique exercise of his or her rationality. The great merit of Blondel's reflection on the necessity of practical mediation for access to the truth[14] is maintained in an integrally personalist perspective in which the intellect and the will are reciprocally connected.

Thus there emerges the need to overcome a twofold theoretical limitation proper to the modern tradition and shared with autonomous ethics: intellectualism and naturalism. Emphasizing the distinction of the faculties, intellectualism tends to assert a primacy of reason, independent from the will and the person's affective dispositions. For it, moral truth is deduced from metaphysical truth and the *ought* from the *is.* According to an essentialistic and naturalistic interpretation of the scholastic adage, "action follows being" *(operari sequitur esse),* speculative reason carries out a metaphysical analysis of human nature and discovers the order inscribed in it by God the Creator, which human per-

---

12. See Angelini, *Il senso orientato,* pp. 420-25.

13. Thomas Aquinas, *De malo,* q. 6: "Unde et ipsum bonum, in quantum est quaedam forma apprehensibilis, continetur sub vero quasi quoddam verum; et ipsum verum, in quantum est finis intellectualis operationis, continetur sub bono ut quoddam particulare bonum."

14. Maurice Blondel, *Action (1893): Essay on a Critique of Life and a Science of Practice,* trans. Oliva Blanchette (Notre Dame: University of Notre Dame Press, 1984).

sons would thus have the task of accomplishing by means of their will.[15] This is in consonance with the Stoic perspective expressed in the maxim *living according to nature.* These are the lines followed by the Spanish scholasticism of the sixteenth century (with proponents such as Gabriél Vásquez and Francisco Suárez), and, in our own days, also by Josef Pieper and others.[16] To the extent that this position is concerned with safeguarding the objectivity of moral truth, apparently offering a sure protection against widespread subjectivism, it is often completely identified with the position of the Catholic tradition in general and that of St. Thomas Aquinas in particular. And yet, Aquinas's thought, as has been thoroughly demonstrated, is quite different from it.[17]

In the crisis of metaphysics, the intellectualist position will be tempted to deduce moral values from empirical facts as are documented by the human sciences (psychology, sociology, cultural anthropology, etc.), thus proposing an unsound passage from what is statistically *normal* to that which is also ethically *normative.*[18] In this regard, we must recognize the element of truth that is present in the argument of the "naturalistic fallacy."[19] The argument, promoted by analytic philoso-

---

15. Josef Pieper, *Die Wirklichkeit und das Gute: Eine Untersuchung zur Anthropologie des Hochmittelalters* (Munich: Kösel, 1963), p. 70.

16. See Martin Rhonheimer, "Die Konstituierung des Naturgesetzes und sittlichnormativer Objektivität durch die praktische Vernunft," in *Persona, verità e morale: Atti del Congresso Internazionale di Teologia Morale (Roma 7-12 aprile, 1986)* (Rome: Città Nuova, 1987), pp. 859-84.

17. Regarding this, see Wolfgang Kluxen, *Philosophische Ethik bei Thomas von Aquin* (Hamburg: Meiner, 1980), pp. 21-71; Giuseppe Abbà, *Lex et virtus: Studi sull'evoluzione della dottrina morale di San Tommaso d'Aquino* (Rome: LAS, 1983); Livio Melina, *La conoscenza morale: Linee di riflessione sul Commento di san Tommaso all'Etica Nicomachea* (Rome: Città Nuova, 1987); Martin Rhonheimer, *Praktische Vernunft und Vernünftigkeit der Praxis: Handlungstheorie bei Thomas von Aquin in ihrer Entstehung aus dem Problemkontext der aristotelischen Ethik* (Berlin: Akademie Verlag, 1994).

18. The indispensable reference to the human sciences in the sphere of morality must always occur through the filter of an appropriate philosophical and theological anthropology that is capable of criticizing possible implicit ideological presuppositions in the sciences themselves and of eliminating the bias of their point of view with the perspective of a "complete human truth." At this level, which is not treated in the context of this chapter, the necessary contribution of philosophical reflection to moral theology can be appreciated. See John Paul II, *Veritatis Splendor*, n. 112.

19. G. E. Moore, *Principia Ethica* (Cambridge: Cambridge University Press, 1993), p. 12. On this see Giuseppe Abbà, *Quale impostazione per la filosofia morale? Ricerche di filosofia morale, I* (Rome: LAS, 1996), pp. 138-41.

phers, is based on what is called "Hume's Law," according to which it is impossible to pass from affirmations about what *is* the case to prescriptions about what *ought* to be done.[20] According to this approach, there is a great divide between facts and values, which ethical logic must respect.

While the expulsion of truth from ethics is erroneous, opening the door to irrational emotionalism, one must still recognize that moral goodness — which concerns being not as essence but as the result of free action — cannot be deduced from any metaphysically necessary component, even if it finds its ontological basis in it.[21] The adage that action follows being *(operari sequitur esse)* is an ontological, not an epistemological principle. Knowledge of the good to be freely achieved (the moral good as opposed to the ontological good) is an originally practical knowledge that occurs within a unique experience that persons have of themselves in their acting. Practical reason, therefore, is not a mere application of speculative knowledge but a specific way of knowing the good that occurs within the dynamic of the acting person's attraction to the good.

However, the element that allows us truly to appreciate the radical nature of the connection between truth and freedom in the practical perspective is formed by the context of interpersonality, within which moral experience is given. The moral good, toward which freedom is oriented, is the good of a communion that is initially given but completely achievable only through human action.[22] Confronted with the person of the other, freedom feels called upon because it is radically indebted and constitutively oriented toward fulfilling love in the communion among persons. The search for the truth about the good that is to bring about the communion among persons has as its necessary condi-

20. David Hume, *A Treatise on Human Nature,* III, I sect. 1 (Amherst, NY: Prometheus Books, 1992), pp. 455-70. The attribution of "Hume's Law" to David Hume is actually based on a misunderstanding: Nicholas Capaldi, *Hume's Place in Moral Philosophy* (New York: Peter Lang, 1990), pp. 55-95.

21. On the relationship between metaphysics and morality see Joseph de Finance, "Aux sources de la métaphysique et de la morale," chapter 5 of his *L'ouverture et la norme: Questions sur l'agir humain* (Vatican City: Libreria Editrice Vaticana, 1989), pp. 111-38.

22. Regarding this I refer to the first part of my *Cristo e il dinamismo dell'agire: Linee di rinnovamento della teologia morale fondamentale* (Rome: PUL-Mursia, 2001) and the study by Juan José Pérez-Soba, *Amor es nombre de persona: Estudio de la interpersonalidad en el amor en Santo Tomás de Aquino* (Rome: PUL-Mursia, 2001).

tion the freedom of recognizing the other as other and of willing the objective good for that other. Freedom's relationship to truth becomes dramatic precisely because freedom is related to the irreducibility of another personal freedom and not to things or concepts that can be grasped, controlled, and manipulated.

Thus we are presented with the inevitability of "believing," which, before it is a theological issue, is one of general anthropology, insofar as it is necessary for gaining access to moral truth.[23] Moral truth is vouched for by a series of convergent evidences that culminate precisely in the interpersonal dimension in which moral truth is given. The consideration of the temporal articulation in which moral experience occurs highlights how the fulfillment of the original promise of good, given to freedom in the encounter with the other, can take place only at the cost of faith, which believes, entrusting itself to the "voice" that is heard even during the hard times of trial. Acting in faith means accepting to obey the commandment on the basis of a rationality that does not consist in the autonomous possession of crystal clear evidence of the reasons for action. Full access to the truth about the good is mediated by a faith that accepts the risk of acting, believing in the original promise and in the invitation that it holds.

3. The Relevance of Christian Faith for Praxis

Let us now move on to consider faith in a properly theological sense, that is, as Christian faith, as the response of the entire person to God who definitively reveals himself in Christ Jesus.[24] The Christian faith possesses the intrinsic efficacy of a new operative principle for existence. Faith is the recognition of the gift that God makes of himself to human beings, redeeming and calling them to participation in the divine life, a gift that shows the absolute gratuity of his love for human persons (see Jn 3:16). Such a revelation is not the simple communication of truth

23. See Angelini, "Il senso orientato," pp. 423-25. See also his more recent and complete work, *Teologia morale fondamentale: Tradizione, Scrittura e teoria* (Milan: Glossa, 1999), pp. 640-51.

24. Vatican Council II, *Dei Verbum*, n. 5: "'The obedience of faith' (Rom. 16:26; see 1:5; 2 Cor. 10:5-6) 'is to be given to God who reveals, an obedience by which man commits his whole self freely to God, offering the full submission of intellect and will to God who reveals,' and freely assenting to the truth revealed by Him."

to the intellect but the offer of a personal relationship that calls upon and involves the entire person: intelligence, will, and affection. Inviting us to respond, God's grace opens the way to an active participation in this gift, renewing human freedom from within and giving it a Eucharistic form.[25] Grace is not a "thing" nor the gift of a fleeting moment, but it is, in itself, a *motus,* a dynamism that, when freely accepted, enters into synergy with the dynamisms proper to human action, reordering them and orienting them toward the supernatural goal of communion with God and with our brothers and sisters in God.

Far from eliminating practical reason and its demands, the Christian faith guarantees its full realization. Although taking the form of obedience, it is an act that fully conforms to reason and that does not exclude the demand for truthful evidence. What is avoided is the intellectualistic prejudice in the interpretation of this demand.[26] It is through practical obedience to God's commandments that faith grants us access to the truth, which is first given only as an initial promise. This is the meaning of Jesus' words to the Jews who had believed in him: "If you remain in my word, you will truly be my disciples, and you will know the truth, and the truth will set you free" (Jn 8:31-32). An intellectual disposition is not enough to know the truth that will set us free. What is needed is the concrete and permanent practice of discipleship that alone verifies the authenticity of the faith proclaimed.

Grace produces the act of faith in us, but the act is also, at the same time *(simul),* a free human act, a choice of our freedom.[27] This faith, which comes from our core, from our heart, is a "faith working through love" (Gal 5:6). Thus we can understand the intimate tie of faith to charity, which is the fulfilled form of the Christian life. If we are gratuitously justified by our faith and not by our works (Rom 5:1; Gal 2:16), nevertheless we will be judged "according to [our] works" (Rom 2:6). Understanding this paradox of Pauline theology means understanding the dynamic of Christian freedom.[28] As a free decision that involves the entire

---

25. For an illustration of the developments of theological anthropology following Vatican Council II's renewal of the concept of "revelation" see Angelo Scola, Javier Prades, and Gilfredo Marengo, *La persona umana: Antropologia teologica* (Milan: Jaca Book, 2000).

26. See Angelini, *Teologia morale fondamentale,* p. 644.

27. See Aquinas, *Summa theologiae,* I-II, q. 113, a. 3.

28. See Heinrich Schlier, *Linee fondamentali di una teologia paolina* (Brescia: Queriniana, 1995), pp. 160-62.

person at a radical level, faith is the Christian's "fundamental choice."[29] It does not remain extrinsic to our concrete choices but enters into them and specifies them through love of charity. It does not rest external and transcendental to particular acts but constitutes their determining principle. In this way one can overcome the extrinsicism characteristic of autonomous ethics, that is, the dichotomy between the fundamental norm and the material norms of action.

On the one hand, as St. Thomas says, "the movement of faith is not perfect unless it is quickened by charity."[30] Living faith generates hope and hope generates charity. On the other hand, charity is the efficient cause of faith inasmuch as the movement of the will is concerned. In this sense, without charity "faith . . . is dead" (Jas 2:26). In the sinner faith remains like a dead body, which has no soul to animate it and to permit it to express itself in the accomplishment of acts conducive to salvation.[31] The act of faith bears with it an intentionality that remains oriented toward God and that tends to express itself in deeds. It is again Aquinas who speaks of a "virtue of the first intention"[32] that lasts and that informs the believer's every choice and desire.

Living faith, animated by charity, provokes a dynamic oriented to corresponding works and choices. That is what St. Paul expresses in his letter to the Galatians when he speaks of "faith working through love" (Gal 5:6) and of the "fruits of the Spirit" (Gal 5:22), which are born in those who allow themselves to be led by him. In his commentary on the Pauline text, Aquinas says that the Christian life consists in charity, the cause of which is the Holy Spirit, who is welcomed by faith and who moves the human heart to do good. Good works are, in reality, an assent to the Holy Spirit. Christian freedom is adherence to the actual grace that moves it to choose the good. In *lectio* VI,[33] Aquinas explains that good works are more properly called "fruits" because they represent the final outcome of the seed of the Spirit, that is, the faith that was sown in

29. See Joseph Ratzinger, "Faith as Knowledge and Praxis — The Fundamental Option of the Christian Credo," in *Principles of Catholic Theology: Building Stones for a Fundamental Theology* (San Francisco: Ignatius Press, 1987), pp. 67-75.

30. Aquinas, *Summa theologiae*, I-II, q. 113, a. 4, ad 1: "Motus fidei non est perfectus nisi sit caritate informatus."

31. See Council of Trent, De Iustificatione, chapter 15 (Denzinger-Schönmetzer, *Enchiridion Symbolorum, definitionum et declarationum de rebus fidei et morum,* 1544).

32. Aquinas, *Summa theologiae*, I-II, q. 1, a. 6, ad 3: "Virtus primae intentionis."

33. Thomas Aquinas, *Super Epistolam ad Galatas lectura,* c. V, l. 6.

us at Baptism. They are the ultimate perfection toward which faith tends and which allows us to merit heaven. This is why they could also be called "flowers," because with their perfume and beauty, they anticipate in hope the greatest of fruits, that is, the beatitude of eternal life.

4. The Exercise of Practical Reason in Believing

In order to bring our reflection to a conclusion, we must now consider the ways that practical reason is exercised, with particular reference to how they are inherent to belief.[34] Moral knowledge, which has "the truth about the good" as its object, is distinguished from both a purely speculative knowledge (which regards being) and a technical knowledge (which regards *making* and not *acting*). The exercise of the practical reason finds expression in two moments. The first is a direct dimension that culminates in the virtue of prudence, and the second is an indirect dimension that takes the form of ethical science.[35] The first type of knowledge is that of virtuous persons and is directed toward accomplishing excellent human acts. As part of a community and a living tradition, educated by the virtues and having become intimately connatural to the good, such persons are capable of judging in the concrete particular what is the conduct appropriate for the multiple and changing circumstances in which they find themselves. Ethical science on the other hand concerns the philosopher and takes the form of a second-level reflection on the exercise of practical reason. Thus, beginning from the principles of natural law and from an evaluation of moral experience, ethics seeks to formulate universal conclusions. Even if incapable of reaching the concreteness of contingent action, it nevertheless represents an indispensable critical point of reference for the prevailing *ethos,* which does not always correspond to the demands of reason or the truth about the good. With reference to Aristotle, it has been justly noted that:

34. Here I return to some reflections that I proposed in a section of my article "'Verità sul bene'. Razionalità practica, etica filosofica e teologia morale: Da *Veritatis Splendor* a *Fides et Ratio,*" *Anthropotes* 15 (1999): 125-43.

35. See Melina, *La conoscenza morale,* pp. 221-31; Antonio Da Re, "Il ruolo delle virtù nella filosofia morale," in F. Compagnoni and L. Lorenzetti, eds., *Virtù dell'uomo e responsabilità storica: Originalità, nodi critici e prospettive attuali della ricerca etica della virtù* (Cinisello Balsamo: Edizioni San Paolo, 1998), pp. 55-79.

Practical philosophy places the *ethos* under discussion, even if it legit-imizes it as the basis of an ethics that is valid for virtuous persons. It could, in fact, be shown that — in regard to an entire series of funda-mental problems in ethics such as the supreme human good, the fam-ily, slavery, the use of riches, etc. — Aristotle often assumes, on the basis of practical philosophical considerations, positions that are in conflict with the prevailing *ethos*.[36]

As a consequence, practical reason, with its twofold expression in ethical science and in prudence, calls upon the virtues in a different de-gree, depending on the form it takes. If universal scientific knowledge of morality does not necessarily require the actual presence of the moral virtues in the person who seeks to attain it, prudence, which is the ulti-mate perfection of practical reason, cannot exist without the moral vir-tues. In principle, to acquire ethical science it is enough hypothetically to presuppose the human person's rational inclination to the good and deduce particular consequences from it. In its concrete application, however (and morality is fulfilled in determined judgments on concrete action), it is impossible to hit the mark without a suitable virtuous pre-disposition. On the other hand, it must be noted that also for the effec-tive exercise of universal moral knowledge the presence of the virtues is *practically* necessary to possess the evidence of the principles. In this sense, it is again Aristotle who sustained that whoever lives according to the passions is not a suitable listener to the lessons of ethics.[37] This im-plies that ethical science always has a more global than analytical aspect in which the reason that is at work is stimulated by the affectivity and nourished by a connatural knowledge, which it brings to critical aware-ness.[38] Thus we can understand Aquinas's observation that a society's bad customs can obscure and almost erase the principles of morality.[39] A people's *ethos* can come to deform the original moral sense of that people's members, causing them to lose the evidence of moral princi-ples and thus compromising not only their practical judgments but also their scholarly research.

36. Enrico Berti, *Aristotele nel Novecento* (Rome: Laterza, 1992), p. 219, cited in An-tonio Da Re, "Il ruolo delle virtù," p. 68.

37. See Aristotle, *Ethica Nicomachea*, 1.7, 1098b.

38. See Rafael Caldera, *Le jugement par inclination chez saint Thomas d'Aquin* (Paris: Vrin, 1980).

39. See Aquinas, *Summa theologiae*, I-II, q. 94, a. 4.

The human person, who has a nature, is at the same time also more than his or her common nature. Since persons are not merely exemplars of a species, their moral task is not only that of respecting the general moral norms. What is at stake here is not simply achieving the universal aspect of our nature but corresponding to a unique and very particular call that comes from the personal relationship that every human being has with God. Already at the level of universal moral norms elaborated by ethics, the constitutive limit of these very norms emerges. Concrete moral action does not have universal and unchanging essences for its object but choices that regard singular and contingent realities, which can vary in many ways because of the particular circumstances within which they are realized. Human actions regard singular and contingent things, which vary infinitely and cannot be subsumed under an identical general species.[40] In this sense, the universal norm is always the fruit of an abstraction that grasps the common species but leaves aside what is particular. This is why Aquinas clearly saw the *insufficiency of moral science as such* to give the ultimate direction to human action. In fact, according to the Aristotelian understanding, only universal and necessary realities — which allow for permanent connections to be determined among them — can be the object of scientific knowledge.[41] Human actions, instead, which are the object of moral knowledge, are realities that are variable in infinite ways, and thus cannot be arrived at on the level of science.[42] As regards concrete actions considered in their contingency, a demonstrative universal and necessary knowledge cannot be had of them. It is not possible to establish univocal connections by which to deduce necessitating conclusions from first principles. Concrete actions can be the object of advice but not of demonstration.

Attempting to come as close as possible to concrete action, modern ethics of the law, which inspired post-Tridentine Catholic manualist morality, developed a casuistry that offered paradigms to be applied to

---

40. See Thomas Aquinas, *Sententia libri Ethicorum,* VI, 1. See also Stephen A. Dinan, "The Particularity of Moral Knowledge," *The Thomist* 50 (1986): 66-84.

41. See Hans-Georg Gadamer, "Il problema ermeneutico e l'etica di Aristotele," chapter 4 of his *Il problema della conoscenza storica* (Naples: Guida, 1974), pp. 61-73.

42. See Aquinas, *Sententia libri Ethicorum,* VI, 3; Aquinas, *Summa theologiae,* I-II, q. 94, a. 5. On these aspects see Melina, *La conoscenza morale,* pp. 171-72, pp. 225-31; Klaus Hedwig, "Circa particularia: Kontingenz, Klugheit und Notwendigkeit im Aufbau des ethischen Aktes bei Thomas von Aquin," in *The Ethics of St. Thomas Aquinas* (Vatican City: Libreria Editrice Vaticana, 1984), pp. 161-87.

typical cases, making use of induction and beginning from moral experience. Using models that reflect an accumulated ethical experience, casuistry thus tried to compensate for the inevitable abstractness of the universal norm.[43] Nevertheless, the "case" inevitably remains an impersonal generalization that still does not adequately grasp the uniqueness of the situation, nor will it ever be able to do so. Casuistry must at any rate leave space for conscience to render the final judgment without leave of appeal. In this way conscience, in the name of the action's concrete singularity and the person's inalienable freedom, tends to oppose itself systematically to the law and the abstract universality of its precepts. In this type of hermeneutic model, human action is considered "from the outside" and is then placed in an extrinsic relationship with moral norms. Casuistry takes recourse to techniques of a substantially juridical application of the law to the case.

The concurring teaching of *Veritatis Splendor* (60-63) and *Fides et Ratio* (98) recalled the constitutive reference of conscience to a "truth about the good." This is a truth which precedes conscience, which it must honor, and which is the basis of its very dignity. However, this reference to the "truth about the good" requires a fundamental change of perspective for morality, a change that emphasizes the interior action from the point of view of the acting person. This is the point of view of the virtues, for which the culmination of practical reason is not the judgment of the conscience but the virtue of prudence.[44]

This is why practical reason is perfected in a form of knowing that is not scientific, namely in prudence, which alone is able to know the contingent precisely in its contingency and particularity. This is the virtue that, perfecting practical reason, allows it to grasp what is right in the concrete, overcoming the shortcomings of science. It is an intellectual virtue because it resides in practical reason, but it is also a moral virtue because it presupposes the rectitude of the appetite concerning the final end and the proximate ends. It is precisely on the strength of this mixed nature that prudence predisposes a person connaturally to know the moral truth about the contingent and particular realities of action, providing action with effective direction in their regard. Scientific moral

---

43. See Klaus Demmer, "Erwägungen über den Segen der Kasuistik," *Gregorianum* 63 (1982): 133-40.

44. Regarding this see Servais Pinckaers, "Rediscovering Virtue," *The Thomist* 60 (1996): 361-78.

knowledge is thus more properly adapted to its object when it is structured as a reflection on the moral virtues and not mainly as an elaboration of norms. Nevertheless, prudence is not an isolated and incommunicable knowledge, detached from and opposed to that of moral science.[45] There is a science even of contingent things, which are never so particular as not to have universal and immutable aspects. Moral science as practical science can therefore, in light of the first principles of morality, express a normative judgment on these universal elements of action.

However, the need for the personal singularity of moral truth, to which the contemporary mentality is particularly sensitive, is completely realized in the *sequela Christi,* presented by *Veritatis Splendor* as *"the essential and primordial foundation of Christian morality"* (VS 19). It is in the encounter with Christ that the rational creature receives a unique name, a task, and a mission and thus, according to Hans Urs von Balthasar's anthropological perspective, becomes truly a "person" in the theological sense.[46] In following Christ, the spiritual subject is ever more personalized. The contingency of the call implied in the vocational circumstances demands the full appreciation of the virtue of prudence. It is prudence "in Christ," the real participation in his wisdom through the gifts of the Spirit, which make us attentive and sensitive to each of the suggestions of our Friend and which give us the ability to act in correspondence to the supernatural goal that has been gratuitously granted us.[47]

If the perfection of practical reason is found in the virtue of prudence, for Christians it is concretely realized in the new dimension of their being "in Christ" through faith, hope, and charity. Thomas explicitly affirms that there can be no true prudence without charity.[48] In fact, only charity allows human persons to be oriented toward their true final

45. On this subject see the work by Daniel Nelson, *The Priority of Prudence: Virtue and Natural Law in Thomas Aquinas and the Implications for Modern Ethics* (University Park, PA: Pennsylvania State University Press, 1992), which systematically compares a deformed idea of the natural law with an ethics of virtue. The result is an inductive understanding of prudence that is quite different from Aquinas's true thought.

46. Hans Urs von Balthasar, *Theo-Drama: Theological Dramatic Theory,* vol. 2: *The Dramatis Personae: Man in God,* trans. G. Harrison (San Francisco: Ignatius Press, 1990), pp. 377-81.

47. Aquinas, *Summa theologiae,* I-II, q. 108, a. 4: "Sed Christus maxime est sapiens et amicus"; see Romanus Cessario, *The Moral Virtues and Theological Ethics* (Notre Dame: University of Notre Dame Press, 1991), pp. 60, 76-79.

48. Aquinas, *Summa theologiae,* I-II, q. 62, a. 2.

end, which is the condition for the exercise of prudence. Even more, according to Paul's letter to the Philippians, the capacity for discernment results from the abundance of charity: "that your love may abound still more and more in knowledge and all discernment — ἡ ἀγάπη ὑμῶν . . . περισσεύῃ ἐν ἐπιγνώσει καὶ πάσῃ αἰσθήσει" (Phil 1:9). In joining us to God as the goal of our desire, charity allows us also better to understand the value of human realities as paths to obtaining that end. This is why Augustine defines prudence as "a love that discerns"[49] and why Aquinas clarifies that love exercises discernment in that it compels the reason to discern.[50]

A suggestive comment that Origen makes in reference to the Book of Exodus (Ex 7:10-13)[51] places Christian prudence in relationship with *wisdom,* illuminating its original, or rather, paradoxical character in respect to human forms of sagacity. Aaron's staff, which changes into a serpent and devours the other serpents of the Egyptian magicians, is interpreted as Christ's cross, true wisdom (see 1 Cor 1:18). Upon coming in contact with earthly realities, this wisdom turns into a serpent, that is, into true prudence (see Mt 10:16), and destroys the many forms of false prudence that are of a purely human nature. True Christian prudence is not an expression of human caution but of the light of divine wisdom made manifest in Christ's cross and projected onto earthly realities. In its primary aspect, the gift of wisdom refers to the supernatural knowledge of divine things due to the infusion of the Holy Spirit; however, in reference to human realities and the human good, it turns into prudence and operates as such.[52]

Beyond the law, though never against the law, practical reason is fulfilled in the gifts of the Spirit and, particularly, in the gift of *wisdom,* which not only introduces divine realities to our knowledge but also allows us to judge human realities starting from charity.[53] It is also a participation in the supreme wisdom of the cross, spoken of in Paul's first letter to the Corinthians, a wisdom that conquers all human prudence with God's wise foolishness. It is the gift of *counsel* that corresponds to

---

49. Augustine, *De moribus Ecclesiae catholicae*, 1.15.25.

50. Aquinas, *Summa theologiae*, II-II, q. 47, a. 1.

51. Origen, *In Exodum homiliae*, IV.

52. See Aquinas, *Summa theologiae*, I, q. 1, a. 6; II-II, q. 47, a. 2, ad 1.

53. See John Paul II, *Fides et Ratio*, n. 44; Aquinas, *Summa theologiae*, II-II, q. 45, a. 1-2. Also concerning this theme see José Noriega, *"Guidados por el Espíritu": El Espíritu Santo y el conocimiento moral en Tomás de Aquino* (Rome: PUL-Mursia, 2000).

the virtue of prudence at the level proper to it, predisposing reason to being directly regulated and moved by the Holy Spirit in the discernment of the good regarding particular and contingent things.[54] This openness to the Spirit's suggestions, however, does not negate the rational and human level of prudence but rather aids and perfects it, respecting its natural light. Natural prudence is thus assumed and oriented toward its true objective in the supernatural perspective.

Practical reason then — in both forms that it takes on, i.e., as prudence and as ethical science — provides us with the foundational knowledge of the truth about the human good. Therefore, it offers an indispensable contribution to theological knowledge. While theological knowledge is founded on higher principles and thus certainly transcends and verifies natural practical rationality, the former can never contradict the latter's constitutive dynamics and must therefore incorporate it within its own structure. Reason can thus develop the exercise of its practical dimension in the light of faith, which fulfills the dynamism of human action in Christ beyond our every expectation.

54. Aquinas, *Summa theologiae,* II-II, q. 52, a. 1-2.

PART TWO

The Christological Fullness of Action

• IV •

Faith and the Moral Life: The Ways for Moral Theology to Overcome Extrinsicism

The Christian who lives by faith has the right to justify his moral actions on the basis of his faith. Since faith's content — namely, Jesus Christ, the revealer of a love that is triune and divine — has adopted both the form and the guilt of the First Adam, as well as the constrictions, perplexities, and crises of the latter's existence, the Christian is in no danger of failing to find the First Adam, and hence his own ethical problems, in the Second.[1]

In this famous text presented to the International Theological Commission in December 1974, Hans Urs von Balthasar reasserted the intrinsically Christian nature of morality, basing its connection to the faith on the Christocentric level, pointing to the correspondence between the first and the second Adam. The fullness of the Christological faith offers the most suitable perspective for illuminating from within the decisions of the life of human persons, who were created in Christ and are forever destined to Christ, so as to be "sons in the Son" (VS 18), according to Emile Mersch's meaningful expression, which *Veritatis Splendor* takes up again.[2] At the same time, the Christocentric horizon does not eliminate but rather requires a proper study of the human dimension of moral action, paying due attention to its specific, fundamental, and inescapable problems, so as to avoid being inconclusive.

1. Hans Urs von Balthasar, "Nine Propositions on Christian Ethics," in Heinz Schürmann, Joseph Ratzinger, and Hans Urs von Balthasar, *Principles of Christian Morality,* trans. G. Harrison (San Francisco: Ignatius Press, 1986), p. 77.

2. Emile Mersch, *The Theology of the Mystical Body* (St. Louis: Herder, 1955), p. 325.

1. The Problem of Extrinsicism and Its Roots

The necessity of ensuring the vital synthesis of faith and morality was also felt strongly during the Second Vatican Council, to the point that the Council Fathers affirmed: "One of the gravest errors of our time is the dichotomy between the faith which many profess and their day-to-day conduct" (GS 43). These words, which primarily reflect a pastoral concern, can also be well applied to the situation of post-Tridentine moral theology, which in its manualistic approach separated morality from dogmatics and spirituality, focusing on the topics of law and obligation, conscience and sin.

Does not the root of the separation between faith and everyday life, which was denounced by the Second Vatican Council, perhaps also lie in the minimalistic understanding of morality that characterizes the manualist tradition, in the mere juxtaposition of the human person's supernatural goal and the ethical demands of the natural law, and in the extrinsicism and positivism of ecclesiastic law? Even before the Council, Servais Pinckaers had outlined the structure of a renewal for moral theology through a *"ressourcement"* that was not limited to the rediscovery of the great texts of the biblical and patristic tradition but was first of all a rediscovery of the living source of the faith and of the gift of the Spirit, into which the dynamism of action is grafted.[3]

What steps are necessary to truly achieve such a renewal of moral thought, capable of overcoming the limits of the manualist tradition? The fact that the faith remained external to morality was not something accidental to be remedied by giving the traditional casuistic structure a superficial biblical paint job or by simply adding some theological premises to it. Although it grasped the problem and pointed in the right direction, Fritz Tillmann's pioneering attempt in the 1930s nonetheless also demonstrated the insufficiency of a "material Christocentrism" and the need for a much deeper elaboration of theological and anthropological categories from within the moral perspective.[4] How should we think of human action and how should we think

3. Servais Pinckaers, *Le renouveau de la morale: Études pour une morale fidèle à ses sources et à sa mission présente* (Paris: Téqui, 1979), pp. 13-25.

4. See Fritz Tillmann, *Die Idee der Nachfolge Christi* (Düsseldorf: Schwann, 1934). The limitations of his attempt were revealed by Louis Bertrand, *Christ and Moral Theology* (New York: Alba House, 1967). For a general outline of the question see chapter 5, "Bilancio e prospettive del cristocentrismo in morale," of my *Cristo e il dinamismo*

of the faith in a way so as to avoid their remaining two dimensions extrinsic to one another?

Thirty years after the Council and after half a century of attempts to renew moral thought, John Paul II's encyclical *Veritatis Splendor* denounces once again as one of the two decisive factors of the crisis in which Catholic moral theology still finds itself the "opinion . . . frequently heard which questions the intrinsic and unbreakable bond between faith and morality" (VS 4). The other factor is the attempt to detach "human freedom from its essential and constitutive relationship to truth" (VS 4).

In effect, those attempts at renewal, although worthy and admirable in many respects, at times have reached dead ends and positions contrary to "sound doctrine." Fundamentally, the question of the intimate and vital unity between Christian faith and moral action was unresolved or had found solutions that were not completely satisfying. As faith remained external to morality in the post-Tridentine manualist tradition, so it did in the so-called "new morality."[5] The reason for this is to be found in certain presuppositions that are inadequate both in the way they understand human action and in the manner in which they reflect theologically on the faith in its connection to action. We can comprehend these insufficiencies by looking at two currents that have dominated the recent panorama of Catholic moral thought: proportionalism and autonomous morality, of which one can also find various forms of crossbreeds.

Proportionalism seeks an argument that justifies the rectitude of human actions on the basis of a calculation of the pre-moral goods and evils that derive from them.[6] Separating a person's *goodness* from the

---

dell'agire. Linee di rinnovamento della Teologia Morale Fondamentale (Rome: PUL-Mursia, 2001), pp. 91-111.

5. Regarding this see Romanus Cessario, "Casuistry and Revisionism: Structural Similarities in Method and Content," in *"Humanae vitae": 20 anni dopo, Atti del II Congresso Internazionale di Teologia Morale* (Milan: Ares, 1989), pp. 385-409.

6. For a presentation of the theory and the debate see Bernard Hoose, *Proportionalism: The American Debate and Its European Roots* (Washington, DC: Georgetown University Press, 1987). Given the relevance the text has had for the debate, I would also like to indicate the essay by Josef Fuchs, *"Intrinsece malum: Überlegungen zu einem umstritten Begriff,"* in W. Kerber, ed., *Sittliche Normen: Zum Problem ihrer allgemeinen und unwandelbaren Geltung* (Düsseldorf: Patmos, 1981), pp. 74-91. Servais Pinckaers also weighs in on the discussion in his *Ce qu'on ne peut jamais faire: La question des actes intrinsèquement mauvais. Histoire et discussion* (Fribourg-Paris: Editions Universitaires Fribourg/Du Cerf, 1986).

rightness of that person's acts, this theory reduces the objective moral judgment to a consideration of the external act from a technical perspective. Insofar as what matters is the rightness of the act, "acting" is reduced to "making," and the person is separated from his or her acts. In this way too, the perspective of a properly moral finality is abandoned.

In this sense, proportionalism and casuistry substantially share the same exterior approach to human action, the latter considering morality an accidental quality of the exterior act deriving from its comparison with the law.[7] By measuring the morality of action on the basis of its conformity to the law and of the rules of the law's application, as does casuistry, or on the basis of its consequences, as does proportionalism, both theories look at action from without, thus separating it from the finalistic dynamism of intentionality and isolating it like a crystallized atom. Hence we can well understand how faith remains extrinsic to ethical reflection, a reflection that is limited to the normative dimension.

On the other side, we need to deal with the radical objection to the influence of faith on morality that is raised by the so-called "autonomous morality" inspired by Kant.[8] According to this position, the rational and free dignity of action is respected only when the human person gives the moral law to him- or herself, without receiving it from any external authority. In this way, faith can have a general and formal influence upon subjective motivations, but it has nothing to say about the determination of an action's material content. At this level, reason alone is competent. Therefore, a reference to God can in no way serve as a criterion for concrete moral discernment. Naturally, what on this view has to be excluded even more specifically is a reference to the God who has revealed his will in Tradition and Sacred Scripture, which are authentically interpreted in the Church by the magisterium. In this perspective, what is "specifically Christian" is completely absorbed in what is "authentically human."[9] Faith is limited to subjectively and formally inspir-

---

7. See, for example, Dominicus Prümmer, *Manuale Theologiae Moralis secundum principia S. Thomae Aquinatis* (Freiburg im Breisgau: Herder, 1935), I, II, cap. III, a. 1, n. 9, pp. 67-68.

8. The reference here is to Alfons Auer, *Autonome Moral und christlicher Glaube* (Düsseldorf: Patmos, 1971).

9. See the texts by Josef Fuchs, "Morale autonoma ed etica di fede," in Josef Fuchs, *Responsabilità personale e norma morale* (Bologna: Dehoniane, 1978), pp. 45-76; and Sergio Bastianel, *Autonomia morale del credente: Senso e motivazioni di un'attuale tendenza teologica* (Brescia: Morcelliana, 1980).

ing an action that receives its determining content from autonomous reason common to all human persons. This is why, from the point of view of exterior action, nothing distinguishes a Christian from a non-Christian. In the words of Karl Rahner: "to be a Christian is simply to be a human being, and one who also knows that this life which he is living, and which he is consciously living, can also be lived even by a person who is not a Christian explicitly and does not know in a reflexive way that he is a Christian."[10]

We have thus come to the ultimate root of the extrinsicism between faith and morality. It lies in a theological problem raised historically by Lutheranism: the relevance of human works in view of salvation. If the sinner's justification before God occurs through the gratuitous attribution of divine justice, which God concedes the sinner by faith in Christ's merits, then persons are saved only by the act of trusting abandonment, while their works contribute nothing. According to the Father of the Reformation, "good works do not make a good man, but a good man does good works."[11] Before God, therefore, it is faith alone that determines the identity of persons and not their works, with respect to which the Christian is now free. Ethics thus comes to lose every decisive relevance for salvation. It becomes a worldly affair that has to do with social and political relationships. It becomes a science that regulates communal life in view of the earthly good of society. Morality is thus reduced to a secular problem, that is, the calculation of what promotes society's exterior and temporal welfare.[12]

Identifying the deep historical and theoretical roots of the extrinsicism between faith and the moral life — here only hinted at in summary fashion — also outlines the task of a moral theology that truly

10. Karl Rahner, *Foundations of Christian Faith: An Introduction to the Idea of Christianity* (New York: Crossroad, 1989), p. 430.

11. Martin Luther, *On Christian Liberty* (Minneapolis: Augsburg Fortress, 2003), p. 39.

12. See Berthold Wald, *Genitrix virtutum: Zum Wandel des aristotelischen Begriffs praktischer Vernunft* (Münster: LIT, 1986). Giuseppe Abbà, *Quale impostazione per la filosofia morale? Ricerche di filosofia morale,* vol. 1 (Rome: LAS, 1996), shows how the theological utilitarianism of the Scottish Anglican Clergy was the first example of utilitarian ethics and constituted the decisive link for the passage to classical philosophical utilitarianism. Thus it can also be seen how the presupposition for accepting proportionalism in Catholic moral theology was precisely the secularization of ethics that came about by the acceptance of the Protestant separation between "the order of salvation" *(Heilsethos)* and "the worldly ethical order" *(Weltethos).*

desires renewal. First of all, it means understanding human action in a new way, in its finalistic dynamism and as an expression of the person. Second, it means seeking an understanding of the faith that allows us to see it as an authentic operative principle. These are the two steps, then, to be accomplished in the following reflection.

2. The Perspective of the Dynamism of Action

At precisely this point we are able to appreciate the contribution of the perspective developed by Aquinas in the second part of his *Summa theologiae*.[13] This is what some moral scholars of Fr. Pinckaers's school have done in the past decades. Naturally, it was necessary to overcome neo-scholasticism's reductive approach to Thomist moral thought, an approach that brought presuppositions to Aquinas's work that were proper to modernity, emphasizing mainly the treatises on the law and on conscience and, secondarily, those on acts, which were considered with respect to their imputability. What was necessary instead was to rediscover St. Thomas's global point of view on human action in all its originality and innovative force as he introduced it in the *prima secundae* of his *Summa theologiae*.

At the root of the movement that provokes human action lies the unique attraction of the good. This attraction is made possible by affective union, which is the elementary level of the experience of love. This experience implies that there is an initial enrichment of the person who bears within him- or herself a promise of fulfillment and happiness. This is certainly not just any kind of happiness, but authentic happiness, which alone can appease human desire and which can come to meet us only as a gift, a gift that surpasses every human expectation and at the same time corresponds extraordinarily to what is in our heart. The loving vision of God, in beatific communion with him — this is the answer brought by Christian revelation to the question of happiness that is at the root of human action. Faith in Christ, by which we acknowledge and accept such a surprising answer, is therefore at the most intimate heart of the dynamism of action. It becomes a light that directs our funda-

---

13. Servais Pinckaers, "Morale de l'obbligation et morale de l'amitié," in *Le renouveau de la morale*, pp. 26-43. Also Giuseppe Abbà, *Lex et virtus: Studi sull'evoluzione della dottrina morale di San Tommaso d'Aquino* (Rome: LAS, 1983), pp. 142-225.

mental intentionality toward the goal of life. Faith offers human free-dom the perspective of its fulfillment in communion with God and the ideal of a good life in communion with others, our brothers and sisters, because they are children of the same Father. The human will, then, is not primarily the faculty of choosing indifferently one thing over an-other. Rather, it is the energy of love that, through action, seeks to reach the Beloved.

The intimate connection between faith and the moral life is thus not established from without — by a normative imposition regarding single deeds — but from within, that is, from within the dynamism of action itself, which is substantially a dynamism of love aiming at the commu-nion with the Beloved and, in him, with other persons. It therefore be-comes clear that love cannot content itself with the minimum required by the law, but in every single act seeks the excellence that contains an anticipation and foretaste of communion. Beyond the respect of limits, Christian morality promotes the creativity of love and the personal and unique response that each of us is called to give to the Love that has re-vealed itself to us.

Such creativity and excellence, however, demand a perfection of hu-man freedom that is not given naturally. Instead, it must be patiently built and developed in synergy with divine grace. The perspective of the acting person demands a focus on the interior principles of action and on the affective dimension, which sustains and characterizes the dyna-mism of action. Very much in contrast to an autonomistic understand-ing of freedom, what must be valued here is precisely its historical and creaturely condition. The movement of action springs forth from the encounter with reality, from the attraction that reality provokes, and from the passions that are consequently stirred in us. These are a re-source for action and not an obstacle to it, because they contribute to its construction. However, they must find a light and an orientation in or-der not to be destructive. They must be formed and integrated into the perspective of the truth about the good of the person, that is, they must become virtues.

If freedom is fundamentally a capacity for love, then the moral vir-tues are the strategies of love.[14] They are not habits that limit the possi-bilities of choice but qualities that allow freedom to fulfill itself as a gift

---

14. Paul J. Wadell, *The Primacy of Love: An Introduction to the Ethics of Thomas Aqui-nas* (Mahwah, NJ: Paulist Press, 1992), p. 90.

within the concrete and varied choices of the moral life. Understood from this perspective, the moral virtues do not enclose us within a search for individualistic self-perfection but rather open us to a dynamic of communion that has for its goal the gift of self in charity.[15]

The concept of integration helps us to understand what is referred to here.[16] This concept refers to a multiplicity of operative dynamisms that must be guided and led back to unity in order to produce action that truly corresponds to the person and that is capable of expressing the person in his or her movement toward the goal. This unity will be both dynamic and hierarchic. It will be a dynamic unity because precisely in the movement of action all the factors that make action possible must converge — affections, motivations, capacities, and circumstances. It will be a hierarchic unity because it will be based on the primacy of the meaning of action in view to its end.

Personal unity, which is expressed in the totality of the act of love, will therefore follow a twofold line of development in order to arrive at integration.[17] On the one side, there is the affirmation of the truth about the good, inasmuch as reason directs the affections to attain this good. Here, however, it is important to note that practical reason, which grasps the truth about the good of the person, is rooted in the moral virtues themselves, which thus do not play a mere executive role subsequent to knowledge, but one that is constitutive of knowledge in the construction of excellent action.[18] On the other side, integration can come about by means of the bond with the beloved. In fact, through action, greater union with the beloved is sought. In this regard we can fully recognize the role of love, and in particular that of charity, as the guiding principle of our actions. For St. Thomas, prudence is fully a virtue and can properly carry out its decisive function in action only when

15. See José Noriega, "Las virtudes y la comunión," in Livio Melina, José Noriega, and Juan José Pérez-Soba, *La plenitud del obrar cristiano: Dinámica de la acción y perspectiva teológica de la moral* (Madrid: Palabra, 2001), pp. 403-11.

16. Regarding this see Karol Wojtyla, *The Acting Person*, trans. A. Potocki (New York: Springer, 2000), pp. 189-267.

17. Besides the classic study by Conrad A. J. van Ouwerkerk, *Caritas et ratio: Étude sur le double principe de la vie morale chrétienne d'après S. Thomas d'Aquin* (Nijmegen: Janssen, 1956), see also the recent book by Michael Sherwin, *Charity and Knowledge in the Moral Theology of St. Thomas Aquinas* (Washington, DC: Catholic University of America Press, 2005).

18. On this see my essay, Livio Melina, "Verità sul bene: Razionalità practica, etica filosofica, e teologia morale," in *Cristo e il dinamismo dell'agire*, pp. 53-67.

charity is present, establishing the acting person's orientation toward the final end.[19]

In this way the interpersonal dimension becomes relevant to the very heart of action, which is why we can speak not only of a "morality of the first person" but also of a "morality of the second person."[20] Thus the door is opened wide to understanding the role of friendship — and of friendship with Christ, that is, charity — in the construction of action. A "morality of friendship" is precisely what Fr. Pinckaers had begun to speak of many years ago.

3. Faith as a New Operative Principle

Now we must develop a second series of reflections, which will allow us to grasp the value of faith as a "new . . . criterion for . . . acting" (VS 88), in the words of the expression used by John Paul II. The biblical word that will shed a guiding light on our reflection comes from Paul's letter to the Galatians: "faith working through love" (Gal 5:6).[21]

Our point of departure can be the return to the general anthropological figure of faith that is situated at the root of action and that at the same time constitutes the presupposition for understanding the Christian faith in the specific sense.[22] Moral experience arises from the gift of a first encounter with the good and from the attraction that this good awakens in us. In its initial givenness, however, this good is offered to us as a simple promise. It appears to us as a suitable object of aspiration, but it does not present itself as a given fact that is completely comprehensible to us, tangible to our senses and within the grasp of our concepts. Between our action and the attainment of the happiness that we

---

19. See Thomas Aquinas, *Summa theologiae,* I-II, q. 65, a. 2; as well as II-II, q. 47, a. 13.

20. The term comes from Paul Ricoeur, "Sympathie et respect: Phénoménologie et éthique de la seconde personne," *Revue de métaphysique et de morale* 59 (1954): 380-97; the presence of such a perspective in Aquinas is documented in the study by Juan José Pérez-Soba, *Amor es nombre de persona: Estudio de la interpersonalidad en el amor en Santo Tomás de Aquino* (Rome: PUL-Mursia, 2001).

21. On this see Heinrich Schlier, *Lettera ai Galati* (Brescia: Paideia, 1966), pp. 241-43 (orig. German: *Der Brief an die Galater: Übersetzt und erklärt von H. Schlier,* Meyers Kommentar VII [Göttingen: Vandenhoeck & Ruprecht, 1962]).

22. Regarding this see Giuseppe Angelini, "Il senso orientato al sapere: L'etica come questione teologica," in G. Colombo, ed., *L'evidenza e la fede* (Milan: Glossa, 1988), pp. 387-443.

hope for yawns a gap that only the risk of faith can surmount. Maurice Blondel explored the mystery of human action, showing that evidence is given only in action itself at the cost of the supreme risk of faith.[23] In this way, he managed to overcome an intellectualistic understanding of moral truth that considers moral truth to be given prior to action and independently of the person's affective dispositions.

This is even more evident in biblical narrative, where the promised fulfillment infinitely surpasses human capacities and the reach of action. In the figure of Abraham, faith is expressed as trusting obedience to the word of him who can fulfill the promise, who can grant a son coming from a sterile woman, who can even raise that son from the dead (see Heb 11:8-19). The proportion between human action and its fulfillment is not empirically given but mediated by the obedience of faith, which is based on God's faithfulness. Truth is not a purely rational dimension or the property of a concept, but it is God's faithfulness to his word in the history of a covenant. The attainment of the fullness that we hope for is promised to us in symbolic anticipation and by the word of him who calls, promises, and asks us for obedience in order to accomplish his plan.

Biblical faith is never a purely theoretical believing, but it is always and necessarily expressed in action. In Sacred Scripture, believing means acting: leaving one's home country, accepting to carry out a sacrifice, leaving Egypt, obeying the words of the covenant. Only in action can we express our faith in God because "not everyone who says to me, 'Lord, Lord,' will enter the kingdom of heaven, but only the one who does the will of my Father in heaven" (Mt 7:21). This is why Jesus' great moral discourse, the Sermon on the Mount, ends with the admonishment that a solid construction of one's life is based on the unity between listening and putting what has been heard into practice; otherwise one would be building on sand rather than rock (see Mt 7:24-27). The true disciple who follows Jesus is the one who expresses his faith in practice. Here, let us note, however, that the wise man who builds his house upon the rock is first of all Christ himself, who in building his Church lays as foundation the incontestable unity of faith and the moral life.[24]

---

23. See Maurice Blondel, *Action (1893): Essay on a Critique of Life and a Science of Practice,* trans. Oliva Blanchette (Notre Dame: University of Notre Dame Press, 1984).

24. Joseph Ratzinger, *To Look on Christ: Exercises in Faith, Hope, and Love* (New York: Crossroad, 1991), pp. 57-62.

Thus we return once more to the Christological dimension of the faith as the foundation of its unity with life. It is precisely the definition of faith presented in the conciliar constitution *Dei Verbum* that recalls the crucial personalist and existential dimension of the faith. The Council Fathers say, "'The obedience of faith' . . . 'is to be given to God who reveals, an obedience by which man commits his whole self freely to God, offering the full submission of intellect and will to God who reveals,' and freely assenting to the truth revealed by Him" (DV 5). Without denying the dimension pertaining to the content of the truth to be believed — which is recognized by the "submission of intellect and will" — the Second Vatican Council emphasizes the more fundamental personalist aspect of the faith, which implies the abandonment of the whole person to God who has revealed himself in the person of Jesus.

The Christian faith, therefore, takes the specific shape of a relationship with Jesus — recognized as the Father's Son and the way to reach him — and is expressed in a personal abandonment and in obedience to him, in a path of discipleship that becomes praxis and is expressed in action. But how does faith become an operative principle?

"Faith begets hope and hope charity," Aquinas affirms, in harmony with the tradition that precedes him.[25] The unity of the person in his or her acting is the principle that allows us to understand the relationship between the three theological virtues, among which faith has the precedence of origin. Still, in their personal significance faith and hope find their ultimate support in charity, since it is only in charity that the fullest meaning of virtue — that of uniting us to God — is achieved.[26] In this sense, we understand the assertion that love is the mother and root of all the virtues, being their very form. Aquinas even goes so far as to say that without charity, faith is not truly a virtue. In fact, it is charity that gives unity and complete meaning to the entire moral life. And not just that: even as regards the order of the generation of the theological virtues, faith is preceded by a germinal and imperfect form of love, which then — once the act of faith and hope has been accomplished — can be assumed and perfected in charity.[27]

We can thus see the unique significance of affective union, which

---

25. See Aquinas, *Summa theologiae,* I-II, q. 66, a. 6, which cites the *Glossa.*

26. See Aquinas, *Summa theologiae,* I-II, q. 62, a. 4: "Ordine vero perfectionis, caritas praecedit fidem et spem, eo quod tam fides quam spes per caritatem formatur, et perfectionem virtutis acquirit."

27. See Thomas Aquinas, *Quaestio disputata de caritate,* q. 1, a. 3c e, ad 12.

has a direct connection to grace.[28] According to St. Thomas, it is precisely faith in Christ that opens the possibility of the intimate presence of the Spirit, who becomes the guide for our acts. This is the specific and primary element of the new law.[29] The dynamic of the integration of the affectivity, which was already implied in the Aristotelian concept of virtue, is hence brought to perfection in a specifically supernatural dimension. Faith, aroused by a first, imperfect love, recognizes by a gift of the Holy Spirit the good that constitutes the goal of its aspirations and its love — communion with God. Thus it is the deepest source of the dynamism of Christian morality. In fact, it establishes our actions' ultimate goal and thus animates their intentionality from within. Together with Fr. Romanus Cessario, we can say that "the act of faith constitutes such an entelechy in action" as to inform the entire dynamism of the virtues.[30] Through love and the entire organism of the moral virtues, faith thus becomes a true operative principle, which guides Christian action and confers a supernatural value on it.

The act of faith, produced in us by grace, is also at the same time (*simul* in Aquinas's words)[31] a free human act, a choice of our freedom. *Veritatis Splendor* puts it this way: "Faith is a decision involving one's whole existence" (VS 88). Or with Joseph Ratzinger we can say that faith, in establishing life within the horizon of a relationship with the Thou of God, is a Christian's fundamental option.[32] The act of faith implies an intentionality that remains oriented toward God and tends to be expressed in deeds. It is again Aquinas who speaks of a "virtue of the first intention"[33] that remains and that informs the believer's every desire and every choice. In fact, our first free act establishes the ultimate horizon of our choices and thus configures on the intentional level the dynamic of action that is then developed through the virtues.[34]

28. See Pérez-Soba, *Amor es nombre de persona*, pp. 587-625.

29. See Aquinas, *Summa theologiae*, I-II, q. 106, a. 1.

30. Romanus Cessario, *The Moral Virtues and Theological Ethics* (Notre Dame: University of Notre Dame Press, 1991), p. 24.

31. Aquinas, *Summa theologiae*, I-II, q. 113, a. 3.

32. See Joseph Ratzinger, *Principles of Catholic Theology: Building Stones for a Fundamental Theology* (San Francisco: Ignatius Press, 1987); Juan José Pérez-Soba, "La fe como 'elección fundamental'," in Melina, Noriega, Pérez-Soba, *La plenitud del obrar cristiano*, pp. 201-15.

33. Aquinas, *Summa theologiae*, I-II, q. 1, a. 6, ad 3: "Virtus primae intentionis."

34. See Aquinas, *Summa theologiae*, I-II, q. 89, a. 6; on this see Jacques Maritain, "The Immanent Dialectic of the First Act of Freedom," in *The Range of Reason* (New

*   *   *

Now we can finally gather the results of the path we have completed in order to understand faith's intrinsic connection to the moral life. The paths taken by moral theology, not without interruption and dispersion, have been able to explore more adequately both the specifically moral meaning of action and the personal dimension of the act of faith.

On the basis of the rediscovery of authentic Thomist doctrine as well as the contributions from phenomenological reflection and the so-called action theory,[35] moral theologians have become acutely aware of the originality of the moral perspective,[36] of the specific nature of practical reason, and of the virtues as constitutive principles of action. This new approach allows us to discern the possibility of an intimate relationship between the moral life and faith, precisely because this approach knows how to appreciate the light that the faith gives to human intentionality, which animates the entire practical dimension.

Besides, theological reflection has freed the faith from an intellectualistic reduction, both as virtue and as act, resituating it within the personalist horizon of a relationship that commits the entire person of the believer to the person of Jesus. Grasped within the dynamic horizon of the growth of charity, faith appears as the Christian's fundamental choice, which elicits a response that implies one's entire life and which remains as an orientation in action.

Assuming charity and the virtues as necessary mediations of the working of the faith, as suggested here, allows us to avoid the two competing ways of one-sidedly and extrinsically opposing faith and morality. On the one hand, there is the aesthetic absolutization of the moment of faith, which does not take seriously the dynamic of action and practical reason and thus remains inconclusive, an abstract anthropological affirmation that is not mediated at the level of the principles proper to action. On the other hand, there is an approach that closes the ethical perspective into a kind of self-sufficiency that confines the horizon of

---

York: Scribner, 1952), chapter 6; and Cornelio Fabro, "La dialettica d'intelligenza e volontà nella costituzione esistenziale dell'atto libero," in *Riflessioni sulla libertà* (Rimini: Maggioli, 1983), pp. 57-85.

35. On this subject I would like to indicate Gertrude E. M. Anscombe, *Intention* (Oxford: Blackwell, 1957).

36. See Martin Rhonheimer, *La prospettiva della morale: Fondamenti dell'etica filosofica* (Rome: Armando, 1994).

faith to something that simply adds to subjective motivation or to something that is merely decorative. Neither position offers the basis for a true moral theology but, respectively, gives place to either a theological anthropology that abandons action to the intuition of subjective conscience, or to a rational ethics that is sufficient in itself, even if it can possibly be completed by a theological addition.

From the perspective of the "faith that works through love," suggested here, it is instead possible to fully honor the main task that Joseph Ratzinger drew up for moral theology, namely that of thinking "the collaboration of human and divine action in the full realization of the human person."[37]

---

37. Joseph Ratzinger, *La via della fede: Le ragioni dell'etica nell'epoca presente* (Milan: Ares, 1996), p. 98; see also the essays by Joseph Ratzinger, "Il rinnovamento della teologia morale: prospettive del Vaticano II e di *Veritatis splendor*," and Antonio Cañizares Llovera, "L'orizzonte teologico della morale cristiana," in Livio Melina and José Noriega, eds., *Camminare nella Luce: Prospettive della teologia morale a partire da Veritatis Splendor* (Rome: Lateran University Press, 2004), pp. 35-45 and pp. 47-61.

V

Christ as the Fullness of the Human Good and Morality

"Why do you call me good?" (Mk 10:18, Lk 18:19). The question about the good to be done in order to have eternal life that the rich young man puts to Jesus is not addressed to any teacher whatever but, according to Mark and Luke's narration, to the "good" teacher.[1] In this way, the evangelists clarify the reason why that question was addressed to Jesus. The young man had seen in him much more than an expert in the law or a simple example to imitate. His ability to suitably respond to the question about the good was presumed to come from his intimate personal quality of familiarity with the Good. The apparent denial expressed in Jesus' first response means, fundamentally, a much more substantial invitation to discover the depth of the experience of encounter by which the very question had been provoked: "No one is good but God alone" (Mk 10:18, Lk 18:19). In his encounter with Jesus, a fullness of the good was revealed to the rich man, a fullness that can have its ultimate root only in God, but that is at the same time also a manifestation of the human good that attracts the person and tends to permeate his free action. The path of the good is the only one that can lead to eternal life.

The invitation to look to Christ in order to find the fullness of the moral good is constantly reiterated in recent Church teaching, so for instance in reference to the desired renewal of moral theology.[2] *Gaudium et Spes,* in a passage of clearly Christocentric inspiration, affirms: "Christ,

---

1. According to the version of the Ephrem (C) manuscript and other witnesses, Matthew 19:16-19 should also include the reference to Jesus as the "good teacher."
2. See John Paul II, *Veritatis Splendor,* nn. 8, 117.

the final Adam, by the revelation of the mystery of the Father and his love, fully reveals man to man himself and makes his supreme calling clear" (GS 22). It is in the perspective of the faithful's "supreme calling in Christ" that the conciliar decree on priestly formation,[3] too, invited scholars to perfect moral theology.

Now, the "fullness of the human good," as Jesus' questioner well understood, has to do with the person's identity in that it is freely pursued and achieved by action.[4] We will now seek to shed new light on this issue, placing ourselves within a theological perspective, or better, an explicitly Christological one. Exploring the assertion that gives the title to this chapter, we will study two fundamental questions that will be the central points of this exposition.

In the first place, what is it that the reference to Christ allows us to grasp about the fullness of the human good entrusted to action that goes beyond a merely rational consideration? It is the question of the newness unveiled in Christ, a question that obviously also implies the problem of the justification and the appropriate modalities of such a Christocentric reference.

In the second place, how can the Christocentric dimension also integrate the necessary objective reference to the "nature of the human person and his acts" (GS 51) in the practical perspective of the dynamism of action? This is the question of how to integrate the rational dimension relative to determining the "goods for the person" into Christian action.

The theological question of moral Christocentrism is posed as the foundational hermeneutical horizon within which the problems of the "good of the person" and the "goods for the person" can find their ultimate clarification and the context for a suitable relationship. This is a verification of the possibility for and the modalities of a Christocentric

3. Vatican Council II, *Optatam Totius*, n. 16. Regarding this see Philippe Delhaye, "Les points forts de la théologie morale à Vatican II," *Studia Moralia* 24 (1986): 16-18.

4. The personalist nature of the human good demands that it depend only on self-determination without conditioning on the part of factors that are extraneous to freedom: "The final perfection of persons is an act of the person: the act through which persons — and no one else in their place — fulfill and actualize themselves"; Carlo Caffarra, "*'Primum quod cadit in apprehensione practicae rationis'* (I-II, q. 94, a. 2): Variazioni su un tema tomista," in *Attualità della Teologia Morale: Punti fermi — problemi aperti, Studies in Honor of Rev. P. J. Visser, CSSR,* Studia Urbaniana 31 (Rome: Urbaniana University Press, 1987), pp. 143-64.

foundation of natural law reinterpreted in personalist terms according to the coordinates of the acting person's practical perspective that is situated within the dynamism of action.

1. The Manifestation of the Fullness of the Human Good in Christ

The first of the questions just proposed has accompanied and troubled moral reflection during the last century, ever since the limits of a traditional manualist approach appeared in plain light. In fact, when constituting itself as an autonomous discipline,[5] moral theology established rather weak and extrinsic connections with Christology, preferring to position itself in reference to pure obligation defined on the basis of the rational principles of natural law, of the Ten Commandments, and of the precepts of the Church, leaving the task of clarifying the evangelical dimension of Christian life to spirituality (ascetical and mystical theology).[6] Moreover, moral theology was mainly conceived in view to preparing priests for the ministry of confession. Hence it was focused on practical applicability, an emphasis that tended to give it a legalistic and casuistic form of expression, void of intrinsic organization and integration.

a. First Approach: The Exemplarity of a Personal Model

It was the merit of Fritz Tillmann and his followers and collaborators in the first half of the last century to have sought to introduce a clear Christocentric reference into moral theology, which served as the theological and systematic principle from which reflection started.[7] For Tillmann, moral theology as the scientific exposition of the principles

---

5. See Johann Theiner, *Die Entwicklung der Moraltheologie zur eigenständigen Disziplin* (Regensburg: Pustet, 1970).

6. See Servais Pinckaers, "Qu'est-ce que la spiritualité?" *Nova et vetera* 1 (1990): 7-19.

7. Fritz Tillmann, *Die Idee der Nachfolge Christi* (Düsseldorf: Schwann, 1934); Theodor Steinbüchel, *Religion und Moral im Lichte christlicher personaler Existenz* (Frankfurt: Knecht, 1951). For a critical summary see Johannes Reiter, *Modelle christozentrischer Ethik: Eine historische Untersuchung in systematischer Absicht* (Düsseldorf: Patmos, 1984); Alberto Bonandi, "Modelli di teologia morale nel ventesimo secolo," *Teologia* 24 (1999): 89-138, 206-43.

of the Christian moral life must show "the immediate connection of ethical doctrine to the person of the Lord."[8] The essential elements of his proposal are clearly derived from Scheler: the principle of personal exemplarity *(Vorbildprinzip)* and the idea of the person's commitment toward this model.[9]

The particularity of a person we are meant to follow serves as a catalyst in the vital perception of values. The Jesus paradigm thus offers a "normative personality" *(normierende Persönlichkeit)* in relation to good and evil. Tillmann proposes a perfect identity between "that which is good" and "that which is conformed to Christ" *(christusförmig),* and correspondingly between "that which is evil" and "that which is contrary to him" *(christuswidrig).*[10] Of course, the personal ethical model should not be imitated in an extrinsic fashion but rather creatively assimilated as a basis for our own original formation.

The great progress that this new Christocentric approach marks in reference to both the naturalism of the late scholastic tradition and Kantian formalism lies in the personal character of the model *(Vorbild)* that serves to determine the moral good. The moral good is no longer defined as the fulfillment of the functions of the human operative faculties as it is the case in a naturalistic approach that attempts to determine the moral without taking personal freedom into account and that therefore deduces what is morally good from a metaphysical analysis of the constitutive principles of human nature. On the other hand, the moral good is not reduced to a purely formal element either, as if freedom, in its absolute rational autonomy, had as its only rule the dependence upon itself.[11] The category of the model grasps the good in its essential and profoundly personal dimension. It regards being and not simply doing; it appeals to the heart and not only the reason; it concerns the individual

8. Tillmann, *Die Idee der Nachfolge Christi,* pp. 10ff.: "Die unmittelbare Bindung der Sittenlehre an die Person des Herrn."

9. Max Scheler, *Formalism in Ethics and Non-Formal Ethics of Values: A New Attempt Toward the Foundation of an Ethical Personalism* (Evanston, IL: Northwestern University Press, 1973).

10. Tillmann, *Die Idee der Nachfolge Christi,* p. 12.

11. See André Léonard, *Le fondement de la morale: Essai d'éthique philosophique générale* (Paris: Cerf, 1991), pp. 128-29; Juan José Pérez-Soba, "Operari sequitur esse?" in Livio Melina, José Noriega, and Juan José Pérez-Soba, *La plenitud del obrar cristiano: Dinámica de la acción y perspectiva teológica de la moral* (Madrid: Palabra, 2001), pp. 65-83.

person in his or her existential concreteness and not just the fulfillment of general rules.[12] Nevertheless, this initial attempt at a Christocentric basis for moral theology still remains fragile and substantially incomplete, exposed to objections of noteworthy philosophical and theological weight.[13]

In the first place, a Christological basis of the moral good leaves open the question of universality. Hence, Kant maintained that examples had only an exhortative and no foundational value in the moral sphere.[14] We are thus invited to reflect on how this Christological basis of morality can be absolute — which is theologically speaking indispensable — and how one can respond to the Enlightenment objection according to which it is impossible to base universal and absolute truth upon singular historical events.[15] In what sense does assuming Christ as the reference point for defining the human good not render Christian morality something entirely specific and particular, invalidating from the start its claim to express universal truths that correspond to the demands of reason?[16]

12. It was above all Theodor Steinbüchel who developed this last perspective, emphasizing the concrete and individualized character of the precept *(Gebot)* along the lines of the current of thought called "situation ethics," which was then condemned by the magisterium (see Denzinger-Schönmetzer, *Enchiridion Symbolorum, definitionum et declarationum de rebus fidei et morum,* 3918-21). Regarding this see Alberto Bonandi, *Sistema ed esistenza: Il pensiero morale di Theodor Steinbüchel* (Brescia: Morcelliana, 1987).

13. See, for example, those advanced by Louis-Bertrand Gillon, "La théologie morale et l'éthique de l'exemplarité personnelle," *Angelicum* 34 (1957): 241-59, 361-78.

14. Immanuel Kant, *Groundwork of the Metaphysics of Morals* (Cambridge: Cambridge University Press, 1997), p. 21: "Imitation has no place at all in matters of morality, and examples serve only for encouragement, that is, they put beyond doubt the practicability of what the law commands and make intuitive what the practical rule expresses more generally, but they can never justify setting aside their true original, which lies in reason, and guiding oneself by examples."

15. See Gotthold Ephraim Lessing, "Sopra la prova dello Spirito e della forza," in M. F. Sciacca and M. Schiavone, eds., *Grande antologia filosofica,* vol. 15 (Milan: Marzorati, 1968), pp. 1557-59, cited in Angelo Scola, "Cristologia e morale," in *Questioni di antropologia teologica,* 2nd ed. (Roma: PUL-Mursia, 1997), p. 108.

16. This is the response to the moral Christocentrism advanced by the supporters of autonomy. Franz Böckle, *Fundamentalmoral* (Munich: Kösel, 1977), p. 234: "Die christologische Konzentration widersetzt sich einer normativen Verallgemeinerung." See also: Charles C. Curran, *The Catholic Moral Tradition Today: A Synthesis* (Washington, DC: Georgetown University Press, 1999), p. 31: "I also have problems using Jesus Christ as the stance because this approach has been used by some in the past to ground a very narrow Christology or Christomonism that gives little or no independent room or importance to the human."

This is the first task that the Christocentric approach of the "personal model" leaves unfinished.

In the second place, insofar as Tillmann and his followers immediately appeal to biblical citations that regard the inner motivations for action, their Christological approach does not succeed in penetrating to the concrete material content of action. In effect, when it comes to offering normative indications, Tillmann simply refers to the natural law as expounded in traditional manuals. For him, therefore, the Christocentric element refers only to the transcendental, subjective, and interior aspect, while the universality of an action's objective content must be ensured by reason. From this point of view, too, one can speak of an incomplete Christocentrism, which requires a better integration of the moment of content, i.e., the moment of the concrete "goods for the person" within the perspective of the revelation in Christ of "the good of the person."

We must therefore follow these two paths of inquiry: in the first place, how a single person can be the revelation of an absolute and universal human fullness; in the second place, what is the original type of human fullness of the good that Jesus Christ reveals to us in his actions?

b. The Filial Fullness of Christ's Action

Not every reference to Christ on the part of theological reflection suffices to qualify it as Christocentric. Even approaches that are rigorously based on the autonomy of practical reason can accept generic references of an exemplary kind. In order to come closer to the precise meaning in which to understand the Christocentric perspective here, we can recall the definition given by Giacomo Biffi in the context of dogmatic theology, but with a specific application to morality: Christocentrism "is the vision of reality that makes the humanity of the incarnate Son of God the foundational ontological principle of the whole creation, in all its levels and dimensions."[17] On the other hand, it is important to specify that the focus of Christocentrism is primarily methodological, in the strict sense of the word: It does not claim to account for the whole material content of theology, absorbing it into Christology (Christo-

17. Giacomo Biffi, *Approccio al cristocentrismo: Note storiche per un tema eterno* (Milan: Jaca Book, 1994), p. 11.

monism), but "it indicates the point of view from which to contemplate the form of Revelation."[18]

From the specific perspective of moral theology we must hence ask ourselves how Christ, who in his humanity as the incarnate Son of God is the foundational ontological principle of all reality, can also be the principle for understanding the fullness of the human good to be accomplished in action. This question, which remained unexplored in Tillmann's reflection, stands at the very beginning of our inquiry. In order not to remain outside the free dynamism of action, we must understand Christ's action in its singular humanity and, in it, contemplate the fullness of the good that it reveals.[19]

The rich young man of the Gospel narration understood Jesus to be the "good teacher,"[20] the manifestation of a "fullness of life" that can only come from his personal communion with the Father, the only one who is truly good. His human existence, entirely like ours except for sin, manifested the Son's perfect obedience to God's will, an expression of his communion with the Father in the Holy Spirit. Christ's human actions are the manifestations of a perfect docility to the Spirit (see Lk 4:1) and thus reveal the face of the Father, to whom they refer in the praise that they stir up in those who are their astonished witnesses (see Lk 4:15). His miraculous healings, his tender embrace of the little ones and the sick, his concern for the crowds, his attention to the very least, and, above all, the forgiveness offered to sinners reveal the Father's merciful face.

Jesus' response to Philip, "whoever has seen me has seen the Father" (Jn 14:9), also refers specifically to his action: "the Son can do

---

18. Angelo Scola, *Hans Urs von Balthasar: A Theological Style* (Grand Rapids: Eerdmans, 1995), pp. 59-60. See also Hans Urs von Balthasar, *La mia opera ed Epilogo,* trans. G. Sommavilla (Milan: Jaca Book, 1993): "Christ himself stands in the true theological center, in relation to which the world and creation receive their structure. . . . The one and only existential figure of Christ forms the center of history" (p. 55); Christ, the *universale concretum,* is the sole point that opens up unto the universal and cosmic Logos (p. 57).

19. See the perceptive contribution offered in this sense by José Noriega, "El camino al Padre," in Melina, Noriega, Pérez-Soba, *La plenitud del obrar cristiano,* pp. 157-68.

20. The original meaning of attributing the title of διδάσκαλος ἀγαθός to Jesus in respect to the meaning that successively came to characterize the Pharisaical "rabbi" is well argued in Martin Hengel, *The Charismatic Leader and His Followers,* trans. J. C. G. Greig (Edinburgh: T. & T. Clark, 1981). In this sense, the *sequela* that Christ proposes appears as a call to share his destiny, welcoming the announcement of the approaching kingdom, rather than as an invitation to enter into a relationship that joins the disciple to the master, the expert in the Torah.

nothing of his own accord, but only what he sees the Father doing; for whatever he does, that the Son does likewise" (Jn 5:19). Whoever contemplates Christ, above all in his form of a servant, thus reaches the Father, the radical source of all goodness. The very love for one's enemies that Jesus not only preaches to his disciples (Mt 5:43-48) but also practices in giving his life in the supreme act of his existence and in the form of the redemptive sacrifice on the cross (see Rom 5:8; Phil 2:6-8; Jn 13:1-20) makes manifest the perfection of the Father's love: "For God so loved the world that he gave his only Son" (Jn 3:16; Mk 15:39).[21]

Christ, therefore, does not propose himself as an absolute model except insofar as he is a divine person and the image of the Father. Only when his divinity is recognized can the universal and absolute character of his human action be understood and accepted. Only then can he, in the words of von Balthasar, be understood as the "concrete personal norm" of the moral life. In this way, the problem of the opposition of heteronomy and autonomy, which is inevitable in the face of a merely human exemplar, is overcome.[22]

The ethical principle of imitation, therefore, must be based on the principle of the unique image that Christ is of God. As Son, he resembles the Father and makes him manifest through his actions. This is exactly why he can claim to be imitated and followed. Beyond the conformity of simple obedience that is characteristic of the Old Testament, there emerges here something that is new and particular to the gospel. The justification of love for our enemies offered in Matthew ("that you may be children of your heavenly Father," Mt 5:45) prescribes the kind of likeness whereby the Son is similar to the Father and which allows us to discover in the Son the traits of the Father.[23] It is in precisely this sense that Augustine, in his commentary on the Sermon on the Mount, interprets this Gospel text Christologically and in view to imitation: "Therefore He does not say, 'Do those things, because you are sons' but 'Do those things, that you may be sons.' But

---

21. See Réal Tremblay, "Le Père, clé de voûte de la vie morale," in *L'élévation du Fils: Axe de la vie morale* (St. Laurent, Québec: Fides, 2001), pp. 99-117.

22. Hans Urs von Balthasar, "Nine Propositions on Christian Ethics," in Heinz Schürmann, Joseph Ratzinger, and Hans Urs von Balthasar, *Principles of Christian Morality,* trans. G. Harrison (San Francisco: Ignatius Press, 1986), pp. 77-81.

23. On the theme of the image of God as an ethical principle, see Ceslas Spicq, *Théologie morale du Nouveau Testament,* vol. 2 (Paris: Gabalda et C., 1970), pp. 688-744, which has abundant bibliographic references.

when He calls us to this by the Only-begotten Himself, He calls us to His own likeness."[24] Also according to the Apostle the principle of filiation is the ultimate basis of our imitation of God in Christ Jesus: "Therefore be imitators of God, as beloved children. And walk in love, as Christ loved us and gave himself up for us, a fragrant offering and sacrifice to God" (Eph 5:1-2).

The fullness of Jesus' action, therefore, is a filial fullness in the imitation of the Father, above all in his perfect charity with which he gratuitously loves even sinners: "So be perfect, just as your heavenly Father is perfect" (Mt 5:48). In Christ "dwells the whole fullness of the deity bodily" (Col 2:9) because "in him all the fullness was pleased to dwell" (Col 1:19). The Father's action, therefore, in which the human and divine principle converge in the person of the Son, is understood in terms of πλήρωμα, filling human action with the fullness of divine life and, through it, the world.[25]

c. The Revelation of the Human Good in Its Personalist Fullness

Christ's action is the perfect expression of his filial communion with the Father. It is precisely when his action reveals the mystery of love that it also manifests a new fullness regarding the human good, a fullness that puts our freedom in motion and that is entrusted to it. Theological reflection on the human dimension of Christ's action has been very rich, in both late Eastern patristics and medieval scholasticism. It was still oriented toward clarifying Christological problems — as in the discussion with monothelitism as well as in discussions over the sacraments. Moral reflection has profited from it only in a limited way. In a necessarily brief manner, referencing accredited studies, I will show the fruitfulness that this inquiry holds for a suitable theory of action from a specifically moral perspective.

Thomist theory has contemplated the *"acta et passa Christi in carne"* as mysteries through which salvation is earned (meritorious causality), is taught (exemplary causality), and is communicated (efficient causal-

24. Augustine, *De sermone Domini in monte,* 1.23, 78-79.
25. This is how it is expressed by Juan José Pérez-Soba, "La persona y el bien," in Melina, Noriega, Pérez-Soba, *La plenitud del obrar cristiano,* pp. 293-318, subscribing to the exegesis on πλήρωμα by José María Casciaro Ramírez, *Estudios sobre cristología del Nuevo Testamento* (Pamplona: Eunsa, 1982), pp. 291-307.

ity).[26] These mysteries hold a *virtus,* an operative dynamism, that is permanently effective on all three levels just mentioned. Now, the theological principle that is the basis of the absolute meaning of Christ's action is that of *"caro (Christi) instrumentum divinitatis,"*[27] which Aquinas derives from St. John Damascene. If God himself is the efficient cause of grace, he uses Christ's humanity almost like a united instrument *(instrumentum coniunctum),* which then prolongs its efficacy in the Church's sacraments.[28] The use of the word "instrument" here should not deceive us. Aquinas was well aware of its analogical function. In fact, he often added the cautionary correction *"quasi* instrumentum,"[29] clarifying that the function of Christ's humanity is not merely the passive one of an inanimate instrument utilized by divine nature. The mysteries of which we speak, precisely to enjoy a meritorious, exemplary, and efficient causality, are actions that are fully human, the fruit of freedom and love.

Behind this observation made by Aquinas certainly lies the wealth of the Eastern Fathers' Christological reflection. In particular, an important step for understanding the personalist dimension of action in relation to its natural presuppositions was accomplished by Maximus the Confessor on the occasion of the monothelite controversy.[30] In effect, Maximus demonstrated both the human integrity of Christ's free acting and his personal and divine character as the Son of God. Meditating on the episode of Christ's agony in the garden — in particular on his supreme act of self-offering to the Father that Christ carries out in the words of his prayer, "My Father, if it is possible, let this cup pass from me; yet, not as I will, but as you will" (Mt 26:39) — the great saint

26. Regarding this see Inos Biffi, *I misteri di Cristo in Tommaso d'Aquino,* vol. 1: *La costruzione della teologia* (Milan: Jaca Book, 1994), pp. 371-404.

27. John of Damascus, *De fide orthodoxa,* 1.3.15 (*Patrologia graeca* 94.1049a).

28. Thomas Aquinas, *Summa theologiae,* III, q. 62, a. 5: "Principalis autem causa efficiens gratiae est ipse Deus, ad quem comparatur humanitas Christi sicut instrumentum coniunctum, sacramentum autem sicut instrumentum separatum."

29. Thomas Aquinas, *De veritate,* q. 27, a. 3; q. 29, a. 5; Thomas Aquinas, *Compendium theologiae,* c. 212.

30. Regarding this see R.-A. Gauthier, "Saint Maxime le Confesseur et la psychologie de l'acte humain," *Recherches de Théologie Ancienne et Médiévale* 21 (1954): 51-100. For the decisive importance of St. Maximus — known through St. John of Damascus — on Thomas's thought, see Juan José Pérez-Soba, *Amor es nombre de persona: Estudio de la interpersonalidad en el amor en Santo Tomás de Aquino* (Rome: PUL-Mursia, 2001), pp. 321-36.

of Constantinople coins the concept of θέλησις to indicate that freedom is rooted in Christ's integral human spiritual nature. At the same time, however, the gnomic act of choice is attributed to the βούλησις, which is proper to the divine person of the Son.[31] The human nature assumed by the Son is the integral expressive instrument of his divine person that is freely shown in his deeds. In this way, not only Christology but also the hermeneutic of human action takes a crucial step, accomplishing a dynamic and integrated interpretation of the connection between person and nature. Even if the will's natural dimension is the indispensable foundation of the freedom of action, it is not yet enough to explain it: spiritual nature founds but does not determine freedom. Action that is truly free not only implies the determination of the spiritual faculties (reason and will) but also involves the personal subject taking a stance.

On the other hand, the final determination of freedom only occurs in reference to the will of a person: the beloved, the Father. Through the mediation of John Damascene, Aquinas accepts Maximus the Confessor's analyses of the human act, distinguishing between *voluntas ut natura* (corresponding to θέλησις) and *voluntas ut ratio* (corresponding to βούλησις).[32] He explains the dynamic integration of the two dimensions of willing in the interpersonal experience of love: "Reason considers something willed in its relation to the will of a friend."[33] *"Agere autem propter finem non est naturae, sed personae,"*[34] Aquinas again affirms in a context of Christological reflection. By its very nature then, the human act demands to be a personal act, and only with the appearance of the beloved is it complete in its final determination.

In the meditation on Christ's action, therefore, the personal fullness of human action is highlighted, a fullness that action acquires in the context of an interpersonal dimension, namely when its ultimate goal is another person. We can now continue our inquiry into the fullness of the human good revealed in Christ, studying no longer only the subjec-

31. Maximus the Confessor, *Disputatio cum Pyrrho* (Patrologia graeca 91.317c).

32. Marcello Gigante, "Thelesis e Boulesis in S. Tommaso," *Asprenas* 26 (1979): 265-73.

33. Aquinas, *Summa theologiae,* III, q. 18, a. 5, ad 2: "Conformitas voluntatis humanae ad voluntatem divinam attenditur secundum voluntatem rationis, secundum quam etiam voluntates amicorum concordant, inquantum scilicet ratio considerat aliquod volitum in ordine ad voluntatem amici." For this insight I am indebted to Pérez-Soba, *Amor es nombre de persona,* pp. 333-36.

34. Thomas Aquinas, *Super Epistolam ad Romanos,* I, l. 3.

tive but also the objective aspect of action, that is, the good understood as the will's goal.

The first characteristic by which something presents itself as good in the dynamic of action is that of corresponding to a desire. "The good is what all desire," Aquinas affirms, taking up the celebrated Aristotelian definition found at the beginning of the *Nicomachean Ethics,* which situates the *ratio boni* within the context of appetibility.[35] Aquinas, however, also introduces the idea of "perfection," thus widening the horizon within which to understand this fundamental experience. What is perfect also presents itself as lovable and desirable, not simply in that it satisfies a desire but because it manifests a preciousness that is attractive and worthy of admiration.[36] This was precisely the experience that we have looked at earlier in the rich man's dialogue with Jesus. And this is also the way Jesus himself summarizes his moral teaching contained in the Sermon on the Mount recorded in Matthew's Gospel: "So be perfect, just as your heavenly Father is perfect" (Mt 5:48).

This perfection of the good that we catch sight of in Jesus has its ultimate origins in the Father, and it enjoys a new and unique characteristic: it is made manifest in communication and in the gift.[37] This is how Luke presents it: "Be merciful, just as your Father is merciful" (Lk 6:36). The fullness that fascinates us and that we seek through our actions thus consists in imitating the integral gift that God, in his goodness, gives to each person, good or bad, without excluding anyone.[38] The Father's perfect goodness, his very fullness of life, is expressed in the absolute gratuity of a love that gives without measure and without discrimination, a love that is always open to forgive even those who are bad.

In this way Thomas can also accept and integrate the neo-Platonic definition of the good, *bonum diffusivum sui,*[39] transforming the idea in a way so as no longer to interpret it within an emanationist context,

---

35. Aquinas, *Summa theologiae,* I, q. 5, a. 1, in reference to Aristotle, *Ethica Nicomachea,* 1.1 (1094a): "Bonum est quod omnia appetunt."

36. Joseph de Finance, *Saggio sull'agire umano* (Vatican City: Libreria Editrice Vaticana, 1992), pp. 71-96.

37. See Giuseppe Segalla, *Un'etica per tre comunità: L'etica di Gesù in Matteo, Marco e Luca* (Brescia: Paideia, 2000), pp. 49-50.

38. See Tremblay, *L'élévation du Fils,* pp. 101-4, who relies on the exegesis of Joachim Gnilka, *Das Matthäusevangelium,* I (Freiburg im Breisgau: Herder, 1988), pp. 191ff.

39. See Julien Peghaire, "L'axiome 'bonum diffusivum sui' dans le néoplatonisme et le thomisme," *Revue de l'Université d'Ottawa* 2 (1932): 5-30.

but rather within an authentically personalist one: "It belongs to the essence of goodness to communicate itself to others."[40] Communication, in fact, implies otherness as an exterior and personal reference, which is necessary for the diffusion of goodness. Moreover, communication includes an act of free will that characterizes the movement of the diffusion of the good in personalist terms.[41] As has been shown,[42] the originality of Thomas's approach consists precisely in integrating into love as a complete act both the dimension of desirability — and thus of final causality — and that of the communication of good to the beloved: "Love consists chiefly in the lover wishing good to the loved one."[43] Thus also the moment of the appetibility of the good, indispensable for the natural dynamics of the will, takes on a new character in that it is inserted in the context of an interpersonal communication: "Good is loved inasmuch as it can be communicated to the lover."[44]

Thus, when contemplated in Christ, human action is not born of a lack or a need that craves for its satisfaction. Rather, it is the superabundant fruit of the fullness of a love that wants to communicate itself to the point of embracing all, to fill everything with the same fullness of the Father's love: "I have come to set the earth on fire, and how I wish it were already blazing!" (Lk 12:49). The Holy Spirit is this fire and the intrinsic principle of this fruitful communication, indwelling the dynamism of Christ's action, making it both a pleasing offering to the Father and a service of redemptive love for Christ's brothers and sisters in humanity.[45] It is precisely as *communicatio Christi* that the

40. Aquinas, *Summa theologiae,* III, q. 1, a. 1: "Pertinet autem ad rationem boni ut se aliis communicet, ut patet per Dionysium (IV cap. *de Div. Nom.*). Unde ad rationem summi boni pertinet quod summo modo se creaturae communicet. Quod quidem maxime fit per hoc quod naturam creatam sic sibi coniungit ut una persona fiat ex tribus, verbo, anima et carne, sicut dicit Augustinus (XIII *de Trin.*). Unde manifestum est quod conveniens fuit Deum incarnari." See Reginald Garrigou-Lagrange, "The Fecundity of Goodness," *The Thomist* 2 (1940): 226-36.

41. See Jean-Pierre Jossua, "L'axiome *'bonum diffusivum sui'* chez s. Thomas d'Aquin," *Recherches de Science Religieuse* 40 (1966): 127-53.

42. Pérez-Soba, *Amor es nombre de persona,* pp. 349-60, 546-72.

43. Thomas Aquinas, *Summa contra gentiles,* 3.90: "In hoc enim praecipue consistit amor, quod amans amato bonum velit."

44. Aquinas, *Summa theologiae,* I-II, q. 28, a. 4, ad 2: "Bonum amatur inquantum est communicabile amanti."

45. Von Balthasar, "Nine Propositions," 77-81.

Holy Spirit is the principle of life also in us and the ladder for our ascent to God.[46]

It can thus be said that analyzing action within a Christological context has allowed patristic and scholastic thought to grasp new personalist dimensions in the understanding of the good and to produce with Aquinas an original synthesis of the Aristotelian and neo-Platonic traditions. Gathering the results of the reflection developed to this point, we can affirm that exploring the uniqueness of Christ's action as the human action of a divine person has brought to light new qualities of the human good. The filial fullness of his unique relationship with the Father has shown itself to be open to participation in discipleship and imitation. Moreover, situated within the context of Trinitarian relationships, the personalist and communicative character has appeared as the ultimate truth of action. With this, the emphasis on "transcendence" — if you want, on the Christocentric fullness of the good — comes to a conclusion. Now we must ask how this fullness is inherent to the human dynamism of action and how it transforms it. This is the second phase of our reflection, that is, the moment of "integration."

2. The Integration into Human Action of the Good Manifested in Christ

The unique encounter with Christ, while it reveals the fullness of the human good, is also, at the same time, a personal call to bring this good about. When the call is answered, it provokes the polarization of life in a personal relationship with Christ, the "living and personal Law" (VS 15). This relationship gives birth to a new perception of the "good of the person" and the "goods for the person" that constitute the objective content of moral intentionality determined by practical reason. The integration into action of the fullness of the good made manifest in Christ — the object of the second section of this chapter — poses a series of crucial questions for moral theology: How are the religious and the moral elements connected in this experience? How can the person's indispensable uniqueness be safeguarded in an approach that proposes an exemplary point of reference? How is the ra-

---

46. That is how, in the ecclesial context, Irenaeus expresses it in *Adversus haereses,* 3.24.1.

tional and objective character of ethics taken up in the new dynamics of Christian action?

The first two questions will be addressed in treating the connection between the "good of the person" and vocation. The last section of the chapter, titled "Goods for the Person in Christ," will be dedicated to the third question.

a. Vocation: "The Good of the Person" in Christ

Prior still to any particular specification in terms of the states of life, Christian existence itself in its entirety must be defined as a "vocation." In fact, if a believer's experience cannot be understood without reference to a personal and historical relationship, then the category of vocation appears proper to express the entirety of Christian life as a permanent and daily response to a call. This call is not heard only at one particular moment in time but is progressively drawn out as the believer becomes more like Christ in a process that gives historical circumstances interpreted by faith the specific value of signs.[47] The call, therefore, is the very essence of Christian life. It implies a living relationship with the living God who, in Christ, is not a mere object of knowledge or worship but a person who intervenes in history, who makes his voice heard and who calls us by name.[48] The divine call represents the breaking in of an absolute imperative into a person's life, asking to be obeyed unconditionally as the expression of the Lord's will.

Nonetheless, the notion of vocation has a specific moral relevance that is distinct, though not independent, from its religious one.[49] In fact,

47. Angelo Scola, Javier Prades, and Gilfredo Marengo, *La persona umana: Antropologia teologica* (Milan: Jaca Book, 2000), pp. 322-24; Angelo Scola, *Gesù destino dell'uomo: Cammino di vita cristiana* (Cinisello Balsamo: Edizioni San Paolo, 1999), pp. 105-17. The relevance of the concept of vocation for the moral and spiritual life, taken together, is also explicit in Charles-André Bernard, *Vie morale* (Rome: PUG, 1973), pp. 225-71.

48. Hans Urs von Balthasar, "The Call," in *The Christian State of Life* (San Francisco: Ignatius Press, 1983), pp. 391-504; Antonio Sicari, *Chiamati per nome: La vocazione nella Scrittura* (Milan: Jaca Book, 1979); Paolo Martinelli, *Vocazione e stati di vita del cristiano: Riflessioni sistematiche in dialogo con H. U. von Balthasar* (Rome: Edizioni Collegio S. Lorenzo da Brindisi, 2001).

49. On the relationship between the two dimensions, the study by Bernhard Häring is classic and still valid: *Das Heilige und das Gute* (Krailling: Wewel, 1950), pp. 62-72.

while it establishes the person in an absolute relationship with the transcendent, it also determines that person's moral identity, that is, the human good entrusted to action, which is the "good of the person."[50] This good can be defined as the perfection of the person that depends exclusively upon the exercise of the person's freedom that determines itself. It expresses the person's original and unique value in reference to the immanent character of his or her actions and their moral dimension. The good of the person, therefore, is incommensurable in respect to all other exterior goods that are attainable through action. "For what will it profit a man, if he gains the whole world and forfeits his life? Or what shall a man give in return for his life?" (Mt 16:26). The person's vocation in Christ allows us to have a better idea of the good of the person, offering both an interpersonal context for its determination and the content that qualifies it in light of the "ideal" of a good life.

The Christological form of the vocation (see Gal 4:19) implies a call to more and more adopt a filial profile in Christ. The growth of our very existence occurs on the basis of a progressive assimilation to Christ: "until Christ be formed in you" (Gal 4:19). The believer's identity comes from his or her relationship in Christ to God's paternity, in whose benevolent plan our status as adopted children has a primacy even with respect to redemption (see Eph 1:3-6).[51] Being "sons in the Son" is above all a gift, which, however, demands to be dynamically fulfilled by our freedom, which in our acting imitates the Father and thus becomes more like him and reveals him ever more.

Since the divine call always surprises us in a condition of sin, the positive response, which is only possible through grace, takes the form of a conversion. In it, freedom fully grasps the initial gift and, by means of it, dynamically unites human actions. The communication of grace is brought about in friendship with Christ. In this way, at the heart of conversion there is an interpersonal moment: Conversion can in no way be reduced to the person's progressive maturation according to a dynamic

50. On the concept of the "good of the person" in its relationship with the "goods for the person," see also chapter 3 of my *Sharing in Christ's Virtues: For a Renewal of Moral Theology in Light of Veritatis Splendor,* trans. William E. May (Washington, DC: Catholic University of America Press, 2001), pp. 59-91: "An Ethics Founded on the Truth about the Good of the Person."

51. See Tremblay, *L'élévation du Fils,* pp. 30-33, who bases his exegesis of Ephesians 1:3-6 on Chantal Reynier, "La bénédiction en Éphésiens 1:3-14: Élection, filiation, rédemption," *Nouvelle Revue Théologique* 118 (1996): 182-99.

of growth in the virtues. It is precisely this factor of not being able to be objectified that renders the need for conversion in the Christian life permanent and progressive.[52]

The call addresses us in our irreducible singularity. We are called by name, or rather, it is precisely the call that gives each of us a personal name. As von Balthasar affirms, the human being as a spiritual subject becomes a person thanks to God's call, receiving the mission for which he or she has been created.[53] Only he who has created and called human persons, choosing them and elevating them to communion with him, can say who they truly are. Within Christ's incomparable oneness, therefore, the space for analogous calls and personalizing missions is opened. In their singularity *(Einmaligkeit)* these calls and missions, far from leading to individualism, are the paths to communion and universality.

From a specifically moral point of view, the person's vocation provokes a concise perception of personal goods understood in a practical and human way. According to Emmanuel Mounier, a vocation is the living and creative principle of a personal relationship with God that allows the gradual integration of our actions and the unification of the person.[54] An ideal of the good life is thus formed in an original synthesis that determines the content of the final end from a practical point of view: an intentional order of human perfection that gives happiness — as the formal goal of action — a determined form, a form that is worthy and proper, capable of serving as the principle of excellent acts that conform to it.[55]

---

52. See Carlo Caffarra, *Living in Christ: Fundamental Principles of Catholic Moral Teaching* (San Francisco: Ignatius Press, 1987), pp. 199-205.

53. See Hans Urs von Balthasar, *Theo-Drama: Theological Dramatic Theory,* vol. 3: *Dramatis Personae: The Person in Christ,* trans. G. Harrison (San Francisco: Ignatius Press, 1993), pp. 202-14, 263-82. Regarding this see Ellero Babini, *L'antropologia teologica di Hans Urs von Balthasar* (Milan: Jaca Book, 1988), pp. 173-83.

54. See Emmanuel Mounier, "Manifeste au service du personnalisme," in *Œuvres,* vol. 1 (Paris: Éditions du Seuil, 1961), p. 528: "Cette unification progressive de tous mes actes, et par eux de mes personnages ou de mes états est l'acte propre de la personne. Ce n'est pas une unification systématique et abstraite, c'est la découverte progressive d'un principe spirituel de vie, qui ne réduit pas ce qu'il intègre, mais le sauve, l'accomplit en le recréant de l'intérieur. Ce principe vivant et créateur est ce que nous appelons en chaque personne sa vocation."

55. See Giuseppe Abbà, *Felicità, vita buona e virtù: Saggio di filosofia morale* (Rome: LAS, 1989), pp. 51-53.

b. *"Goods for the Person" in Christ*

We are left with the final step of our reflection, which regards the integration of the "goods for the person" into the dynamics of action understood Christologically. The expression "goods for the person" indicates those particular goods that are the object of our choices and that naturally attract us, inclining us to attain them. These are the goods of being and life, of sexual complementarity and procreation, of life in society, and of the knowledge of truth.[56] In shaping action, human freedom does not start from indifference but from spontaneous fundamental orientations toward that which presents itself as good and thus provokes us to act in order to attain it. Scholastic theology defined the natural law as the order that reason creates in our human acts, shaping our various inclinations to particular goods in view of the person's integral good. In creating this order, human reason participates in God's eternal wisdom, expressing its designs.[57] Recent Thomist hermeneutic has pointed out the crucial role of the virtues in determining the human good insofar as they permit an initial integration of the natural inclinations in the direction of the person's integral good.[58]

As I have already noted, contemporary personalist reflection has shown how the context in which the ultimate determination of the concrete good of action occurs is the experience of love and interpersonal communication. The will considers something as good insofar as it is communicable to the beloved. In this sense, the expression "goods for the person" indicates that the good that is the object of practical intentionality is not only addressed to the person but is already grasped

---

56. See Aquinas, *Summa theologiae,* I-II, q. 94, a. 2. Here I am following the straightforward and clear presentation suggested by Servais Pinckaers, *Morality: The Catholic View* (Notre Dame: St. Augustine's Press, 2001), pp. 96-111.

57. Joseph de Finance, "La legge naturale," in R. Lucas Lucas, ed., *Veritatis Splendor: Testo integrale e commento filosofico-teologico* (Cinisello Balsamo: Edizioni San Paolo, 1994), pp. 287-98. For a more extensive critical discussion from the perspective of an ethics of virtue see Martin Rhonheimer, *Natural Law and Practical Reason: A Thomistic View of Moral Autonomy,* trans. G. Malsbary (New York: Fordham University Press, 2000), which is an updated and revised version of the original German *Natur als Grundlage der Moral: Die personale Struktur des Naturgesetzes bei Thomas von Aquin* (Innsbruck-Wien: Tyrolia-Verlag, 1987).

58. See Eberhard Schockenhoff, *Bonum hominis: Die anthropologischen und theologischen Grundlagen der Tugendethik des Thomas von Aquin* (Mainz: Grünewald, 1987).

in its first communicative orientation, directed toward constructing communion with another person. Practical reason, energized by the virtues, has the function of knowing the truth of action so that it may effectively contribute to building communion among persons.[59]

Within the Christocentric context, the "goods for the person" are at the same time confirmed in their fundamental, permanent value and relativized and transformed in relation to the person's supreme call in Christ.[60] Our natural inclinations are the first signs of this vocation to charity. Insofar as they are originally given in creation, they maintain their value, but now they are situated within a dynamic of perfection in charity, which transcends them.[61] Our natural attachment to life takes on a new shape in the perspective of a gift of oneself. Marital love is understood as a sign — the sacrament of God's love for humanity, of Christ's love for the Church, his Bride. At the same time, a new road opens up, that of virginity for the kingdom of heaven, which, while transcending conjugal love, confirms the nuptial meaning of the body, realizing it no longer under the earthly sign of the use of the sexual organs but according to the fruitfulness of a higher order. Sociality, with its rule of justice, is perfected in charity, which does not deny the natural and rational demands of equity but inserts these within the higher horizon of the communion of which the Church is the anticipation. Finally, the search for truth encounters the Truth made flesh. The gift offered by faith does not deny the person's search and the demands of reason but directs these toward a deepening without end.

Some patristic commentaries have understood the beatitudes as the Christological fulfillment of the natural law.[62] Particularly meaningful is St. Ambrose's interpretation. Comparing the four beatitudes recounted by Luke with the eight beatitudes of Matthew's Gospel, Ambrose correlates the first, which were addressed to the crowds on the plains, to the fundamental demands of the law, which have to do with the four cardinal

---

59. See chapter 2 of the present volume, "Acting for the Good of Communion."

60. Here I am revisiting some thoughts already advanced in my book *Sharing in Christ's Virtues*, pp. 84-85.

61. Thus *Veritatis Splendor*, n. 53: "Christ is the 'Beginning' who, having taken on human nature, definitively illumines it in its constitutive elements and in its dynamism of charity towards God and neighbor."

62. Besides Ambrose's homily we can see, in the same sense, that of Augustine, *De sermone Domini in monte;* and that of the Venerable Bede, *In Lucae evangelium expositio* (*Corpus Christianorum Series Latina* 120.136-142).

virtues. On the other hand, he understands the eight beatitudes found in Matthew, which Jesus spoke to his disciples on the mountainside, as the "summit of the virtues" *(summa virtutum)*.[63] These no longer regard the milk fed to children, but the much more substantial food that consists in the new law of charity, which transcends the simple legal prescriptions toward the perfect imitation of Christ.

In fact, properly understood the beatitudes are not normative indications but a kind of "self-portrait" of Christ proposed for his followers to imitate,[64] describing the disciples' fundamental attitudes in relation to human goods and in relation to the trials in which they may find themselves. The beatitudes point out the way to follow Jesus in every act his disciples perform and thus offer a hermeneutic of the moral truth of the person's goods, which "mediates between the principles of natural law and the moral norms of action specific to Christians."[65]

This is a justice that goes beyond that of the Pharisees, that is, beyond a mere respect of the law, and which, far from eliminating the law, perfectly fulfills it in the sense of bringing about the ultimate and original intention of the Father's plan.[66] On the one hand, then, there is an emphasis on the permanent value of the Ten Commandments, a confirmation (purification and clarification) of what is given in the natural law.[67] In fact, what is specifically Christian about normative morality is not found on the level of the negative commandments: what is of strict necessity as the minimum for virtue to respect is already sufficiently es-

---

63. Ambrose, *Expositiones in evangelium secundum Lucam,* 5.46-72 *(Corpus Christianorum Series Latina* 14.151-159). "Hic enim quattuor uelut uirtutes amplexus est cardinales, ille in illis octo mysticum numerum reserauit. Pro octaua enim multi scribuntur psalmi, et mandatum accipis octo illis partem dare fortasse benedictionibus: sicut enim spei nostrae octaua perfectio est, ita octaua summa uirtutum est" (5.49, *Corpus Christianorum Series Latina* 14.152).

64. Joseph Ratzinger, *To Look on Christ: Exercises in Faith, Hope, and Love* (New York: Crossroad, 1991), pp. 54-62.

65. Germain Grisez, *The Way of the Lord Jesus,* vol. 1: *Christian Moral Principles* (Chicago: Franciscan Herald Press, 1983), pp. 627-59.

66. Paul Beauchamp, *La legge di Dio* (Casale Montferrato: Piemme, 2000), p. 138.

67. On the Ten Commandments as an expression of the natural law see Reginaldo Pizzorni, "Comandamenti e legge naturale," *Euntes Docete* 53 (2000): 127-37, with documentation of the thesis from Irenaeus, *Adversus haereses,* 4.16.5 *(Patrologia graeca* 7, 1018) and others; Augustine, *Enarrationes in Psalmos* 57.1 *(Patrologia Latina* 34.673); Aquinas, *De veritate,* q. 14, a. 12, ad 3; Aquinas, *Summa theologiae,* I-II, q. 100, a. 3 and others; and Domingo De Soto, *De iustitia et iure,* II, q. 1, a. 2.

tablished by the old law.[68] On the other hand, the path to an ulterior positive interpretation is opened. The commandments are not to be understood merely as extreme limits to be respected but as paths to be followed in order to fully achieve the moral goods that they safeguard.[69]

The cardinal virtues are Christologically fulfilled in the beatitudes, a fact that has something paradoxical to it, particularly as regards the promised rewards. As Ambrose observes, it implies an assimilation to Christ also in his death and resurrection (see Phil 1:23). On this earthly pilgrimage the beatitude of the heavenly kingdom — the final reward — is already present in the Church as the beginning of the kingdom, but it is hidden under the veil of tears, of apparent defeat, and of persecution.[70]

And yet, it is precisely amidst the contradictions and limits of our earthly condition that Christian action can shine like a city on a hill or a lantern on a lampstand with the light of a new fullness that comes from knowing the Father and from the overabundant gratuity of his love. Thus the filial and personalist fullness of the human good revealed in Christ will be expressed in the disciples' actions, so that people will see their good deeds and glorify their heavenly Father (cf. Mt 5:16).

---

68. See Aquinas, *Summa theologiae,* I-II, q. 108, a. 2.

69. See John Paul II, *Veritatis Splendor,* n. 15.

70. See Ambrose, *Expositiones in evangelium secundum Lucam,* 5.60-61 (*Corpus Christianorum Series Latina* 14.155).

VI

The Church and the Dynamism of Action

1. The Question Concerning Morality as an Ecclesial Question: The Challenge of "Autonomous Morality"

Why is the Church's witness today rejected above all in the sphere of moral theology? Why does her preaching find such great difficulties here? It is regarding this issue and within a perspective of evangelization that the most acute problem of the connection between ecclesiology and moral theology unfolds. Indeed, it is precisely here that the signs of an alternative anthropology emerge. It is not without reason that some speak of a tacit and significant "moral schism" within the Church. A notable number of the faithful have inwardly separated themselves from the magisterium's moral teachings, not only at a practical level but also as regards their convictions. This is not simply the common phenomenon of the divergence between theory and praxis, nor is it just a dissent confined to some particular issues; it is something new in the history of the Church. It is the emancipation of Christian moral conscience from the ecclesial *communio,* which is the result of the radical subjectivization of morality.[1]

On the one hand, it seems that traditional Catholic morality with its severe prohibitions — at least in some of its aspects, such as those regarding sexuality and the conjugal life, bioethics and the defense of life

---

1. On this see Carlo Caffarra, "L'autonomia della coscienza e la sottomissione alla verità," in G. Borgonovo, ed., *La coscienza* (Vatican City: Libreria Editrice Vaticana, 1996), pp. 142-62.

— presents an obstacle to the acceptance of the gospel message. There is therefore the tendency to relegate it to second place or even to stop speaking of it at all in order to emphasize the *kerygma* in its purity and positivity. On the other hand, in relation to the spheres of public morality, social and international justice, ecology, and social communication, a privileged space for dialogue seems to have opened that allows for an encounter with the new ethical questions present in society. There is, however, a certain ambiguity here. The Church is heard in these areas under the condition of putting in parentheses what is specific to the Christian proposal as such and of speaking in the name of a global ethics that is common to all persons of good will.

There are then two apparently antithetical proposals in the sphere of moral theology, which however end up strangely joining in a single figure of Christian life and a new model of the Church. A first alternative holds it to be fully compatible with ecclesial communion to adopt ethical positions that are at odds with the teaching of the magisterium in the areas of marital ethics, sexual ethics, and bioethics.[2] Morality, at least as it is traditionally proposed by Catholic doctrine, could then not be considered the decisive criterion for ecclesial membership. "Ethical pluralism" would be legitimately compatible with the Church's unity.[3] Catholic identity would be safeguarded by an act of faith and by adherence to transcendental Christian attitudes, while determined operative norms would only be relevant for a proper worldly orientation, but not for salvation.[4]

A second alternative on the other hand does emphasize the connection between ecclesial membership and the moral attitudes that characterize its public witness, but reduces these to the commitment to fight for peace, justice, and the environment. Moreover, such ethical behavior should not be considered as specifically Christian, but be tied to a new

2. See Franz Böckle, "*Humanae vitae* als Prüfstein des wahren Glaubens? Zur kirchenpolitischen Dimension moraltheologischer Fragen," *Stimmen der Zeit* 115 (1990): 3-16.

3. Philipp Schmitz, "Ein Glaube — Kontroverse Gewissenentscheidungen," in J. Horstmann, ed., *Gewissen: Aspekte eines vieldiskutierten Sachverhaltes* (Schwerte: Kath. Akad., 1983), pp. 60-76.

4. See Josef Fuchs, "Verità morali — Verità di salvezza," in *Etica cristiana in una società secolarizzata* (Casale Monferrato: Piemme, 1984), pp. 59-78; Josef Fuchs, "Christian Morality: Biblical Orientation and Human Evaluation," *Gregorianum* 67 (1986): 745-63.

humanism, which is the basis for a global ecumenism in which dogmatic differences should be put in their proper limits to make room for the recognition of common ethical values.[5]

These problems have obvious repercussions in the area of ecumenism, where the topic of morality has still not found an adequate space for discussion, at least in the dialogue with the Catholic Church. In fact, between 1992 and 1996 the World Council of Churches dedicated a research series to the issue of *Ecclesiology and Ethics.*[6] At first the Church was spoken of as an intrinsically moral community that not only has an ethics but that is itself an ethical reality. Later the term "moral community" was more prudently avoided, and the Church was spoken of as a *koinonia* that favors a continual process of moral formation. Finally, it was affirmed that "in the church's own struggles for justice, peace, and the integrity of creation, the *esse* of the church is at stake."[7]

On the one hand, therefore, there is the tendency to "de-moralize" the Church when it comes to specific ethical themes relating to the areas of personal morality. On the other hand, there is the outright identification of what makes for ecclesial membership (and ecumenism) with ethical political commitment, prescinding from the dogmatic aspects as if these were secondary and not characteristic of Christian identity. However, in this second tendency ecclesial communion is reduced to the commitment to universal human values, so that ultimately the new morality redefines the nature of the Church and the criteria for membership in her. In any case, the Church has ceased to be recognized as the "mother" of the Christian moral subject, who now defines autonomously his or her ethical identity and criteria for worldly choices.

As can be seen from these brief remarks, the question of morality has become an ecclesial question of primary importance, above all in that it bears on the connection between faith and morality as constitutive of Christian identity. The traditional Catholic teaching, reaffirmed

5. This has been proposed by Hans Küng, *Progetto per un'etica mondiale: Una morale ecumenica per una sopravvivenza mondiale* (Milan: Rizzoli, 1991).

6. Thomas F. Best and Martin Robra, eds., *Ecclesiology and Ethics: Ecumenical Ethical Engagement, Moral Formation and the Nature of the Church* (Geneva: WCC Publications, 1997). For a panoramic presentation and bibliography of the issues see the essay by Basilio Petrà, "Communio ecclesiale e genesi del soggetto morale," in Livio Melina and Pablo Zanor, eds., *Quale dimora per l'agire? Dimensioni ecclesiologiche della morale* (Rome: PUL-Mursia, 2000), pp. 73-97.

7. Best and Roba, eds., *Ecclesiology and Ethics,* "Costly Commitment," paragraph 71.

by *Veritatis Splendor,* presents the Church as a witness to the indissoluble bond between truth and freedom, between faith and morality (see VS 26-27). As the encyclical asserts, "Christian faith . . . is not simply a set of propositions to be accepted with intellectual assent. Rather, faith is a . . . *truth to be lived out,*" "a decision involving one's whole existence," and "a new and original criterion for thinking and acting" (VS 88). It has been opportunely recalled that the first name that the new Christian religion received at its very beginnings and that was deemed appropriate to define it is "the Way," a name frequently used in the Acts of the Apostles (see e.g., Acts 19:9; 22:4; 24:14).[8] Christianity, therefore, is first of all a concrete way of living, a praxis born of faith. It is not a vague collection of ideals that are interpretable in various and contradictory ways according to the subjective tastes of an age or a culture but a precise and recognizable manner of living. Every separation between the confession of faith and the moral life would — according to the first letter of John — constitute the denial of the logic of the incarnation, that is, a new docetism that denies Christ come in the flesh.[9]

2. The Basic Perspective of *Veritatis Splendor*

It is precisely in the face of this challenge that John Paul II's moral encyclical must be read. Underlying all the ethical questions for which *Veritatis Splendor* offers a critical discernment in the light of the "healthy doctrine" is "ultimately the question of the *relationship between freedom and truth*" (VS 84). In its turn, this question can be understood in its foundations and in its implications only if situated within the more radical context of the connection between faith and morality (see VS 88). It is this ultimate, theological horizon that allows us to grasp the full dimension of the tie between freedom and truth both in its theoretical implications and in its historical foundations.[10] Before all else then,

8. See the presentation of the encyclical given by Joseph Ratzinger, "Christian Faith as 'the Way': An Introduction to *Veritatis Splendor,*" *Communio* 21 (1994): 199-207.

9. See 1 John 2:4: "Whoever says, 'I know him,' but does not keep his commandments is a liar, and the truth is not in him." See also Raymond E. Brown, *The Gospel and Epistles of John: A Concise Commentary* (Collegeville, MN: Liturgical Press, 1988), pp. 109-22.

10. Wolfhart Pannenberg, *Ethik und Ekklesiologie: Gesammelte Aufsätze* (Göttingen: Vandenhoeck & Ruprecht, 1977), pp. 55-69.

Veritatis Splendor confronts an understanding of autonomy that severs the connection between truth and freedom because it has first broken the link between faith and morality.

Two characteristics of the claim to autonomy can still be seen here. On the one hand there is an idea of freedom without ties. In this understanding, which has imposed itself with the Enlightenment, freedom is seen as the absolute affirmation of the self and, therefore, as autonomy from the tradition, as the emancipation from the community, and as the independence from any origin.[11] In the end, in the period defined as "postmodernity,"[12] it has even come to be conceived of as the autonomy from truth. Michel Foucault's scornful and provocative words are symptomatic of this situation: "The truth will enslave you." Along the same lines, the Bolognese philosopher Uberto Scarpelli has proposed an ethical project to construct an "ethics without truth."[13]

But perhaps it is also necessary to consider the reasons for this autonomistic position. There is, in fact, also the possibility of a truth that enslaves us, a truth that is extrinsically imposed and contrary to freedom. Here the second possible characteristic of autonomy appears, namely its intellectualistic character that, at times, even the defenders of the objectivity of morality have not known how to avoid. It is the claim to a direct and purely rationalistic access to truth, which thus becomes reified, crystallized, and possessed in abstract concepts and norms and which is then applied to the living reality of action. Regarding this problem, Blondel's lesson remains up-to-date and fruitful.[14] Following the thought of the great master from Aix-en-Provence, *Veritatis Splendor* offers a way out of this blind alley that opposes truth to freedom almost as if these were antithetical terms to choose between.

Assuming the point of view of the practical dynamism of freedom,

11. The noted analyses by Alasdair MacIntyre can be cited here: *After Virtue: A Study in Moral Theory* (London: Duckworth, 1985), and *Three Rival Versions of Moral Enquiry: Encyclopaedia, Genealogy, and Tradition* (London: Duckworth, 1990).

12. Jean-François Lyotard, *The Postmodern Condition: A Report on Knowledge* (Manchester: Manchester University Press, 1984). For a penetrating and prophetic analysis of the issue see, above all, Romano Guardini, *The End of the Modern World: A Search for Orientation,* trans. J. Theman and H. Burke, ed. and intro. F. Wilhelmsen (London: Sheed & Ward, 1957).

13. Uberto Scarpelli, *Etica senza verità* (Bologna: Il Mulino, 1982).

14. Maurice Blondel, *Action (1893): Essay on a Critique of Life and a Science of Practice,* trans. Oliva Blanchette (Notre Dame: University of Notre Dame Press, 1984).

that is, placing "oneself *in the perspective of the acting person*" (VS 78), means overcoming an abstract (separated) understanding of truth and the resulting extrinsicism of freedom. According to the teaching in *Fides et Ratio,* between truth and freedom there exist a circularity and an inseparable connection. "Truth and freedom either go together hand in hand or together they perish in misery" (FR 90).

Here, the theological dimension offers the decisive illumination. The "relationship between freedom and truth is complete, and we understand [its] full meaning" (FR 15) precisely in our encounter with Christ and with his word of salvation. Within the context of Christian revelation, the truth has a "personal" character.[15] This is why, in Christ, the truth gives itself in an interpersonal dimension. *Veritatis Splendor* situates it within the encounter with the rich young man. For us today, the encounter with the truth of Christ always occurs in a communal and ecclesial way. Therefore, at the same time and from the very beginning both freedom and community are called into play in our access to the truth. Freedom is always implicated in the perception of the truth about the moral good, which requires the person's overall dispositions (virtue). The Aristotelian and Thomist axiom, according to which for the virtuous person "that which is really good seems to him to be good,"[16] clearly expresses the surpassing of every ethical intellectualism.

In the words of the French Jesuit Gaston Fessard, we can also say that our access to the truth in the historical situation in which we live has a feminine and nuptial character, or rather, a Marian one that passes through the mediation of the Church.[17] Since truth is the nuptial gift that Christ in the Spirit gives to the Church, his Bride, its acceptance

15. Vatican Council II, *Dei Verbum,* nn. 2-6. According to Henri de Lubac, the Second Vatican Council substituted "an abstract idea of truth for the most concrete possible idea of truth, that is, the idea of personal truth, which has appeared in history and, from the very heart of history, is capable of sustaining it. The idea of this truth in person, which is Jesus of Nazareth, is the fullness of Revelation" (Henri de Lubac, "La rivelazione divina e il senso dell'uomo: Commento alle Costituzioni conciliari *Dei Verbum* e *Gaudium et Spes,*" in *Opera Omnia* 14 [Milan: Jaca Book, 1985], p. 49).

16. Aristotle, *Ethica Nicomachea,* 3.4, 1113a; Thomas Aquinas, *Sententia libri Ethicorum,* III, 10, 88-90: "In singulis videtur ei esse bonum id quod vere est bonum"; see Livio Melina, *La conoscenza morale: Linee di riflessione sul Commento di san Tommaso all'Etica Nicomachea* (Rome: Città Nuova, 1987), pp. 111-12.

17. Gaston Fessard, *La Dialectique des Exercices Spirituels de Saint Ignace de Loyola,* vol. 2: *Fondement — Péché — Orthodoxie* (Paris: Montaigne, 1966), pp. 125-256.

demands Mary's humble *fiat* and one's adherence to the community of believers.

3. The Privileged Ecclesiological Vision of *Veritatis Splendor*

In the perspective of the encyclical, the Church is seen in a privileged way as "Christ's relevance [Lat. *'simultas temporum'* = 'contemporaneity'] for people of all times" (VS 25; see 7, 117). This corresponds to the fundamental inspiration that animates the pontifical document. The moral question is situated within the horizon of evangelization, which is "the most powerful and stirring challenge which the Church has been called to face from her very beginning" (VS 106). Faced with the new challenges of history and the anxiety of men and women in seeking the meaning of life, evangelization is about offering "to everyone the answer which comes from the truth about Jesus Christ and his Gospel" (VS 2); it is a question of making *"this 'encounter' with Christ possible"* (VS 7), an encounter which alone can satisfy the desire of the human heart and for which God has wanted his Church.

Now, according to Kierkegaard's teaching, contemporaneity is the only way to establish an appropriate relationship with Christ.[18] This is why the Church is the present-day possibility of the encounter between the questions that persons have today and the great response that Christ can offer. The mediation of the connection between truth and freedom, in fact, "occurs" historically in the Church. The "truth about the good" — which is the object of people's moral question as well as the object of Christ's response — this "truth about the good" is permanently offered to human freedom by the Church as a communal event. The Church exists in history precisely for this reason, to allow for a living, present-day encounter between human beings, who anxiously ask their questions about meaning, and Christ and his response, which is the only truly proper one.

From these considerations arise the document's other privileged

18. On this see Jean Laffitte, "Contemporanéité du Christ à l'homme de tous les temps dans le premier chapitre de l'Encyclique 'Veritatis Splendor,'" in Graziano Borgonovo, ed., *Gesù Cristo, legge vivente e personale della santa Chiesa: Atti del IX Colloquio Internazionale di Teologia di Lugano (15-17 June 1995)* (Casale Monferrato: Piemme, 1996), pp. 211-23.

ecclesial formulations: the Church as the *sacrament of mystery* (VS 21), as the *event* that mediates Christ's presence today (VS 7), most of all as the competent *witness* before human freedom to the splendor of moral truth (VS 96). The access to the truth about the good on the part of the Christian moral subject is thus mediated by that person's relationship of filial freedom with the Church, who can be a Mother in the Spirit because she is first Christ's immaculate Bride.[19]

4. *Status Quaestionis* Concerning the Ecclesiological Models Used in Moral Theology

Let us now turn to the problem of the relationship between ecclesiological models and moral theology in order to understand the connection between faith and morality from within the discipline of theology.[20] The originality of the approach suggested by *Veritatis Splendor* can be delineated by determining the *status quaestionis* of the debate regarding the ecclesiological models used in moral theology. This is a subject that up to now has not found much expression or received much study,[21] so that it is possible to offer only a very general and rough draft that, however, will be useful for sketching out the question in its essential terms.

19. Jules Mimeault, "Il riferimento a Cristo-verità nella Chiesa," in Livio Melina and Juan de Dios Larrú, eds., *Verità e libertà nella teologica morale* (Rome: Lateran University Press, 2001), pp. 155-73.

20. For an overview of the main ecclesiological models see, among others, Avery R. Dulles, *Models of the Church* (New York: Doubleday, 2002).

21. A few principal bibliographical references are: K. McNamara, "La vita in Cristo e la vita nella Chiesa," in E. McDonagh, ed., *Il rinnovamento della teologia morale* (Brescia: Queriniana, 1967), pp. 110-32; Bernhard Häring, "Il mistero della Chiesa e i suoi riflessi nella morale cristiana," in J. B. Metz, ed., *Orizzonti attuali della teologia,* vol. 2 (Rome: Paoline, 1967), pp. 215-43; Herbert Schlögel, *Kirche und sittliches Handeln: Zur Ekklesiologie in der Grundlagendiskussion der deutschsprachigen katholischen Moraltheologie seit der Jahrhundertwende* (Mainz: Grünewald, 1981); Livio Melina, "Ecclesialità e teologia morale: Spunti per un 'ri-dimensionamento' teologico della morale," *Anthropotes* 5 (1989): 7-27; Josef Georg Ziegler, "Ekklesiologie und Moraltheologie: Ihre Beziehung im 20. Jahrhundert," *Theologie und Glaube* 87 (1997): 321-45, 527-40; Livio Melina and Pablo Zanor, eds., *Quale dimora per l'agire? Dimensioni ecclesiologiche della morale* (Rome: PUL-Mursia, 2000).

a. The Juridical-Doctrinal Model of the Post-Tridentine Manualist Tradition

If we examine the manualist tradition prior to Vatican Council II, we notice immediately how the casuistic form of a morality based on precepts corresponds to a juridical vision of the Church as a *societas perfecta*. Within this horizon, such an ecclesiological approach carries out the function of justifying the authority of the ecclesial magisterium in determining moral norms that are binding in conscience.

This argumentation is directed against modernity's claim of rationalistic autonomy. In his *Dei diritti dell'uomo*[22] (On Human Rights), Nicola Spedalieri, an Italian apologist of the late 1700s, recognizes the existence of rights prior to any revelation. For him, however, reason alone cannot defend such rights. Only a religious society that admits the authority of the Catholic magisterium can guarantee moral order in society. A few decades later, Joseph de Maistre, too, adopted the same apologetic approach:

> You should recall often this chain of reasoning: There is neither public morality nor a national character without religion. There is no European religion without Christianity. There is no Christianity without Catholicism. There is no Catholicism without the pope. There is no pope without the supreme authority that belongs to him.[23]

Such a line of reasoning finds echo in Pius IX's encyclical *Quanta Cura*.[24] The defensive tone of this approach, aimed at confronting both relativism and subjectivism as well as natural reason's claim to autonomy, joins up with the narrow horizon within which the ecclesial dimension is considered. What matters is defending the magisterium's competence in declaring moral norms.

In this way the theological dimension remains extrinsic to the connection between ethics and ecclesiology, falling into a corresponding

22. Nicola Spedalieri, *Dei diritti dell'uomo* (Assisi, 1791); see Giuseppe Ruggieri, "Ecclesiologia ed etica," *Cristianesimo nella Storia* 9 (1988): 1-22.

23. These affirmations are reported in Yves M. J. Congar, "L'ecclésiologie de la révolution française au Concile du Vatican sous le signe de l'affirmation de l'autorité," *Revue de Sciences Religieuses* 4 (1960): 77-114.

24. See Denzinger-Schönmetzer, *Enchiridion Symbolorum, definitionum et declarationum de rebus fidei et morum*, 2890.

heavy moralism. Normative regulation is brought to action from without its proper dynamism, while personal conscience finds itself in a potential fundamental conflict with the ecclesial element, which is understood exclusively in its institutional aspects and perceived within the framework of a fundamental opposition between objective and subjective morality.

In such a theoretical framework — marked by the antithesis between law and conscience, which characterizes a good portion of the moral debates from the time of St. Alphonsus and the moral systems to our own day[25] — the consequent assertion of the autonomy of conscience takes the form of a refusal or at least a restriction of the magisterium's normative competence (at the level of natural law or of determined norms of behavior).

b. The Narrative Model of the "Communitarians"

This current is found above all in the English-speaking world and in Protestant circles (Stanley Hauerwas and Gilbert Meilaender) but not restricted to those (Alasdair MacIntyre, Vigen Guroian, and Paul Wadell).[26] In contrast to the approach of modern rationalism, which is based on the abstract universality of moral reason and its autonomy, these authors are rediscovering the importance of communal traditions and narratives for the formation of the virtuous subject. Ethical rationality is brought back within a determinate historical and communitarian context. The "shipwreck" of the Enlightenment model of autonomous morality and the fact that emotivism and subjectivism are unacceptable, led these authors to rediscover the roots of *ethos* within

25. On this see Servais Pinckaers, *The Sources of Christian Ethics,* trans. M. T. Noble (Washington, DC: Catholic University of America Press, 1995); Louis Vereecke, *Saggi di storia della teologia morale moderna da Guglielmo d'Ockham a sant'Alfonso de Liguori* (Cinisello Balsamo: San Paolo Edizioni, 1990).

26. See Stanley Hauerwas, *A Community of Character: Toward a Constructive Christian Social Ethics* (Notre Dame: University of Notre Dame Press, 1981); Gilbert Meilaender, *Friendship: A Study in Theological Ethics* (Notre Dame: University of Notre Dame Press, 1985); Alasdair MacIntyre, *After Virtue;* Vigen Guroian, *Ethics after Christendom: Toward an Ecclesial Christian Ethics* (Grand Rapids: Eerdmans, 1994); and Paul J. Wadell, *Friendship and the Moral Life* (Notre Dame: University of Notre Dame Press, 1989).

the realm of particular communities in which the ideal of a good life is expressed in exemplary figures and edifying stories. Only in such a context are moral terms and value judgments still meaningful.

Nevertheless, in the absence of a theory of practical reason to ensure the objectivity and universality of the moral values that are cherished by particular religious or ethnic groups, this proposal ultimately lacks criteria for distinguishing between vices and virtues, for preferring one tradition rather than another, or for explaining why one community is superior to another.[27] Applying this ethical model to moral theology, then, one can certainly appreciate the communitarian aspect of ecclesial life and its ethical tradition, but one risks reducing the Church to one ethical community among others, being left without any principle to vindicate her claim to uniqueness and universality.

c. The Ontological Model of the Orthodox Tradition

A strong antimoralist emphasis characterizes the Orthodox position (Christo Yannaras, John Zizioulas, and Vigen Guroian)[28] and, above all, a certain reception of it in Catholic spheres (Luigi Ceccarini).[29] This current of thought wants to be a radical alternative to the moral reflection historically developed in the West, confronting the Latin Catholic tradition very critically. The connection between the Church and the moral subject is established on an ontological and not a normative axiological level. The believer's moral subjectivity has its intrinsic dimension at the level of a new ontology determined by baptism: ecclesial being.

The moral dimension is either immediately deduced from ecclesial being on the basis of the Scholastic axiom *agere sequitur esse*[30] or it is even

27. See Giuseppe Abbà, *Felicità, vita buona e virtù: Saggio di filosofia morale* (Rome: LAS, 1989).

28. Christos Yannaras, *The Freedom of Morality* (Crestwood, NY: St. Vladimir's Seminary Press, 1984); John D. Zizioulas, *Being as Communion: Studies in Personhood and the Church* (Crestwood, NY: St. Vladimir's Seminary Press, 1997); Vigen Guroian, *Incarnate Love: Essays in Orthodox Ethics* (Notre Dame: University of Notre Dame Press, 2002).

29. Luigi Ceccarini, *La morale come Chiesa: Ricerca di una fondazione ontologica* (Naples: D'Auria, 1980).

30. For a critical summary of the connection between ontology and ethics see the es-

completely reduced to it. Morality, therefore, does not merit any particular or specific attention beyond that which is reserved for it in dogmatics. According to this theological understanding, morality has nothing to do with the individual reaching perfection through his or her ethical efforts, but it is rather about adhering to a new ontology, which is already given as sacramental grace in the Church. The Church, who realizes herself above all in the holy liturgy, is seen as the dwelling place of the *ethos.*

In this way, the primacy of ontology at times amounts to the rejection of axiology and of the specific nature of moral considerations. Reflections on the moral dynamism do not have anything specific to add to theological anthropology, which deals with the being of the Christian subject, and are therefore absorbed by it. In some of these theological and pastoral approaches, the aesthetic moment (the wonder at the gift received) replaces the ethical dimension. Any reference to moral effort is then suspected of Pelagianism.

For Christos Yannaras, for example, the gospel is the antithesis of every objective morality, and ethics represents a factor that corrupts the Church. To an ethics without the Church as proposed by modernity, he contrasts a Church without ethics in his vision of orthodoxy.

d. Toward a Dynamic Model

Critical reflection on the preceding models — on the concerns they raise, on the benefits of the approaches developed but also on their respective deficiencies — urges us to develop a new model that safeguards the universality of moral truth proposed by the Church as well as its historical and concrete communitarian character, its ontological and sacramental foundation as well as the dynamic proper to freedom. *Veritatis Splendor* particularly invites moral theologians to emphasize "that dynamic aspect which will elicit the response that man must give to the divine call which comes in the process of his growth in love, within a community of salvation" (VS 111).[31] The model wished for here should thus

---

say by Juan José Pérez-Soba, "Operari sequitur esse?" in Livio Melina, José Noriega, and Juan José Pérez-Soba, *La plenitud del obrar cristiano: Dinámica de la acción y perspectiva teológica de la moral* (Madrid: Palabra, 2001), pp. 65-83.

31. John Paul II's encyclical refers here to an important document by the Sacred Congregation for Catholic Education, *The Theological Formation of Future Priests* (22 February 1976), nn. 95-101.

lay an authentic ecclesial foundation for morality, while placing it in the proper and original perspective of reflection on human action. Let us try to sketch out some of its essential elements.

In the first place, it is a question of "plac[ing] oneself *in the perspective of the acting person*" (VS 78) in order to recognize the original nature of moral experience[32] in which the practical dynamism of freedom arises. It is through acting that the moral subject establishes him- or herself. A moral choice is not a decision made about something exterior but a choice that regards our very selves[33] and which is situated within an interpersonal context. It is precisely from this "perspective of the first person" that the intrinsic connection between person and communion in acting can be understood. In this sense, it is also possible to speak of a "morality of the second person," as does Paul Ricoeur.[34] Through their actions persons seek above all to bring about communion, in which the love that stirred them to act is fulfilled.[35] Desire aroused by love is always at the origin of every movement. Prior to action there is a passion; prior to responsibility there is a gift; prior to freedom there is grace. The original form of the gift that moves to action is an interpersonal encounter that invites us to communion. The constitutively interpersonal dimension of freedom locates action within a framework that is characterized by the progressive steps of presence — encounter — communion.[36]

In this dramatic perspective, the Church is not only the ontological foundation of a new filial being but is also an *event* that occurs and that incites human freedom to take up the path of communion. She is not only teacher but also *mother,* who generates the person to the virtues, which allow the effective accomplishment of communion in history. The sacraments, and in particular the Eucharist, are the gift of a new ac-

32. Regarding this see Juan José Pérez-Soba, *La experiencia moral* (Madrid: Publicaciones de la Facultad de Teología "San Dámaso," 2002).

33. See Iris Murdoch, *The Sovereignty of Good* (London: Routledge, 1980), p. 8.

34. Paul Ricoeur, "Sympathie et respect: Phénoménologie et éthique de la seconde personne," *Revue de métaphysique et de morale* 59 (1954): 380-97.

35. According to Aquinas, the dynamic of action is, in its essence, a dynamic of the love that, beginning with affective union, tends to be fulfilled in real union: Thomas Aquinas, *Summa theologiae,* I-II, q. 28, a. 6. On this topic I refer you to chapter 2 of the present volume.

36. See Maurice Nédoncelle, *Vers une philosophie de l'amour et de la personne* (Paris: Montaigne, 1957).

tion that, through the dynamism of love, permeates and transforms the moral virtues. It is thus also easier to understand moral action's character of witness and mission in the perspective chosen by *Veritatis Splendor:* It is through our moral action that we witness to the truth about the good encountered in Christ in the ecclesial *communio.*

5. Perspectives of Dynamic Correspondence Between Ecclesiology and Filial Anthropology

Within the horizon of the last model just outlined, filial anthropology[37] can be integrated into moral theology in a dynamic form, corresponding to the perspective of the acting person suggested by *Veritatis Splendor* (VS 78). In a filial anthropology the moment of freedom is from the very beginning integrated into the gift of filial grace. The properly ethical character of such a journey is evident. Grace is understood as an interior dynamic principle, as the gift of a new way of acting: "For those who are led by the Spirit of God are children of God" (Rom 8:14).[38] Filial adoption, given in baptism, has a historical and progressive character. It is realized as free conformation to the Son in the Holy Spirit for the glory of the Father. Human freedom is called to take on the shape of the Son's freedom, participating in his virtues, so as to be fulfilled in charity as the gift of self. The new commandment of love (Jn 15:12; VS 20) demands that our freedom is capable of self-possession.[39] The royal dimension of self-dominion[40] is a necessary prerequisite to serving God and neighbor.

Also the formula "sons in the Son" (VS 18), which *Veritatis Splendor* makes its own, bears a dynamic quality. In moral theology this expression speaks of a vocation and a process to achieve it.[41] While we are chil-

---

37. The fundamental outlines of a Christologically based filial anthropology in an ethical perspective have been developed by Réal Tremblay, *L'élévation du Fils: Axe de la vie morale* (St. Laurent, Québec: Fides, 2001).

38. See José Noriega, "Movidos por el Espíritu," in Melina, Noriega, Pérez-Soba, *La plenitud del obrar cristiano,* pp. 183-200.

39. For the philosophical presuppositions of this text see Karol Wojtyla, *The Acting Person,* trans. A. Potocki (New York: Springer, 2000), pp. 105-8.

40. See the patristic comments on the beatitudes, particularly those of Leo the Great, *Tractatus 95: Corpus Christianorum Series Latina* 138A, 582-90; for the Latin Fathers see Mario Spinelli, ed., *Le beatitudini nei Padri latini* (Rome: Paoline, 1982).

41. Even Augustine, the Doctor of Grace, speaks in this way of the Christian's di-

dren of God through the grace of baptism, we are also called to become such on a journey in which the synergy between grace and freedom gives birth to a new virtuous organism, a new principle of action. On this journey, Christians realize their creaturely image, becoming ever more like the Son who gives himself in charity. This is precisely the sense in which the expression "sons in the Son" was coined and used by Emile Mersch: in relation to the theological virtues, which we can live within the Church, Christ's mystical body and the dwelling place of the moral life.[42]

This is the context in which the intimate connection between charity and the moral virtues is situated, which allows us to recognize the dynamic primacy of grace in every human action.[43] At the origin of the free *motus* of our response to God's call lie the gratuitous encounter with Christ and the gift of the Spirit, which bring about affective union, the first level of love (presence), which is directed toward actualizing itself as real union (communion). It is in this freely accepted affective union that the possibility of forming the moral virtues and of a connatural knowledge of the good is given.

The ecclesiological dimension becomes relevant in the time of salvation through the theological virtues. These allow the person to interiorize the dynamic dimension of grace and lead to the formation of the moral virtues, which are equally necessary for the agent to come to full maturity in his or her action. Charity introduces a new measure into human action, a measure that is no longer just human and rational but truly divine and supernatural. What is achieved this way is not just a disposition that is oriented toward the goal but a certain real anticipation of its

vine filiation: "'*Ut sitis filii Patris vestri qui in caelis est*' . . . in quantum ea quae ab illo praecipiuntur implemus. Unde apostolica disciplina adoptionem appellat qua in aeternam haereditatem vocamur, ut coheredes Christi esse possimus. Filii ergo efficimur regeneratione spirituali et adoptamur in regnum Dei . . . ut cum eo tamquam filii vita aeterna pro nostra participatione frueremur. Itaque non ait: Facite ista, quia estis filii, sed: Facite ista, ut *sitis filii*" (Augustine, *De sermone Domini in monte*, I, 23, 78). He thus clarifies the difference between *ut sitis* (so that you may become children) and *ut estis* (because you are already children) based on 1 John 3:1-2.

42. See Emile Mersch, *The Theology of the Mystical Body* (St. Louis: Herder, 1955), which can be considered groundbreaking as well as fundamental for the theme considered here on the ecclesial dimension of Christian moral thought.

43. See Juan José Pérez-Soba, "'La fe que obra por la caridad' (Gal 5, 6): Un anuncio de vida cristiana," in T. Trigo, ed., *"Dar razón de la esperanza": Homenaje al Prof. Dr. José Luis Illanes* (Pamplona: Publicaciones de la Universidad de Navarra, 2003), pp. 677-706.

presence in the action itself. Charity, in fact, is "the friendship of man for God."[44] Receiving the divine gift always implies an ethical dimension and thus the necessity to develop the moral virtues of which charity is the "form and mother."[45] Indeed, without the moral virtues, the dynamism of charity cannot express itself at the level of human action, involving the multiple goods for the person, the objects of our choices.

In this way one can show the ecclesiological role of charity and the other theological virtues within the moral dynamism.[46] The gift of divine charity is shared in the ecclesial communion, which springs forth from it. The Church is not in herself and principally a moral reality. She is born of God's gratuitous gift that allows us to eucharistically participate in the Trinitarian communion. The gift of this original communion is the source of human communion. The full reception of this gift and its manifestation in life imply the moral dynamism of charity and of the other theological virtues, which then promote the growth of the moral virtues at their own level, transforming them. It is charity that makes us children of the Church and allows the faithful to recognize the Spirit in the Church's words on the strength of affective harmony. Beginning from charity, life in the Church favors the development of the human virtues and thus also a connaturality with the principles of the natural law that, in itself, belongs to the rational dimension common to all persons. Moral knowledge is not brought about only at an intellectual level of argument but also and mainly by a harmony of the entire person who lets him- or herself be continually generated and regenerated in communion *(sentire cum Ecclesia)*.[47]

The fullness of freedom thus also implies a certain form of autonomy of the moral subject. This is the part of truth contained in modern ethics. Indeed, what is at stake here is the coming to be of subjects who bear within themselves the principles of their responsible action, insofar as they know its reasons and are its free authors. But this autonomy of the moral subject is really the filial autonomy of the virtuous person. We can be truly free because the Son has made us free to give ourselves,

---

44. Aquinas, *Summa theologiae,* II-II, q. 23, a. 1.

45. This formula is classic in Medieval scholasticism beginning with Peter Lombard, *Libri Sententiarum,* III, d. 23, c. 3, 2, and is attributed to St. Ambrose.

46. In effect, it was from this aspect that Emile Mersch's research developed.

47. See Ignatius of Loyola, "Rule for a True Attitude of Mind within the Church," trans. J. Munitz and P. Endean, in *Personal Writings* (New York: Penguin Books, 1996), pp. 356-58.

giving us a "house" in which to conform ourselves to him. "The slave does not continue in the house for ever; the son continues for ever. So if the Son makes you free, you will be free indeed" (Jn 8:35-36). If Christian freedom is filial freedom, then it needs a dwelling place to be able to grow into its mature dimension, which is love as the gift of self. To the challenge of modernity, which — like the prodigal son in the Gospel parable — searches for a freedom that is far away from home or even for a freedom without any home, John Paul II's encyclical responds in Augustine's words, "do not go looking for a liberation which will lead you far from the house of your liberator!"[48]

At this point, we can identify some privileged ecclesiological associations, beginning with the clues offered by the encyclical, keeping in mind Yves Congar's observation that no concept is in itself adequate to wholly express the Church's essence.[49]

a. Mother and Teacher Because Christ's Bride

Veritatis Splendor uses some ecclesiological titles, clarifying their meaning and reciprocal connections. The Church is not only a merciful *Mother* but also a *Teacher* of the truth insofar as she is first of all "the faithful *Bride* of Christ, who is the Truth in person" (VS 95). Thus, the magisterial and Petrine element of the ministry at the service of moral truth is seen in the light of the more original pneumatological and Marian dimension of the Church.[50] Above all, the Church's horizontal rela-

---

48. It is worth citing the rest of Augustine's comment on Psalm 100 that is recalled in *Veritatis Splendor*, n. 87: "In the house of the Lord, slavery is free. It is free because it serves not out of necessity, but out of charity. . . . Charity should make you a servant, just as truth has made you free . . . you are at once both a servant and free: a servant, because you have become such; free, because you are loved by God your Creator; indeed, you have also been enabled to love your Creator. . . . You are a servant of the Lord and you are a freedman of the Lord. Do not go looking for a liberation which will lead you far from the house of your liberator!" (*Enarratio in Psalmum* 99.7: *Corpus Christianorum Series Latina* 39, 1397).

49. Yves M. J. Congar, *Sainte Église: Études et approches ecclésiologiques* (Paris: Cerf, 1963). The Second Vatican Council will adopt this plural perspective. On this theme see, in particular, the contributions of Joseph Ratzinger, Hans Urs von Balthasar, and Angelo Scola on conciliar ecclesiology gathered in the collective volume *La Chiesa del Concilio: Studi e contributi* (Milan: Istra-Edit, 1985), pp. 9-74.

50. Regarding this see Hans Urs von Balthasar, *The Office of Peter and the Structure of the Church* (San Francisco: Ignatius Press, 1986), pp. 183-222.

tionship with the faithful and all persons is rooted in her vertical relationship with Christ. Her maternal dimension, highlighted by the Second Vatican Council,[51] is not at all opposed to her magisterial function. The truth, capable of guiding freedom, is spousally received by the Church in the Spirit, and it is because of this gift that she also becomes Mother and Teacher of Christians on their moral path. The temptation to reduce the Church's role in moral formation to sociological terms is avoided when we look at her Christological foundation. In the words of Giacomo Biffi, "in substance, ecclesiality is an intrinsic relationship with Christ, a relationship of both connection and conformity."[52]

b. Dwelling Place and Path

Moreover, the Church is seen as the *dwelling place* of Christian life and, at the same time, as a *path* (VS 119). In poetic literature, the home is the original place of intimacy, where life begins, protected and promising, but it is also the instrument for facing the world, helping us to say: "I will be a resident of the world in spite of the world."[53] The Christian's connection with the Church is both genetic and dynamic. We cannot walk toward the Father without dwelling in the Church who is Mother.[54] And at the same time, we can live in the ecclesial dwelling place only in the hopeful expectation of the coming kingdom, which, in order to come, also demands the commitment of human freedom.[55] The connection between the ecclesial dimension and moral action not only concerns the basic ontological level but also the existential and operative level of freedom in its practical dynamism toward fulfillment.

---

51. See Giampietro Ziviani, *La Chiesa madre nel Concilio Vaticano II* (Rome: PUG, 2001).

52. Giacomo Biffi, *La Sposa chiacchierata: Invito all'ecclesiocentrismo* (Milan: Jaca Book, 1998). Biffi, former archbishop of Bologna, argues that we should not be afraid to speak of an ecclesiocentrism in that it is already included in Christocentrism.

53. See the suggestive reflections on "home" by Gaston Bachelard, *The Poetics of Space* (Boston: Beacon Press, 1994).

54. Cyprian, *De unitate Ecclesiae,* 23.

55. This theme will be discussed in further detail in the following chapter.

c. Memory, Presence, and Prophecy: The Church and the Theological Virtues

In the historical perspective of the time of salvation, the Church is also the house built upon the rock, whose supporting pillars are the theological virtues. At the end of his moral teaching recounted by Matthew in the Sermon on the Mount (Mt 7:24-27), Jesus suggests that the connection between listening and doing, between faith and deeds, is ultimately on the ecclesiological (house) and Christological level (Christ, in fact, is the "wise man" who builds his house on rock).[56]

- *Memory:* The Church, the **"People of God"** (VS 2) among the nations, on which shines the face of Christ, is the source of *faith,* the fundamental choice that makes it possible for us to participate in Christ's virtues.
- *Presence:* As the **Body of Christ** (see VS 21) and as *communio sanctorum* (see VS 18-19, 26, 119), the Church is the place of the new commandment and of the Eucharistic nourishment of *charity.*
- *Prophecy:* As the **sacrament of the kingdom** to come, the Church sustains *hope.* She is the community of the beatitudes that witnesses to holiness even unto martyrdom[57] in order to reach the world. The moral life edifies the Church in the perspective of evangelization (see VS 107). Moreover, precisely in her orientation toward the kingdom, the Church is *sacramentum mundi.* She prefigures a world renewed and fulfilled. Thus, the logic inherent to ecclesial communion is directed toward universality.[58]

---

56. On this explanation see Joseph Ratzinger, *To Look on Christ: Exercises in Faith, Hope, and Love* (New York: Crossroad, 1991), pp. 57-59.

57. See Thérèse Nadeau-Lacour, "Il martirio, splendore dell'agire per la vita del mondo," in Melina and Zanor, eds., *Quale dimora,* pp. 161-72.

58. This is the sense in which the expression of the Church "expert in humanity" (VS 5, taken from an address of Paul VI to the General Assembly of the United Nations) and its consonance with the "moral sense present in peoples" and the "great religious and sapiential traditions of East and West" (VS 94) should be understood.

6. Essential Thematic Points for the Connection Between Ecclesiology and Morality

The reflection on the connection between ecclesiology and moral theology has shown itself to be a crucial question both for its theoretical implications and for the practical perspectives relative to the formation of the Christian moral subject, which cannot be taken for granted today. It has brought into relief some themes that are necessary for its clarification, which we can sum up in the following three points: existentiality, universality, and interiority.

In the first place, the generation of the new moral subject through the Church occurs *existentially.* That is, it is brought about through the person's freedom, stirred up by the encounter with another person. Beyond the basic ontological level, as reflected on by theological anthropology, the connection between the Church and moral action has an event-character. Human freedom is moved by an encounter in which the person anticipates a glimpse of the Good for which he or she yearns and which has the power of attraction. It is not by chance that to clarify the moral question, *Veritatis Splendor* adopts the framework of the episode of Jesus and the rich young man. The encounter with Christ is revealed as singular in that it is precisely the moment when we discover our unique vocation to communion with the Father in the Son by the working of the Holy Spirit. Our freedom is thus incited in a unique way and discovers the goal of the dynamism of love that has always dwelled within it. The Church, Christ's contemporaneity with persons of all times, is called to be the place where such encounter becomes possible today, thus also clarifying and sustaining moral experience.

In the second place, modernity with its claim to rational autonomy questions Catholic moral thought about *universality,* an issue it cannot avoid facing. Emphasizing the role of tradition in its particularity, the proposals advanced by the so-called "communitarians"[59] at times risk reducing the ecclesial dimension of Christian morality to a merely sociological level without being able to differentiate between the Church's ethics and that of a sect. In this sense, the "catholic" claim of Christian

---

59. On the debate between communitarians and liberals see, for example, Alessandro Ferrara, ed., *Comunitarismo e liberalismo* (Rome: Editori Riuniti, 1992), and Gino Dalle Fratte, ed., *Concezioni del bene e teoria della giustizia: Il dibattito tra liberali e comunitari in prospettiva pedagogica* (Rome: Armando, 1995).

morality requires the reference to the classical doctrine of the natural law (see VS 43-47). This can be done without leaving the authentically theological dimension: what one needs to do is to join the ecclesiological element to the Christological one.[60] In fact, in this way, the natural law can be understood as an expression of the Father's eternal wisdom made manifest in the Son made human. As part of the creaturely *imago Dei,* our *ratio naturalis* bears the imprint of the first reflections of the universal call to be "sons in the Son," a call that shines in all its fullness in the new law of love made manifest by Jesus: "Christ is the 'Beginning' who, having taken on human nature, definitively illumines it in its constitutive elements and in its dynamism of charity towards God and neighbor" (VS 53). The Church is our Mother and the Teacher of the moral life only insofar as she is the Bride of Christ who is truth in person and who illuminates the path to the good for every person who comes into the world.

Finally, autonomy also implies the *interiority* of the principle of the moral life, which cannot be regulated in a way that is extrinsic to the person's conscience. It is here that Catholic moral thought can fully honor the modern stance and, at the same time, correct its deformations. This means recognizing the filial character of the moral subject, who comes to his or her autonomy within a communion, understood as a new quality of his or her being and acting. Autonomy is not independence but the childship of the virtuous person, who — being a true child in the Church and thus being able to give him- or herself to others — truly becomes autonomous. And it is here that the Spirit, the soul of the Church, plays a principal role. Though from within an irreducible otherness, which reflects that of Christ toward the Father (at the height of his agony in the Garden of Gethsemane he says: "My Father, if it is possible, let this cup pass from me; yet, not as I will, but as you will," Mt 26:39), the Spirit renders the commandment interior to us in love.[61] Thus the same Spirit becomes the new interior law that through charity is the mother and form of all the moral virtues, which perfect the human

---

60. See Angelo Scola, *La fondazione teologica della legge naturale nello "Scriptum super Sententiis" di san Tommaso d'Aquino* (Fribourg: Editions Universitaires Fribourg, 1982); "Christologie et morale," *Nouvelle Revue Théologique* 109 (1987): 382-410; and Inos Biffi, "Integralità cristiana e fondazione morale," *Scuola Cattolica* 115 (1987): 570-90.

61. Hans Urs von Balthasar, "Nine Propositions on Christian Ethics," in Heinz Schürmann, Joseph Ratzinger, and Hans Urs von Balthasar, *Principles of Christian Morality,* trans. G. Harrison (San Francisco: Ignatius Press, 1986), pp. 75-104.

practical dynamisms, conferring a divine measure upon them. The same Spirit, who assists the Church's magisterium in interpreting divine law, also works in the hearts of the faithful who, united in ecclesial communion, recognize in the magisterium the authentic witness of truth.

I would like to end with a suggestive sentence from St. Irenaeus, who points out the Spirit's central role in the humanity of Christ and in the faithful through ecclesial communion:

> Wherefore He did also descend upon the Son of God, made the Son of man, becoming accustomed in fellowship with Him to dwell in the human race, to rest with human beings, and to dwell in the workmanship of God, working the will of the Father in them, and renewing them from their old habits into the newness of Christ.[62]

---

62. Irenaeus, *Adversus haereses,* 3.17.1: "Unde et (Spiritus Sanctus) in Filium Dei Filium hominis factum descendit, cum ipso adsuescens habitare in genere humano et requiescere in hominibus et habitare in plasmate Dei, voluntatem Patris operans in ipsis et renovans eos a vetustate in novitatem." See Luis Ladaria, "La unción de Jesús y el don del Espíritu," *Gregorianum* 71 (1990): 547-71.

• VII •

Christian Moral Action
and the Kingdom of Heaven

The dynamism of human action tends toward a fullness that is always sought but never achieved. Christ's gospel comes to us like a surprising and unexpected announcement of fulfillment. Together with the gift of an entirely gratuitous event that is already occurring in our midst, our aspirations are presented with a new goal beyond every expectation, the kingdom of God. A new promise sustains our action and a new restlessness animates it. From the present moment onward, there is an anticipated fullness that makes Christian action shine forth. If the Church, "the initial budding forth of that kingdom" (LG 5), is the dwelling place of Christian action, she is, to say the truth, quite a strange dwelling place — one that generates restlessness, continually shifting the habitual terms of human aspirations, always inviting toward a beyond. This home is at the same time a path, and residing in it also always means walking along it. What, then, is the condition of Christian action, situated between the *already* of a dwelling place that has finally been found and the *not yet* of our ultimate goal that transcends the reach of every possible action? What is the place of the moral dynamism in the tension between the Church and the kingdom of God?[1]

---

1. Some German scholars have highlighted the importance of the theme dealt with here, showing the correspondence between ecclesiological models and forms of moral theology: Herbert Schlögel, *Kirche und sittliches Handeln. Zur Ekklesiologie in der Grundlagendiskussion der deutschsprachigen katholischen Moraltheologie seit der Jahrhundertwende* (Mainz: Grünewald, 1981) and Josef Georg Ziegler, "Ekklesiologie und Moraltheologie," *Theologie und Glaube* 87 (1997): 321-45, 527-40. In the Italian sphere see Giuseppe Ruggieri, "Ecclesiologia ed etica," *Cristianesimo nella storia* 9 (1988): 1-22.

In response to these questions, one can delineate three principal approaches, which we will use as the basis of our reflection. First, there is the attempt to understand what the irruption of the kingdom means for the dynamism of action: In what way does the absolutely new event of God's definitive action in Jesus restructure the force field in which human action is situated? In the second step, we will explore the polarities in which Christian action is located, in the tension between present and future, between particularity and universality. Finally, in a third step, we will speak about the Church as the dwelling place of hope, that is, as the place in which the tension of action toward the coming kingdom can sustain itself and become fruitful.

1. The Dynamism of Action and the Breaking In of the Kingdom of God

a. The Kingdom as God's Definitive Salvific Act in History

As the announcement of the kingdom of God lies at the heart of Jesus' preaching and mission, his ethical message too is strictly tied to it, as is its consequent interpretation.[2] The initial words of the *kerygma* as related in Mark's Gospel already establish the connection in an absolutely clear way. "The time is fulfilled, and the kingdom of God is at hand; repent, and believe in the gospel" (Mk 1:15).

The concept of the "kingdom of God" is not of a spatial or static nature. Rather, it expresses an essentially dynamic event, the breaking in of God's royal reign into history. At the heart of the announcement lies the action of God who intervenes in order to reign.[3] The precise moment when this will happen is not the topic of Jesus' preaching. He leaves it to the Father to establish. For Jesus, what is important is not so much the moment as the promise of salvation, which is now being made to Israel

2. See Helmut Merklein, *La signoria di Dio nell'annuncio di Gesù* (Brescia: Paideia, 1994). By the same author see also his preceding study that is more specific but that, by Merklein's own admission, is partially surpassed and partially incorporated in the first one cited, *Die Gottesherrschaft als Handlungsprinzip: Untersuchung zur Ethik Jesu* (Würzburg: Echter Verlag, 1984). For a general presentation of the problem and the studies on the relationship between the announcement of the kingdom and Jesus' ethics see Giuseppe Segalla, *Introduzione all'etica biblica* (Brescia: Queriniana, 1989), pp. 163-82.

3. See Merklein, *La signoria di Dio,* pp. 42-43, 64-67.

through the proclamation of the kingdom. In effect, the saying reported in Mark does not only contain an affirmation of the future *eschaton* but, in an eschatological sense, already qualifies the present. In virtue of Jesus' mission, the coming of the kingdom has already begun. God's reign, therefore, is really an event that is already present now, an event that is revealed in Jesus' works and in his preaching in parables, an event that is expressed in his filial prayer to the Father and in the immediate access to the Father's will which Jesus has demonstrated, an event that will have its fulfillment in the paschal mystery of Christ's death and resurrection.

God's kingdom, therefore, is the action of God in history, who comes to save his people, offering complete forgiveness of all sins, renewing his election and inviting us to conversion. What is at stake in the human response to God's eschatological initiative is nothing less than our salvation, whether we lose or find ourselves. The reign of God, who draws near to his people in Jesus (whose name means "God saves"), frees us from the slavery of sin and death, from the sentence that weighs on the human condition because of our rupture of God's covenant; it allows for a new space of freedom. The limitless forgiveness granted us introduces a new intimacy with God, who in his overabundant mercy calls those who were lost to a life of sons and daughters. God's reign thus means the possibility gratuitously granted us of communion between human beings and God, a possibility to which our action always secretly aspires but never succeeds in achieving.

In the face of the announcement of the coming of the kingdom, human action is provoked to take a stance, welcoming or refusing it. What counts is no longer the observance of the Law's precepts but our openness to believing in Jesus' word, entrusting ourselves completely. At this point, however, the question of human action is sharpened and brought to a head. Who can act when it is God himself who intervenes in human history, bringing it to its fulfillment, or rather, offering a fulfillment that is absolutely beyond every natural expectation and possibility? What space remains for human persons to be the protagonists in the theatre of history when God himself has arrived on the scene?[4] With the irruption of God's salvific action, the space for human action seems to be closed definitively.

---

4. See Hans Urs von Balthasar, *Theo-Drama: Theological Dramatic Theory,* vol. 2: *The Dramatis Personae: Man in God,* trans. G. Harrison (San Francisco: Ignatius Press, 1990), p. 17.

And yet the announcement of the kingdom takes the form of the highest incitement of human freedom, as can be seen particularly well in the parables of the kingdom. Indeed, it does not come attracting attention, making people say, "'Look, here it is,' or, 'There it is'" (Lk 17:21). It comes as a small seed that falls on good soil or like a pinch of leaven in a lump of dough. Jesus speaks of the kingdom in parables because it is given to understand its mysteries only to those who open themselves with simplicity to his word and decide to follow him in the intimacy of discipleship (see Mt 13:10-17; Mk 4:10-13). For all that, the parables are not simple allegories, ornaments of a teaching that is already known and clear. They are a call and an invitation to the listeners to express their judgment, to take a personal stance, and to apply the teaching to the situation they find themselves in.[5] One can understand the mystery of the kingdom, hidden in these parables, only if, like the merchant searching for fine pearls, one is ready to risk one's freedom, to sell everything in order to acquire what has been caught sight of (see Mt 13:45-46). Although the seed of the kingdom bears within it the active principle of its development, independent of the sower's care (see Mk 4:26-29), nevertheless, it must be accepted and nurtured in order to develop and bear fruit (see Mt 13:18-23).

b. Fulfillment and Disproportion

After having briefly recalled the essential elements of the announcement of the kingdom of heaven, now we need to consider the radical way in which the irruption of God's eschatological action in Jesus restructures the field of forces in which the dynamism of human action is situated. Our reflection will try to verify correspondences and discontinuities, taking on the perspective of the movement of action, following the analyses made by Aquinas in the *prima secundae* of his *Summa theologiae.*

In the first place, the kingdom of God appears as the overabundant and unpredictable fulfillment of the desire that animates the human dynamism of action. Jesus' announcement presents the human person's communion with God — and in God, the communion with all other

5. See Charles H. Dodd, *The Parables of the Kingdom* (Glasgow: Collins, 1980), pp. 13-28.

persons and the renewal of creation for the glory of God — as an achievable, immanent, and gratuitously given event. The contents of God's reign that is about to come correspond surpassingly, beyond all expectation, with our yearning for the supreme and complete good from which action flows. The principle of the moral dynamism is the good that attracts us. From the theological point of view, this is the divine good revealed in Christ. Still, insofar as it is a principle, its intelligibility cannot be earned except from considering its effects, that is, from the will's *motus* toward it.[6]

At the origin of human action, there is the desire for happiness, which is insuppressible but which finds no suitable object capable of satisfying it. The will's openness to the infinite can never be placated within the ever finite horizon of what is within our actions' reach.[7] In this regard, Aquinas speaks of the *desiderium naturale* to see God as the ultimate object that alone can satiate human aspiration and give it meaning.[8] In this way, the goal that revelation proposes to human persons corresponds to what every human action ultimately tends toward. The ultimate and perfect beatitude can, in fact, exist only in the vision of the divine essence. It is a "natural" desire in the sense that we become aware of it prior to any free decision of the will and insofar as it is at the very root of our *motus,* in accordance with our concrete and historical nature, which from the beginning was created in grace and, therefore, supernaturally elevated.[9] Aquinas affirms: "God alone can satisfy the will of man, according to the words of Psalm 103:5: 'Who satisfies your desire with good things.' Therefore God alone constitutes man's happi-

---

6. See Giuseppe Abbà, *Lex et virtus: Studi sull'evoluzione della dottrina morale di San Tommaso d'Aquino* (Rome: LAS, 1983), pp. 160-73.

7. As we have already seen, the drama of action, always and necessarily tending beyond itself, is expressed in the marvelous pages of Maurice Blondel's *Action (1893): Essay on a Critique of Life and a Science of Practice,* trans. Oliva Blanchette (Notre Dame: University of Notre Dame Press, 1984), pp. 309-29.

8. Thomas Aquinas, *Summa theologiae,* I-II, q. 3, a. 8. Long debated, the question regarding the interpretation of the *desiderium naturale* in Aquinas's thought and the problem of the supernatural is presented in its essential terms and in a trustworthy critical overview in Giuseppe Colombo, *Del soprannaturale* (Milan: Glossa, 1996), pp. 249-331.

9. An interpretation of the *desiderium naturale* in light of the original rectitude spoken of in Aquinas, *Summa theologiae,* I, q. 95, a. 1, is convincingly proposed in Olivier Bonnewijn, *La béatitude et les béatitudes: Une approche thomiste de l'éthique* (Rome: PUL, 2001).

ness."[10] The human being's perfect act is the one by which he or she is united to God in knowledge.

It must be noted that the intellectual character of the beatifying act in no way implies its intellectualistic reduction. In fact, on the one hand, Aquinas defines it in relation to the Johannine term "life": "Now this is eternal life, that they should know you, the only true God" (Jn 17:3). For creatures, life coincides with operation, which realizes the very principle of their being. In this sense, happiness is life because it perfectly actualizes the person's being.[11] On the other hand, it is precisely the primacy of the intellect over the will in the beatifying act[12] — by which the objective aspect of knowledge prevails over the joy that follows from it — that safeguards the ecstatic character of happiness with respect to the eudaemonistic element. Happiness lies first in the encounter and the communion with God, the highest personal good, and only secondarily in the satisfaction derived from it. Happiness, the end of the dynamism of human action, can thus be interpreted in personalist terms as the perfect fulfillment of the expectation of communion with God and others.[13]

We are facing a crucial question here: If this exceeding fulfillment of the communion with God, in which human happiness is made real, is a gratuitously offered gift, how can it also be a goal for our actions? It is absolutely clear that the kingdom of God is not the fruit of human action. Human action can in no way claim to bring about what is a pure transcendental gift, what surpasses every creaturely possibility. In this sense, we can understand the following verse from Mark: "Of its own

10. Aquinas, *Summa theologiae,* I-II, q. 2, a. 8.

11. See Aquinas, *Summa theologiae,* I-II, q. 3, a. 2.

12. See Aquinas, *Summa theologiae,* I-II, q. 3, a. 4. For a suitable interpretation of the Thomist doctrine of beatitude see these essays by Servais Pinckaers in his *Le renouveau de la morale: Études pour une morale fidèle à ses sources et à sa mission présente* (Paris: Téqui, 1979): "Qu'est-ce que le bonheur?" pp. 77-92; "Recherche de la signification véritable du terme 'spéculatif,'" pp. 93-113; and "Le sens de l'amour d'amitié comme 'fait primitif' de la morale thomiste," pp. 256-63.

13. Regarding this see chapter 2 of the present volume where Thomist thought is reread and completed in the personalist perspective, mainly drawing from Maurice Nédoncelle's *La réciprocité des consciences: Essai sur la nature de la personne* (Paris: Aubier-Montaigne, 1942). For a breakdown of love's vertical and horizontal dimensions also see Juan José Pérez-Soba, "Dall'incontro alla comunione: Amore del prossimo e amore di Dio," in Livio Melina and José Noriega, eds., *Domanda sul bene e domanda su Dio* (Rome: PUL-Mursia, 1999), pp. 109-30.

accord (αὐτομάτη) the land yields fruit, first the blade, then the ear, then the full grain in the ear" (Mk 4:28). It is not the sower's action that determines as a principal cause whether the seed will sprout and grow. Whether he sleeps or wakes, the seed develops on its own through its internal energy. This fact indicates the divine principle of the kingdom's development.[14]

In the same sense, Aquinas also affirms that perfect happiness, consisting in the immediate vision of the divine essence, surpasses not only human nature but that of all creatures.[15] And yet, it would not be admissible that nature abandons the human being precisely in what is necessary such as the fulfillment of a natural desire. Thomas observes that this is why God endowed us with freedom, by which it is possible for us to turn to God, so that God himself might make us blessed. Indeed, "what we do by means of our friends, is done, in a sense, by ourselves."[16] The tension between the impossibility and the necessity of action to reach the goal is resolved in the horizon of friendship with God, through his communicating to us a mode of acting made possible in us by the God made friend in Christ.

Hence the kingdom of God has a uniquely personal character. It reaches us in the very person of Jesus.[17] This must not be understood in the sense that the coming of the kingdom is exhausted in him. The reign of God, which in Christ has reached its decisive point, is an eschatology oriented to fulfillment "so that God may be all in all" (1 Cor 15:28). The dynamism of the kingdom is that of the progressive establishment of the body of Christ in historical time, so that Christ might deliver all to the Father. The Christological and ecclesial nature of the salvific event shows that it is precisely within the structure of an interpersonal relationship that the kingdom of God comes to meet us as a proposal of friendship, through which human action is connected to the action of the Friend who renders it capable of reaching its goal.

The first, fundamental act of human freedom is conversion, the turning toward the Friend, as only he can accomplish in us what is im-

---

14. See Dodd, *Parables of the Kingdom*, pp. 131-45.

15. See Aquinas, *Summa theologiae*, I-II, q. 5, a. 5.

16. Aquinas, *Summa theologiae*, I-II, q. 5, a. 5, ad 1, where Thomas refers to Aristotle, *Ethica Nicomachea*, 3.3, 1112b.

17. Among the Church Fathers, those who emphasize the kingdom's Christological dimension are Tertullian, *Adversus Marcionem*, 4.33.8, and especially Origen, *In Matthaeum commentarius*, 14.7, who speaks of αὐτοβασιλεία.

possible for us. The invitation to conversion, the first call that resounds in the *kerygma* of Mark 1:15, thus reaffirms the absolute primacy of God's action in the coming of the kingdom but, at the same time, indicates that free human contribution is indispensable. We can participate in salvation only by a change of our mentality, by renouncing every prideful autonomy and claim of being able to save ourselves through our works, by a reversal of our value judgments, and by transforming our behavior. When the event of God's royal reign irrupts into human action, it should not be thought that it is we who bring it about. Instead, exactly the opposite holds true. It is God's reign that makes itself present to us, that involves us, and that — to the extent that we welcome it by converting and by renouncing our presumed autonomy — occurs also in our very mode of acting.[18]

c. The Insertion of Human Action into the Dynamism of the Fulfillment of the Kingdom in History

God's definitive action for the salvation of human beings, begun in Jesus' preaching of the kingdom to Israel, truly commits human action to a radical conversion. The intervention of God, who forgives the sins of his people, demands that all persons reached by such an announcement overcome the limits of juridical minimalism in their acts. The unlimited readiness to forgive, in contrast to Peter's attempt to establish at least a certain prudential measure (see Mt 18:21-35), does not at all express a voluntaristic radicalism but rather witnesses to the gratuitous event by which a new principle is introduced at the root of action. The precept of love for one's enemies (Mt 5:43-48; Lk 6:27-36) has its basis in the original filial knowledge of the merciful Father, unknown to non-believers but eschatologically granted to the disciples in their intimacy with Jesus.[19] It is here that the eschatological motivation — based on the personal experience that God reigns and wants to reach all persons with his limitless mercy — underlies even the sapiential recognition of his goodness as the provident Father of creation who makes it rain on the just and the unjust alike. The eschatological foundation of moral action is

18. See Merklein, *La signoria di Dio*, p. 148.
19. Jean Laffitte, *Le pardon transfiguré* (Paris: Editions de L'Emmanuel-Desclée, 1995), pp. 147-62.

not opposed to or exclusive of the creaturely one but rather assumes it, manifesting its ultimate meaning.

But how is human action inserted in the dynamism by which the kingdom grows in history toward its fulfillment? The parables of the kingdom point to a strange dialectic of continuity and discontinuity between human action and the final, divine reward. The parable of the wicked tenant farmers (Mk 12:1-8) shows that the vineyard owner expects fruits from his tenants, and that of the talents (Mt 25:14-30) establishes a direct and proportional continuity between the diligence with which one invests what one has been given and the final retribution. Only those who have worked assiduously in the master's absence will be able to take part — to the degree of their industry — in his eschatological reign, entering into his joy.[20] On the other hand, however, the parable of the laborers who were called at different hours to work in the vineyard and who were then paid the same wage breaks the structure of a rigid, retributive justice. This parable shows the free divine generosity and the absolute primacy of the gratuitous gift of a vocation, which alone is the basis from which human persons can finally set out to do something useful in the vineyard, which is the kingdom.

God's action, therefore, does not exclude human action but rather includes it, giving it a new foundation and a new goal. It is like the rock upon which the human work can be built; it is like the horizon toward which it can be directed. Von Balthasar speaks of a twofold aspect in which divine action relates to human action, making space for it and accompanying it: "God is latent in creation and accompanies it" *(Latenz und Begleitung)*.[21] God, while remaining hidden in a secret presence, does not cease to take us by the hand and to accompany us. Hiding himself and his glory, as the inconspicuous advent of the kingdom implies, God creates the space in which human freedom can be exercised. God's hiddenness, motivated by his love, is the supreme respect for human freedom, a freedom that can also refuse his gift and lose itself. On the other hand, divine providence never ceases to accompany and sustain human action, guarding it and helping it in ever new and fitting ways in its recurring disorientation.

If Christian action is called to participate in God's dynamism of

---

20. On these parables, see again Dodd, *Parables of the Kingdom,* pp. 93-98, 108-14. For the following see pp. 91-92.

21. Von Balthasar, *Theo-Drama,* vol. 2, pp. 271-84.

love that has entered history, it finds its secret source and its efficacy in the Eucharist, the permanent actualization of Christ's paschal self-giving. The Eucharist is the hidden seed of the kingdom that is to come, the dynamic energy that lets us participate in Jesus' charity, the source and form of all the virtues.[22] It is the bread for the journey, directed toward the final banquet of the kingdom, and at the same time it expands the kingdom's boundaries to reach all for whom Christ's body was given and his blood was shed.

2. The Crucial Polarity of Christian Action

If the irruption of the kingdom does not obstruct the dynamism of human action, neither does it resolve its constitutive tensions. Rather, one can say that in a certain sense it increases the dramatic character of action, given the urgency of conversion in the face of the beginning of eschatological time. New tensions arise and new polarities appear in the sphere of action. Everything, however, is embraced by the definitive context of the "already" of the gift and the "not yet" of its fulfillment. The dynamism of action is animated by hope, by which — through the cooperation of human freedom — the seed of divine grace will mature to its fullness.

a. In the Tension Between Church and Kingdom

The orientation of action toward its fulfillment is now inserted within the context of the dynamic relationship between the Church and the kingdom of God. The free acceptance of the Christian message about the salvific event of God's reign brought about in Christ gives birth to a new human companionship in the world and in history, the Church. Thus from the very beginning, divine and human action are intimately joined. God's initiative of gathering into a single, new people the scattered children of the remnant of Israel and those chosen of the nations meets up with the willingness and openness of the human response. At

---

22. On this see my text: Livio Melina, *Sharing in Christ's Virtues: For a Renewal of Moral Theology in Light of Veritatis Splendor,* trans. William E. May (Washington, DC: Catholic University of America Press, 2001), pp. 150-54.

the origin of the building up of Christ's mystical body lies an act of faith, indissolubly and simultaneously human and divine,[23] whose genetic model, unsurpassable and perfect, lies in Mary's consent to the angel's message, a consent that makes possible the incarnation of the Son of God by the working of the Holy Spirit.

In this way, there is a complex relation of immanence and transcendence, of actual presence and future finalization between the Church and the kingdom. On the one side, the Church is already "the initial budding forth of the kingdom" (LG 5) that is mysteriously present in her.[24] On the other side, the kingdom of God transcends the Church, constituting her final goal toward which she tends. This is why, as von Balthasar asserts, "the Church is an *open* space, a dynamic concept from the outset. For all its visibility, the earthly Church is but the movement of the Kingdom of God into the world, in the sense of an eschatological totality."[25]

Moral action, which welcomes and expresses the announcement of the kingdom in our life, thus becomes a factor in the building-up of the Church and contributes to her growth toward the kingdom. In fact, intimately related to the Eucharist, the offering of our bodies — that is, of our concrete acts — becomes "a living sacrifice, holy and pleasing to God," a "spiritual worship," which visibly gives birth to the sacramental body of Christ in the world (see Rom 12:1-2). As in docility to the Spirit and in hierarchic harmony we invest our personal gifts as "God's fellow-workers" and "God's building" (1 Cor 3:9), the Church, the Body of Christ, is built up.

In the great final vision of the wedding of the Lamb, the Book of Revelation describes the Bride dressed in a simple white garment of resplendent, pure linen. John observes: "The linen represents the righ-

23. See Aquinas, *Summa theologiae,* I-II, q. 113, a. 3.

24. For a concise and competent reading of the conciliar ecclesiology regarding the relationship between the Church and the kingdom I refer you to Gérard Philips, *La Chiesa e il suo mistero nel Concilio Vaticano II: Storia, testo e commento della costituzione* Lumen gentium (Milan: Jaca Book, 1982), pp. 90-93, 473-510. Also see the contributions by Joseph Ratzinger, "L'ecclesiologia del Vaticano II" (pp. 9-24); Hans Urs von Balthasar, "Il grande respiro della *Lumen gentium*" (pp. 25-38); and Angelo Scola, "L'essenza della Chiesa nella *Lumen gentium*" (pp. 39-74), gathered in the collective volume, *La Chiesa del Concilio: Studi e contributi* (Milan: Istra-Edit, 1985).

25. Hans Urs von Balthasar, *The Theology of Karl Barth,* trans. J. Drury (New York: Reinhart & Winston, 1971), p. 183, with a reference to Karl Barth's *Die kirchliche Dogmatik,* III (Zurich: Evangelischer Verlag, 1942), pp. 542-43.

teous deeds of the holy ones" (Rev 19:8). Thus it is precisely through Christian action in time that the resplendent linen is woven, the garment that will clothe the Church for eternity.[26] Taking in human freedom and assuming the contribution of action, the event of the kingdom grows in history until Christ delivers his kingdom to God the Father so that "God may be all in all" (1 Cor 15:20-28).

b. The Twofold Polarity of Christian Action

Situated within the sphere marked by the dynamic tension between the Church and the kingdom, Christian moral action is characterized by the polarities created within this very relationship. With the event of the kingdom in Jesus Christ, two fundamental dialectics pass through history and are reflected in the drama of action. These are the diachronic temporal polarity between present and future and the horizontal synchronic polarity between particular and universal.

i. The Diachronic Polarity Between Present and Future

In *Lumen Gentium,* the Second Vatican Council affirms: "While she slowly grows to maturity, the Church longs for the completed kingdom and, with all her strength, hopes and desires to be united in glory with her king" (LG 5). Indeed, the "saving and eschatological purpose" that is proper to the Church "can be fully attained only in the future world" even if the Church "is already present in this world" (GS 40). Thus Christian action is always propelled toward an ulterior goal beyond all temporal accomplishments. Nevertheless, this goal is truly anticipated in the present and not a mere promise. The new covenant differs from the old precisely in the movement from figures and simple promises to the realities and the incipient fulfillment.[27] Christ's redemptive action, brought about in his passion, death, and resurrection and made permanently present in the Eucharistic mystery, is already the effective presence of the kingdom in the "today" of the Church.

26. See John Paul II, *Incarnationis Mysterium,* 29 November 1998, n. 10.

27. See B. Lemeer, "De relatione inter Regnum Dei et Ecclesia in doctrina S. Thomae," *Studi Tomistici* 13 (Vatican City: Libreria Editrice Vaticana, 1981): 339-49.

Thus we can also understand the relationship of continuity and distinction between earthly progress, which is the fruit of human labor, and the kingdom of God, which is God's gratuitous work that will bring history to its eschatological fulfillment. The Council Fathers affirm in *Gaudium et Spes*:

> The values of human dignity, brotherhood and freedom, and indeed all the good fruits of our nature and enterprise, we will find them again, but freed of stain, burnished and transfigured, when Christ hands over to the Father: "a kingdom eternal and universal, a kingdom of truth and life, of holiness and grace, of justice, love and peace."[28] On this earth that Kingdom is already present in mystery. When the Lord returns it will be brought into full flower. (GS 39)[29]

ii. The Polarity Between Particular and Universal

In the history of the world, the Church always presents herself as a particular group among many other human associations. Although the Church's numerical proportions may have been relatively vast in certain historical eras, she always remains a "little flock" (Lk 12:32). Nonetheless, in virtue of her intimate connection to the kingdom that she announces, the Church is "the universal sacrament of salvation" (LG 48) for all humanity.[30] Precisely insofar as she already bears within herself the seeds of humanity's universal destiny, the Church is catholic, directed to each and every person:

> This character of universality which adorns the People of God is a gift from the Lord himself whereby the Catholic Church ceaselessly and efficaciously seeks for the return of all humanity and all its goods under Christ the Head in the unity of his Spirit. (LG 13)

It is in the relationship between the "few" who make up the visible Church and the "many" who remain, for the time being, excluded that

28. Preface for the Feast of Christ the King.

29. Regarding this see also John Paul II, *Laborem Exercens*, n. 27.

30. See John Paul II, "L'universalità della Chiesa," catechesis of 5 April 1995: "The Church is catholic, the universal sacrament of salvation, because in her, by the working of the Holy Spirit, the Kingdom of God is anticipated," *La Traccia* 5 (1995): 403.

the Church's true catholic dimension is manifested, its dynamism directed toward universality. In fact, in this way it becomes clear that the election into the Church is always an election in view and in favor of all the others. The few are the starting point for saving the many. Being elected to participate in the Church always implies a missionary task.

In the tension generated by this structural polarity, ecclesial morality cannot be a closed morality like that of a sect. Instead, it is dynamically open to all, tending toward the horizon of the universal. As Joseph Ratzinger clearly affirms in one of his earliest works, Christian brotherhood "must always remember that it is only one of two sons."[31] Here, the evocative reference is to the recurring biblical image of the "two brothers," in which the election of the younger brother always remains oriented to the hope that the elder brother will also return. This is why love and Christian brotherhood cannot be limited only to our "brothers" in the faith but must always turn to the other brother in the hopeful expectation that he too will finally accept the invitation and return home. Christians, therefore, are brothers and sisters among themselves, not against the many who are outside, but precisely in function of them.

This is also the sense in which we must interpret the norm that Jesus taught about not saluting only our brothers and sisters, as do the Gentiles who do not know the Father (see Mt 5:47). The novelty of the life of the community that is born from the announcement of the kingdom consists in the fact that, knowing the Father's limitless love and his universal salvific will, it does not delimit the horizon of its fraternity in an exclusive sense.

Thus we can see the ultimate basis of the claim to universality proper to the Christian morality that the Church proposes and lives. It is precisely in virtue of the reference to the kingdom of God that this claim is justified. The eschatological future of complete salvation, which is implied therein, has for its content the fulfillment of creation according to the original divine plan. The object of Christian ethics is thus a path of true humanity. In this sense, one can share Wolfhart Pannenberg's thesis that the concept of the kingdom of God — understood as the place of communion between human persons and God and as the fulfillment of creation in that it establishes the connection between the

---

31. Joseph Ratzinger, *The Open Circle: The Meaning of Christian Brotherhood* (Lanham, MD: Sheed & Ward, 1966), p. 115.

idea of good and the idea of God — is important not only for Christian moral theology but also for philosophical ethics as such.[32]

3. The Church, Dwelling Place of Hope

After the breaking in of the kingdom into human history, Christian action, which is grafted into its dynamism, is an action in hope.[33] The gift welcomed is an energy that matures, involving our freedom and transforming us and the world. Now action has a dwelling place that, at the same time, is also a path to our definitive homeland. In fact, although the Church is the "house of God" (1 Tim 3:15), Christians still profess that their "citizenship is in heaven" (Phil 3:20).

In his commentary on the story of Martha and Mary who welcome Jesus into their home (see Lk 10:38-42), Augustine does not identify the two sisters with the active and contemplative forms of life, respectively, as has become customary in later interpretations. Rather, he relates them to the two conditions of Christian life: Martha is the action that unfolds in time and that is necessary while we live in history, whereas Mary is the contemplative rest that can be realized forever only in the heavenly kingdom.[34] Looking at Augustine's interpretation in the light of our previous reflection, we can say that Christian action in history is somehow called to welcome Christ, building up the ecclesial dwelling

---

32. See Wolfhart Pannenberg, *Grundlagen der Ethik: Philosophisch-theologische Perspektiven* (Göttingen: Vandenhoeck & Ruprecht, 1996), in particular chapter 4 on the kingdom of God and ethics. An ample discussion of the book between diverse moralists with a reply by the author was hosted in a forum of the journal *Anthropotes* 13 (1997): 203-47, 483-92. On this theme see also the proceedings of the First Colloquium organized by the International Area of Research on the Status of Moral Theology, in which Pannenberg participated, discussing his position: Livio Melina and José Noriega, eds., *Domanda sul bene e domanda su Dio* (Rome: PUL-Mursia, 1999).

33. If charity is the summit in the order of perfection, still hope has precedence in the order of generation: "spes introducit ad caritatem" (Aquinas, *Summa theologiae*, II-II, q. 17, a. 8), "fides generat spem, et spes caritatem" (Aquinas, *Summa theologiae*, I-II, q. 66, a. 6). Nevertheless, in the same faith that is at the origin of hope and of Christian action there exists the seed of charity that develops through the dynamism of hope. On all this see Charles-André Bernard, *Théologie de l'espérance selon saint Thomas d'Aquin* (Paris: Vrin, 1961); Pinckaers, "La nature vertueuse de l'espérance" and "Le *De Spe,* la *Somme* et autres oeuvres," in *Le renouveau de la morale,* pp. 178-220, 221-40.

34. Augustine, *Sermones,* 103.1-2 (*Patrologia Latina* 38.613-615).

place on earth, while in the future kingdom God himself will offer us as a reward an eternal dwelling place where we can rest in perfect communion with him, the Supreme Good.[35]

a. The Hope of the Kingdom, the Soul of the Christian Moral Dynamism

The Christian moral dynamism is thus animated by our hope of the kingdom: "every one who thus hopes in him purifies himself as he is pure" (1 Jn 3:3). A human action proportionate to the kingdom is at the same time a prophecy of perfect communion and its beginning realization. In this regard, insofar as we are seeking to understand the various dimensions of the relationship between human action and the kingdom, it will be very beneficial to review Thomas's teaching on the beatitudes, on merit, and on reward.[36]

First of all, we must emphasize the absolute disproportion of all human action in respect to the communion with God in which beatitude consists. Because this beatitude is a good that surpasses every created nature, it is impossible for human action to be the efficient cause of its attainment. It is only through God's action *(solo Deo agente)* that human persons are rendered happy, if we speak of perfect beatitude.[37] Nonetheless, to acquire this beatitude, it is fitting for human beings to dispose themselves by means of some movement of their freedom, with which they tend toward it. The various works by which we dispose ourselves in time to accept the gift of beatitude are called "merits."[38] Merit, therefore, is a quality of human acts by virtue of which they are by grace proportionate to the ultimate end of supernatural beatitude.

As we have previously noted, in the *tertia pars* dealing with Christology, Aquinas explains the reason why the arrangement of merit is fit-

---

35. If human action "welcomes" Christ, freely accepting the seed of the kingdom as its new principle, it must also be noted that more properly speaking the human dynamism of action is "welcomed" into the dynamism of the Spirit, transformed by it and led to its fulfillment.

36. On this, besides the study by Olivier Bonnewijn already cited, see also the study by Joseph P. Wawrykow, *God's Grace and Human Action: "Merit" in the Theology of Thomas Aquinas* (Notre Dame: University of Notre Dame Press, 1995).

37. See Aquinas, *Summa theologiae,* I-II, q. 5, a. 6.

38. See Aquinas, *Summa theologiae,* I-II, q. 5, a. 7.

ting, observing that what we receive also on our own merit we receive in a more noble fashion than what we receive as a pure gift. In fact, those who obtain something on their own merit, in a certain way possess it through themselves and thanks to themselves.[39] Once again, however, how can we reconcile the theological demands of the absolute gratuity of the gift with the moral demands of the action's proportion to the end?

The infinite transcendence of divine causality is exalted by including the contribution of human action as a secondary, disposing cause for the acquisition of the supernatural gift of beatitude, which Christ alone can merit for us as the primary, efficient cause. Christ's redemptive action, insofar as it is *gratia capitis* (the grace of the head), is the cause of the merit of the other members of the Body: acting as the head of the Body, that is, the Church, he also merits for us and, in our every action, continues to merit in us.

For Aquinas the Christian's meritorious action rooted in Christ is, at the same time, *spes beatitudinis* (that is, merit as a claim that gives us the hope of happiness)[40] as well as *beatitudo spei* (that is, merit as the happiness of hope, as the beginnings of happiness, given as a reward in the very dynamism of hope).[41] Thus the two fundamental dimensions of the relationship between human action and future happiness are outlined: merit *(meritum)* in its proper sense and reward *(praemium)*. These two dimensions correspond exactly to the two polarities that are inherent to action ever since the breaking in of the kingdom and of which we have spoken above. Merit refers to a certain preparation or disposition of human action with regard to future happiness, while reward signifies the presence of some imperfect anticipation of this happiness already in this life. It refers to the first fruits that can be fully enjoyed only in the eternal and definitive kingdom.[42]

The category of "merit," however, must be cleansed of any strictly juridical connotation. As has been seen, it is in no way an acquired right but a new quality of our action that comes from the intimate union with

---

39. See Aquinas, *Summa theologiae,* III, q. 19, a. 3, and Ghislain Lafont, *Structures et méthode dans la Somme Théologique de saint Thomas d'Aquin* (Bruges: Desclée de Brouwer, 1961).

40. See Aquinas, *Summa theologiae,* I-II, q. 69, a. 2, which is also the reference for the immediately following exposition.

41. Thomas Aquinas, *Super Evangelium Sancti Joannis lectura,* 20.6.5.

42. See Thomas Aquinas, *Super Epistolam ad Galatas lectura,* cap. 5, l. 6.

Christ and his action. In fact, "the merit of life everlasting pertains first to charity,"[43] through which all the acts of the other virtues are oriented toward the ultimate end of enjoying God in the beatific vision. The impossibility of meriting happiness on our own, although it is an object of natural desire, can be overcome precisely in our free ability — gratuitously offered to us — to turn toward God so he might make us happy. In friendship with Christ, human action is able "to merit" that divine good for which desire powerlessly yearns and toward which the movement of our action is directed. With regard to merit, as we have already seen, Aquinas cites the Aristotelian idea of friendship as an *alter ego*: "For what we do by means of our friends, is done, in a sense, by ourselves."[44] Now, it is precisely insofar as merit is ultimately rooted in charity, that is, in an interpersonal relationship of friendship with Christ, that the category is definitively freed not only from legalism but also from any suspicion of selfishness.[45]

As previously noted, the category of "reward" introduces the idea of an anticipated remuneration, an incipient participation in the final beatitude, already beginning with action in history. It is connected to the gospel theme of the "beatitudes," which in the Thomist perspective refers to the supreme excellence of action, also integrating its meritorious aspect and elevating it to an even higher level.[46] In fact, Aquinas's out-

43. Aquinas, *Summa theologiae,* I-II, q. 114, a. 4: "Et ideo meritum vitae aeternae primo pertinet ad caritatem."

44. Aquinas, *Summa theologiae,* I-II, q. 5, a. 5, ad 1: "Quae enim per amicos possumus, per nos aliqualiter possumus."

45. In this sense, the just concerns expressed by Marc Ouellet ("Domanda sul bene, risposta di Cristo," in Melina and Noriega, eds., *Domanda sul bene,* p. 144) are honored.

46. It is certainly the merit of Servais Pinckaers, *The Sources of Christian Ethics,* trans. M. T. Noble (Washington, DC: Catholic University of America Press, 1995), pp. 145-63, to have highlighted again the structural importance of the beatitudes not only in the gospels but also in patristic and Thomistic moral thought. After an almost total oblivion, the theme of the beatitudes begins to reappear here and there in essays of moral theology: Romano Altobelli, "Dall'etica delle virtù all'etica delle beatitudini," *Rivista di Teologia Morale* 115 (1997): 389-94; Renzo Gerardi, *Alla sequela di Gesù: Etica delle beatitudini, doni dello Spirito, virtù* (Bologna: Edizioni Dehoniane, 1998). The Associazione Teologica Italiana per lo Studio della Morale (Italian Theological Association for the Study of Moral Theology) dedicated its 1998 national convention to this theme ("The Beatitudes and the Moral Life"). The proceedings of this conference have been published in: Francesco Compagnoni and Salvatore Privitera, eds., *Vita morale e beatitudini. Sacra Scrittura, storia, teoretica, esperienza* (Cinisello Balsamo: Edizioni San Paolo, 2000). Usually, these treatments are limited to examining the evangelical values proposed by the

standing insight is to understand the beatitudes precisely from the point of view of the dynamics of action. For him, they are not a quality of being or moralistic precepts. Instead, they are those human acts in which the virtues have reached their supreme perfection through the gifts of the Spirit. Thus, in these excellent acts a foretaste of beatitude *(inchoatio beatitudinis)*[47] is given. It could be said that the beatitudes are those human acts that, participating in Christ's action through the Spirit, welcome the mystery of the kingdom into themselves. Within the paradox of an apparent defeat, amidst tears and persecution, human action already hides within itself the seeds of the beatitude of the kingdom. Anticipating the final end, the beatitudes nourish hope and therefore the dynamism by which action reaches toward its transcendent goal.

b. The Church's Historical Communion, Sustenance of Our Hope

On the basis of St. Paul's affirmation that "the kingdom of God is not a matter of food and drink, but of righteousness, peace, and joy in the Holy Spirit" (Rom 14:17), Aquinas, in his treatise on the new law in the *Summa theologiae,* affirms that the kingdom of God consists principally in interior acts.[48] In his commentary on the Letter to the Romans, regarding the text cited above, he further clarifies that "the kingdom of

---

beatitudes, understanding them as a reference to specifically Christian precepts on the virtues without, however, grasping their structural value for a theological understanding of action. For Aquinas, the beatitudes are those acts that, in themselves, integrate the excellence of the virtues and the gifts of the Holy Spirit.

47. Aquinas, *Summa theologiae,* I-II, q. 69. Article 1 reads: "Beatitudo est ultimus finis humanae vitae. Dicitur autem aliquis iam finem habere, propter spem finis obtinendi, unde et philosophus dicit, in I Ethic., quod *pueri dicuntur beati propter spem;* et apostolus dicit, Rom. VIII, *spe salvi facti sumus.* Spes autem de fine consequendo insurgit ex hoc quod aliquis convenienter movetur ad finem, et appropinquat ad ipsum, quod quidem fit per aliquam actionem."

48. Aquinas, *Summa theologiae,* I-II, q. 108, a. 1, ad 1: "Regnum Dei in interioribus actibus principaliter consistit, sed ex consequenti etiam ad regnum Dei pertinent omnia illa sine quibus interiores actus esse non possunt." On the ecclesiological dimensions of Thomist moral theology, in the treatise on the *lex evangelica,* see Servais Pinckaers, "L'Eglise dans la Loi nouvelle: Esprit et institution," Chapter III/2 in *L'Évangile et la morale* (Fribourg: Editions Universitaires Fribourg, 1990), pp. 207-22.

God is said to be that by which God reigns in us and that by which we come to his kingdom."[49] It is, therefore, mainly considered from the interior point of view: inner justice and the peace and spiritual joy that come from it. St. Thomas interprets these last three elements evoked by St. Paul as the three progressive steps through which God's reign is brought about in human interiority. First there is justice as the expression of the harmony in our relationships with God and neighbor. Its effects are inner and social peace. Finally, there is the joy caused by the Spirit that derives from the perfection of the work accomplished and that gives us a foretaste of heaven.

In the gradual assertion of the kingdom within human action through the new law of the Spirit, the Church is a historical community and the sustenance of hope. The ecclesial dimension of this progressive transformation certainly also has an exterior and disciplinary aspect, although it is principally interior and spiritual. In effect, there are exterior ways of acting that are opposed to the justice, peace, or joy of the kingdom, standing in contrast to the dynamics of hope. These must be forbidden also through exterior precepts of the Church. This is the "written" dimension of the new law, on which the binding judgment appertains to the Church and especially to her hierarchical ministry.[50] From apostolic times, some behaviors have been judged to be incompatible with the kingdom:

> Do you not know that the unrighteous will not inherit the kingdom of God? Do not be deceived; neither the immoral, nor idolaters, nor adulterers, nor sexual perverts, nor thieves, nor the greedy, nor drunkards, nor revilers, nor robbers will inherit the kingdom of God. (1 Cor 6:9-10)[51]

---

49. Thomas Aquinas, *Super Epistolam ad Romanos lectura*, cap. 14, l. 3: "Regnum autem Dei dicitur hic id per quod Deus regnat in nobis et per quod ad regnum ipsius perveniamus. . . . Et inde est quod regnum Dei principaliter consideratur secundum interiora hominis, non secundum exteriora (see Lk 17:21)."

50. See Edward Kaczynski, *La legge nuova: L'elemento esterno della legge nuova secondo San Tommaso* (Rome: Vicenza, 1974).

51. Other lists of behaviors that exclude from the kingdom can be found in the Pauline letters: Romans 1:29-31; 1 Corinthians 5:10-11; 2 Corinthians 12:20-21; Galatians 5:19-21; 1 Timothy 1:9-10. In *Veritatis Splendor*, n. 81, John Paul II also makes explicit reference to these texts as a foundation of the Church's magisterial authority to propose determinate norms that are absolutely binding.

The ecclesial community has the authority to declare exterior acts and behaviors that destroy justice and communion to be incompatible with the kingdom.

The Church, however, is effective above all in the interior dimension in which she accompanies Christians in their action, sustaining the hope in the kingdom that animates them. In fact, in her teachers, she is a guide for the path; in her saints, she is the visible anticipation of the peace and joy in which the kingdom consists and to which human action aspires. Augustine defines the Church, precisely insofar as she is the mother of all Christians, also as the *morum regula* — the rule of morals — not just in the sense of the magisterial function of her ministry but also and above all through her very life of communion.[52] Like a mother, the Church is not limited to generating Christian life but is also concerned about nourishing it and causing it to grow toward the kingdom. She accomplishes a complex maternal task in the Christian moral life: she offers the sacraments that nourish Christians *(praebens sacramenta);* she teaches and guides them on the path of virtue *(praedicans);* she encourages and educates them with examples of a holy life *(ostendens exempla);* and with her communal life she favors the true movement of the *delectatio,* orienting it toward the fruits of the Spirit, for which she refines the faithful's taste. For the great Bishop of Hippo, therefore, ecclesial life is a school of the virtues in view of the kingdom.

4. Conclusion

We thus come to conclude our reflection dedicated to the new condition of Christian action, which contains the seed of the kingdom or, as perhaps it is better said, which inserts into the dynamism of the kingdom the dynamism of its very action. Every action of the Christian is like an invocation, "may your kingdom come!" Each action reaches toward a fulfillment that only the Father can grant.[53] At the same time it is an ac-

---

52. Augustine, *De moribus Ecclesiae catholicae,* 1.4.30.63. On this see also my contribution, Livio Melina, "Ecclesialità e teologia morale: Spunti per un 'ri-dimensionamento' teologico della morale," *Anthropotes* 5 (1989): 7-27.

53. Augustine, *De sermone Domini in monte.* In this masterful comment on the Sermon on the Mount in Matthew 5–7, which will remain fundamental for the systematization of Catholic moral thought, in particular for Aquinas, Augustine places prayer at the

tion in peace, because it witnesses to an initial gift that is already present and that gradually bears fruit in excellent acts animated by the Spirit of Jesus.

Thus Christian moral action, welcoming in itself the seed of the kingdom, is born of a fullness and tends toward its fulfillment. It receives its sure basis and its transcendent goal from the irruption of God's reign, which is real and effective in Christ's action and present in the Church's sacraments. Desire and promise, which are the soul of the natural dynamism of human action, are preceded by the gift of a love without limits or boundaries, which urges for a response and bursts open the confines of human action.

It is within the historical community of the Church that we participate in the dynamism of the love of God, who brings his creation to fulfillment and, notwithstanding sin and death, leads us to our goal, to the beatific communion and the renovation of all things. Only remaining in love can we walk toward the goal of the kingdom. We have used the expression "the Church as the dwelling place of hope." In light of the reflections made, we can conclude that the Church can truly be a dwelling place that welcomes and promotes the dynamism of action only if she is first of all the path to the fulfillment of the kingdom of God, toward which she is oriented and in function of which she exists.

---

foundation of the moral journey, connecting the seven petitions of the Our Father to the acquisition of virtue, to the reception of the gifts, and to the participation in the beatitudes, all realities that lead back to the number seven.

Action, the Epiphany
of an Ever Greater Love

"Let your light so shine before men, that they may see your good works and give glory to your Father who is in heaven" (Mt 5:16). These words of Jesus about the disciples' good works as an epiphany of the Father's glory are located by Matthew the Evangelist at the very heart of the Sermon on the Mount, where they serve as the link between the beatitudes, which precede them, and the moral teaching of the New Law, which fills out their concrete specifics.[1] These words indicate that the actions of Jesus' followers are called to shine forth and fulfill a revelatory function for the whole world: to manifest the Father's glory and to bring human beings into communion with him.

How then do human actions give glory to God? What does this mean for our understanding of the operative dynamism in which the synergy between the divine and the human is realized? We will attempt to answer these questions in three moments: first, by meditating on superabundance, the sign that, according to the New Testament, points to the breaking in of the kingdom of God on earth and the effectiveness of the divine presence in our world; next, we will reflect on the leading role of the Spirit in human action; and finally, we will be able to understand the Christian's excellent actions as the expression of agapic rationality, going beyond the human measure of practical reason without contradicting it.

---

1. Cf. also 1 Peter 2:12; on this subject, see Luis Sanchez Navarro, *La Enseñanza de la Montaña. Commentario contextual a Mateo 5-7* (Estella: Verbo Divino, 2005), pp. 56-57, and by the same author: "El Padre en la 'enseñanza de la Montagna' (Mt 5-7): Estructura y teología," *Revista española de teología* 65 (2005): 197-210.

1. A Superabundance That Gives God Glory

The Old Testament already attests to the fact that the human actions of God's covenant people are called to manifest the glory of God. In the book of Deuteronomy, the observance of the Law in the face of other peoples expresses Israel's wisdom and intelligence and manifests God's singular closeness to his chosen people (cf. Deut 4:6-8).[2] The servant's obedience to the law merits a blessing from the Lord, a blessing of abundance and wealth, and this blessing returns in praise to the Creator and Redeemer. The people of Israel are like a beloved vineyard from which God expects fruit in due time. Jesus also takes up this image, speaking severely of the obligation to bear fruit at the exact time that the master requires it (Mk 11:12-14, 20ff.); using a different metaphor for this same teaching, he refers elsewhere to the necessity of repaying the deposit with interest (cf. Mt 25:14-30). For his assiduous care for the vine and for all the good he has entrusted to them, God is not satisfied with words of thanks; he demands scrupulous responsibility and true fruitfulness in their actions.

In the New Testament, however, giving glory to God does not consist in the observance of the law alone or in lip-service, but in the disciple's very existence, inasmuch as it is henceforth grafted onto the God who has given himself personally to humanity in his own Son. The Old Testament images are transformed to express the new reality: the vineyard is no longer just a collective symbol that is the object of the farmer's care; in Christ the Vine, it becomes a planting in which we are personally inserted, and his living sap flows into the branches that we are. God is no longer just the object of the believers' praise, but the intrinsic principle of their very existence.[3]

In the Gospel of John, the disciples are the branch of the vine that, grafted onto Jesus, bears much fruit to the glory of the Father (Jn 15:8). As the Son glorifies the Father with his works, so also the disciples are drawn in and placed in the sphere of glory between the Father and the Son, such that the Spirit, the sap of life, can make the new life of love

---

2. Cf. Norbert Lohfink, *Höre, Israel! Auslegung von Texten aus dem Buch Deuteronomium* (Düsseldorf: Patmos Verlag, 1965).

3. On the subject and what follows, see Hans Urs von Balthasar, *The New Covenant*, vol. 3 of *The Glory of the Lord: A Theological Aesthetics* (San Francisco: Ignatius Press, 1990), pp. 389-431.

spring up within them, making them able to glorify the Father in deed and in truth.

Action is thus understood as a fruit (καρπός) arising from a divine gift, and human freedom has permitted this gift to bear fruit through its own active collaboration. It is precisely in this way that human actions give glory to God. The possibility to bear abundant fruit entails undergoing the suffering of being pruned (Jn 15:2) and reliving the mystery of the grain of wheat, which can only produce much fruit when it falls into the earth and dies (Jn 12:24). Only the utter availability of the Son, who seeks not his own glory, but gives himself totally to the point of letting himself be entirely dispossessed, makes this surprising fruitfulness possible to the glory of the Father. Inserted into the Trinitarian life and filled with divine nourishment, the branches can bear the multitude of fruit the Father expects from them; what is more, their fruit can become the principle of further fruitfulness.

We are now before the distinctive character that, more than any other, reveals the divine quality of the sap permeating the disciples' actions: superabundance (περίσσευμα). This is the mark of God, the manifestation of his glory. The first of Jesus' signs in the Gospel of John, the miracle at Cana (Jn 2:1-11), is significant in this respect.[4] The extraordinary quantity of wine (520 liters) that Jesus provides at the very moment the banquet was nearing its end, as well as its exceptional quality, go well beyond what was necessary and even simply fitting to continue a wedding feast. These characteristics manifest the glory of the God who on the sixth day fulfills the creation and the election by beginning the new humanity in the community of the disciples that is destined to fill the whole earth.[5] Superabundance is the expression that the season of scarcity and dearth has definitively passed away, revealing a new fullness that is lavished out copiously and unreservedly, like a generous fountain that does not fear going dry, but continuously gives of itself. In this way, a divine "always more" appears, which, from the merely human point of view, seems a foolish and incomprehensible prodigality.

The same excess is found in the multiplications of the loaves (Mk 8:8; Mt 14:20), in which the divine intervention goes beyond reasonable

4. This is what Benedict XVI observes in his *Jesus of Nazareth,* trans. Adrian Walker (New York: Doubleday, 2007), p. 252.

5. On this subject, see Bruno Ognibeni, *Il matrimonio alla luce del Nuovo Testamento* (Rome: Lateran University Press, 2007), pp. 69-80.

proportions and the need to satisfy the crowd. It is even more generous when the need is less. The episode of Simon the Pharisee and the sinful woman who appears at his banquet highlights the contrast, this time in the case of human action and not that of Jesus, between the parsimony of the host and the uncalculated outpouring of the woman, who spreads a precious ointment along with her tears, scandalizing one who reasons with a mentality of philanthropic utilitarianism (Lk 7:36-50). The uncalculated outpouring reveals a new principle breaking into human acting, and according to this principle the categories of means and end, projects and programmed execution of acts become inadequate — if they were ever adequate to begin with. The determination of a goal fixes *a priori* a limit on action and consequently establishes adequate means according to a reasonable proportion; in the same way, the end, assigning a conclusion to the work undertaken, measures the process of execution and controls the phases of its progressive realization.

In what respect does superabundance give glory? It is more than just a matter of showcasing one's power to overcome limitations, or a display of wealth by someone who can blithely squander it. Prodigality is not an end in itself, nor is it meant to humiliate others. The episode of the sinful woman brings to the fore the ultimate reason for the sign: superabundance manifests love. She has not loved little, but much; she has loved without measure, and for this reason much has been forgiven her. The circle of divine love has been realized and fostered through the generous collaboration of the woman, who by corresponding with her love to the prior love of God has merited it still more.

The gospel breaks into the human reality of action the way a new wine demands new wineskins. If the new principle of love, penetrating into human action, leads one to go beyond the utilitarian scheme of action, in the same way the manifestation of divine love in Jesus constrains us to go beyond the explanation of love as a tendency of the appetite simply to its own satisfaction. Divine love is not poverty seeking what it lacks. If that were all there is to love, Aristotle would be right in saying that loving does not befit a God, but only man.[6] Love, however, is superabundance of good freely communicating itself in a gift.[7] The fullness of

6. Cf. Aristotle, *Ethica Eudemia,* VII, 12, 1245b 14-15; Kevin Flannery, "Un aristotelico può considerarsi amico di Dio?" in Livio Melina and José Noriega, eds., *Domanda sul bene e domanda su Dio* (Rome: PUL-Mursia, 1999), pp. 131-37.

7. Cf. Livio Melina, José Noriega, Juan José Pérez-Soba, *Camminare alla luce dell'amore. Fondamenti della morale cristiana* (Siena: Cantagalli, 2008), pp. 124-33.

divine love, in which human beings participate, becomes in them the principle of a new generosity that overcomes all limitations.

For the Apostle Paul, grace's act of superabundance (ὑπερπερισσεύειν, Rom 5:20) existentially translates into the law of "always more" in the fruitful gift of himself for the disciples who are entrusted to him in his mission (cf. 2 Cor 1:4-5). This is an overflowing of faith in mutual love (cf. 1 Thess 3:12), which always keeps growing. Even the gesture of the collection for the poor of Jerusalem, an expression of fraternal charity, is thus a gift of abundance that returns in praise to God by manifesting the new principle of grace (χάρις) that inspired it (2 Cor 8–9). In the superabundance of fraternal charity, the Spirit is the one who gives glory to the love of the Father and the Son by making love spring up in the disciples.

2. The Leading Role of the Spirit in Human Acting

Sacred Scripture unequivocally attests, then, to the primacy of divine action in the human actions of the justified. The children of God "are led by the Spirit of God" (Rom 8:14);[8] "for God is at work in you, both to will and to work" (Phil 2:13). Now we must examine, through theological reflection, the meaning of this leading role of the Spirit in human acts with respect to the natural operative dynamisms.

A Father of the Eastern Church can put us on the right track. In reference to John 4:14, "the water that I shall give him will become in him a spring of water welling up to eternal life," St. Cyril of Jerusalem puts it this way:

> Why did He call the grace of the Spirit water? Because by water all things subsist; because water brings forth grass and living things; because the water of the showers comes down from heaven; because it comes down one in form, but works in many forms. . . . So it is one in the palm-tree, and another in the vine, and all in all things; and yet is one in nature, not diverse from itself; for the rain does not change itself, and come down first as one thing, then as another, but adapting itself to the constitution of each thing which receives it, it becomes to each what is suitable.[9]

8. Cf. José Noriega, *Guiados por el Espíritu. El Espíritu Santo y el conocimiento moral en Tomás de Aquino* (Rome: PUL-Mursia, 2000).

9. Cyril of Jerusalem, *Catechesis XVI on the Holy Spirit,* in *The Early Church Fathers and Other Works* (Edinburgh, 1867), no. 12: PG 33, 931-35.

Cyril compares the Holy Spirit to water that adapts to different plants to bear many forms of fruit. To understand how the Holy Spirit's leading role in human actions comes about, this text suggests two questions: (1) How does the Spirit adapt to the demands of human action, inserting himself into it without causing it to lose its proper nature as a true *"actus humanus"*? (2) How is human action transformed by the Spirit so as to contribute to the human person's divinization?

Many different answers have been given to these questions throughout history, and some of the answers have at times diminished the human character of Christian action to the point of losing it entirely. The "spiritualistic" interpretation of Peter Lombard, which served as the matrix for further explanations, understood the Holy Spirit as the immediate principle of action, underemphasizing the role of its human dimension.[10] The Lutheran and Reformed conception of *agapē* moved in the same direction, totally separating divine action from human action, denying the affective dynamics of charity and the very idea that charity might be understood as a virtue.[11] The idea that *agapē* would become a stable capacity at the disposition of the human operative faculties is perceived by Protestants as tainted with Pelagianism.

This approach, shared by Kierkegaard, Nygren, and Barth,[12] is also that of Paul Ricoeur, according to whom the gospel brings into the world of morality an "economy of superabundance" and free gift, a logic of the excessive and the unforeseen, that is in dialectic tension with the human perspective determined by simple justice.[13] Justice is concerned with the Golden Rule's demands of reciprocity and symmetry and tends to establish relations of equity that are universally valid on the basis of mutually acceptable rationality. With the gospel, on the contrary, we enter a world of dissymmetry above every capacity of human virtue.

Along the same lines, Jean-Daniel Causse speaks of the gesture of *agapē* as a moment "above ethics," in which ethics is suspended.[14] Di-

10. Cf. Peter Lombard, *Sententiae,* I, 17, chapter 1, n. 143.

11. A well-known classic is Anders Nygren's *Agape and Eros* (Philadelphia: Westminster Press, 1953).

12. In addition to Nygren's work, see Søren Kierkegaard, *Works of Love* (Princeton: Princeton University Press, 1995); Karl Barth, "Agape and Eros," in *Church Dogmatics: A Selection* (New York: Harper Torchbooks, 1961), pp. 173-93.

13. On this matter, see Paul Ricoeur, *Amour et justice* (Tübingen: Mohr, 1990).

14. Cf. Jean-Daniel Causse, *L'instant d'un geste. Le sujet, l'éthique et le don* (Geneva: Labor et fides, 2004).

vine superabundance could only enter the world when human beings lose control of their own actions and let the power of the gift they have received act in them. This is not a stable dynamism, then, present in history as qualifying a new ethical subject, but rather the instantaneous breaking in of a divine element in human actions. Ultimately, *agapē* is the divine power of gift *in se* and not a human act. In this sense, however, it remains substantially extrinsic to human acting and its dynamisms, a gift that can be welcomed only in an instant and in a void.

Protestant thought remains unable, therefore, to take up the newness of *agapē* within the human dimension of action. Such an approach sees freedom as torn between the demands of divine love and the experience of sin, unwilling to consider freedom apart from the scandal of evil. Reconciliation is always in a future that is still to come and not given within human action, but only in the hope for some "other" intervention. This conception takes place after sin, but before forgiveness.[15] Now, however, forgiveness is a fact; it has already happened and is present in human history. This is the proof of the gratuitousness and fullness of the superabundant gift of God, which has introduced a new possibility into human life. Forgiveness is what transforms the humanly unthinkable into something possible. The memory of the superabundance of love received cannot put limits on gratuitousness; it is free to express itself according to the new logic of the gift. Hope is therefore not purely waiting for a future intervention by God that is yet to take place, but rather it is a trusting expectancy and an active cooperation of one's freedom with a gift already initially given and straining toward its fulfillment.

Since Peter Lombard's interpretation has produced a dialectic and extrinsicistic account of the leading role of the Spirit in human operative dynamisms, it would be worthwhile to return to the debate of that time so as to reconnect with a second line of theological development that has proposed the role of the Spirit as going through the mediation of charity as a virtue, certainly an infused virtue, but one that acts as a true human operative principle.

Alexander of Hales had already set himself apart from the Master of the Sentences by showing how the dynamics of love imply a certain original receptivity on the part of human beings that involves their free-

---

15. About this, see Albert Chapelle, *Les Fondements de l'Éthique. La symbolique de l'action* (Brussels: IET, 1988), 106-8.

dom.[16] It was St. Thomas Aquinas, however, who, continuing this same approach, introduced the decisive factor by showing how the action of divine grace receives its ultimate explanation in the light of friendship, that is, in an interpersonal context: "Charity is a certain friendship of man for God."[17]

Charity presents itself, therefore, as a virtue, as a principle of human operation, that nevertheless has its own specificity: it originates in God's gift of initial personal union with him, a union that must be developed through action. Friendship permits us to maintain the full transcendence of the gift, while also showing its progressive interiorization, just as in the experience of love the lover is transformed by affective union with the beloved, whose imprint, the principle of a specific form of knowledge by connaturality,[18] is borne more and more deeply by the lover.

If charity is a certain friendship with God, on this basis it will be possible to understand the action of the Spirit in a nonextrinsic manner. Love configures the whole intentional system of the acting subjects, orienting them to the last end and determining the virtuous ends of actions in the light of this end.[19] Through friendship with God given to them in the Spirit, Christians receive an initial participation in eternal beatitude, the knowledge of God and communion with him (cf. Jn 17:3). This enables the operative dynamisms of the virtues to be structured with a view to the last end by creating an affective connaturality that becomes a source of light for our actions. For this reason, there is a need for the moral virtues, assumed into charity and transformed by it. By means of charity, the Spirit enters into the affective dynamics of love and permeates the moral virtues; charity becomes "the mother and form of the vir-

16. Cf. Alexander of Hales, *Summa Theologica,* Lectio 2, Pars III.

17. Thomas Aquinas, *Summa theologiae,* II-II, q. 23, a. 1: "Caritas amicitia quaedam est hominis ad Deum." Regarding this text, cf. Antonio Prieto Lucena, *De la experiencia de la amistad al misterio de la caridad. Estudio sobre la evolución historico-teológica desde Elredo de Rieval hasta Santo Tomás de Aquino* (Madrid: Facultad de Teología S. Dámaso, 2007).

18. Cf. Rafael Tomas Caldera, *Le jugement par inclination chez Saint Thomas d'Aquin* (Paris: Vrin, 1980); Marco D'Avenia, *La conoscenza per connaturalità in S. Tommaso d'Aquino* (Bologna: Ed. Studio Domenicano, 1992).

19. Cf. José Noriega, "'Sentite de Domino in bonitate.' Prospettive sulla relazione tra moralità e spiritualità," in Livio Melina and Olivier Bonnewijn, eds., *La Sequela Christi. Dimensione morale spirituale dell'esperienza cristiana* (Rome: Lateran University Press, 2003), pp. 199-213.

tues." The gifts of wisdom and counsel are most particularly a superabundance of charity (cf. Phil 1:9: "that your love may abound more and more, with knowledge and all discernment").

The Paschal logic of expropriation as the condition for authentic appropriation, which, as we saw, is the condition for bearing fruit, remains necessary even in this interpretation of action. The attitude of letting God work in us, thereby acknowledging the primacy of original divine love and the action of the Spirit, does not become a quietism extinguishing every *élan* of action by wrongly anticipating the goal, which is still far away.[20] It is rather a stimulus to intensify even more the tension toward the fulfillment of that which God's free gift has still only anticipated. Every great action begins, in fact, with a passion. The affective dynamics in which charity is rooted entail that God's action be so deeply imprinted in the innermost fibers of human beings and so saturate their sensibility as to orient them to free action that is able to foster ever greater communion with the beloved.

We can now answer our first question, about the modality of the Spirit's leading role in human action: the Spirit inserts himself in action, not immediately so as to be extrinsic to the human element, but by means of charity; he introduces a new proper affection capable of integrating the other affective and operative dynamisms of the virtues and shedding on our actions the new light of divine love. The perspective of friendship permits us to safeguard at once the gratuitous and transcendent character of the gift that comes from another, and also its intimate, progressive realization, through an affective connaturality.

3. Excellent Actions, the Expression of Charity

Our second question, taking us to the heart of the mystery of action as the epiphany of God's glory, is yet to be answered. It demands a return to the biblical theme of superabundance with regard to the theological understanding of human action. How, then, is the superabundance of the gift reflected in action? In other words, how does charity transform human acting, making it a manifestation of divine glory?

20. Cf. Josef Pieper, *Über die Hoffnung,* in *Schriften zur Philosophischen Anthropologie und Ethik: Das Menschenbild der Tugendlehre, Werke,* vol. 4, ed. B. Wald (Hamburg: Felix Meiner Verlag, 1996), p. 275.

Here we come upon what specifies the logic of *agapē*. If we base the moral life on the perspective of normative regulation and on law, our primary task will be to isolate the limits of what can be demanded of human freedom and to establish what is obligatory, the minimum to be observed always and in every case. If, however, the foundation of morality is love, then we must observe a logic of the pursuit of excellence. Love cannot settle for mediocrity; by its nature it always wants the best for the beloved. In this way, we are driven to keep pushing back the limits of what is possible for us, to seek what is "always more," so that the human gesture of gift may express less inadequately what we wish to give.

At this point emerges, in a new form, Blondel's dialectic of the inevitable partiality of the will in action, in the constitutive disproportion between the *volonté voulante (quod procedit ex voluntate)* and the *volonté voulue (quod voluntatis objectum fit)*.[21] For this reason, as this great French philosopher said, "We always have to go further, to be sure not further than we will, but further than we foresaw."[22] Today's context is much different from the dynamics of simple desire that, in its openness to the infinite, denies all its objective determination. It is no longer a question of a void too large to be filled with particular objects, but of a fullness straining to be realized in gestures that are able to express and communicate it more and more. The fullness of divine charity, dwelling in human freedom, tends progressively to broaden action, so that it can be adequated to the Beloved and made capable of receiving him. We must therefore see how charity succeeds in permeating the dynamisms of human operation and broadening them according to this ever greater measure.[23]

We know that for St. Thomas the moral virtues constitute a certain perfection of human persons' natural faculties, maximizing their capacity (*"ultimum potentiae"*),[24] and yet the true perfection of action is only at-

---

21. Maurice Blondel, *Action (1893): Essay on a Critique of Life and a Science of Practice,* trans. Oliva Blanchette (Notre Dame: University of Notre Dame Press, 1984), p. 134.

22. Blondel, *Action (1893)*, p. 137.

23. The German poet Rudolph Borchardt says it well: "What one wants, one cannot give, and one only gives what one must: so one gives a kiss and one would like to give one's life. One gives just a bouquet of flowers because of a garden around the house; one gives a book as a return for the whole world's wisdom. Every gift is just a meaning and an image in a veil. When I sense the fullness, then I know how poor I am"; Rudolf Borchardt, "Mit den Schuhen" (1919), in *Gesammelte Werke: Gedichte* (Stuttgart: Klett-Cotta, 2003).

24. Aquinas, *Summa theologiae,* I-II, q. 55, a. 3.

tained when the Holy Spirit inspires the human operational dynamisms and makes them fruitful through his gifts. In this way, he orders actions to the last end of eternal beatitude, which human reason alone is unable to reach.[25] Perfect action, by means of which we fittingly move toward the last end, is achieved through the beatitudes, which Aquinas interprets as "perfect and excellent acts."[26] They are not just the fruits of the virtues but the outcome of a superabundance arising from the gifts of the Spirit, who works in synergy with human freedom. This original conception of the beatitudes, proper to St. Thomas,[27] who sees them as acts preparing and anticipating beatitude, avoids both a moralistic interpretation, which intends the beatitudes as moral precepts or a program of life to be pursued, and an antimoralistic interpretation, which explains them as pure gifts gratuitously granted or a new ontological condition into which the disciples are inserted by grace independently of their actions.[28]

The connection with the last end of beatitude places the beatitudes in relation to hope. This theological virtue, according to the beautiful image of St. Bonaventure,[29] gives human beings wings, enabling them to keep going beyond the limits of what is humanly possible, since it does not count on human strength alone but is sustained in its impetus by divine assistance. It thus transforms the virtue of magnanimity, making it a Christian virtue by pushing it to broaden its horizons still further, from noble and arduous earthly goods to the new greatness made possible even within difficulties.[30] The beatitudes are therefore the acts of the gifts of the Spirit that bring the Christian virtue of magnanimity to ful-

---

25. Aquinas, *Summa theologiae,* I-II, q. 69, a. 1.

26. Aquinas, *Summa theologiae,* I-II, q. 70, a. 2.

27. On this subject, see once more: Bonnewijn, *La béatitude et les béatitudes.*

28. The relations between grace and *ethos* is well expressed in the following passage from Benedict XVI: "The grace for which he prays does not dispense him from ethics. It is what makes him truly capable of doing good in the first place. He needs God, and because he recognizes that, he begins through God's goodness to become good himself. Ethics is not denied; it is freed from the constraints of moralism and set in the context of a relationship of love — of relationship to God. And that is how it comes truly into its own" (Benedict XVI, *Jesus of Nazareth,* p. 62).

29. Bonaventure, *Sermo XVI, Dominica I Adv., Opera* IX, 40, cited in Joseph Ratzinger, *To Look on Christ: Exercises in Faith, Hope, and Love* (Middlegreen, UK: St. Paul Publications; New York: Crossroad, 1991), pp. 40-65.

30. Cf. Aquinas, *Summa theologiae,* II-II, q. 129; cf. also: René-Antoine Gauthier, *Magnanimité. L'idéal de la grandeur dans la philosophie païenne et dans la théologie chrétienne* (Paris: Vrin, 1951).

fillment; they are the excellent acts Jesus' disciples can perform while following him, broadening their hearts and reason to the standard of God in such a way as to be progressively prepared to receive his fullness. The human desire for happiness is thus saved and opened wide for God by hope, which allows us a foretaste of communion with him in our actions.

The beatitudes, then, are not just "extrinsic" preparation for the supreme act of the beatific vision of God *(merita)*, but they are also in some way a real anticipation thereof, making us share even now as pilgrims — and therefore imperfectly and in a way paradoxically mixed with suffering, tears, and persecution — in the final and eternal beatitude of the heavenly homeland *(praemia)*.[31]

The exegetes, moreover, explain how the "heavenly reward" (μισθός) of which Matthew the Evangelist repeatedly speaks in the Sermon on the Mount is not only for the future but involves the present moment and signifies how the disciple's following of Jesus includes an advance on the filial communion with the Father, in which true rest consists (ἀνάπαυσις).[32] This is not a *quid pro quo* or seeking compensation for required behavior, but rather an active disposing of oneself by the practice of good works to receive the gift of full filial communion, promised by Jesus but also foretasted in his follower's friendship with him. Charity is, in fact, as we have seen, a certain friendship founded on the communication of beatitude.[33]

In this way, we can also grasp the excellence of action according to the Spirit that is proper to the beatitudes. The terminology of St. Thomas in *quaestiones* 69 and 70 of the *prima secundae* abounds in expressions such as *excellens* or *excedens*. The first *(ex-cellere)* indicates the "pushing out" of an inner impulse outwards; the second *(ex-cedere)* means "going beyond" set limitations.[34] The limits crossed in action are those of mere human rationality expressed in the simple "*bonum*

---

31. *Summa theologiae*, I-II, q. 69, a. 2.

32. See on this subject: Luis Sanchez Navarro, "*Venid a mí*" *(Mt 11, 28-30). El discipulado, fondamento de la ética en Mateo* (Madrid: Facultad de Teología San Dámaso, 2004), pp. 307-10; B. Reicke, "The New Testament Conception of Reward," in Oscar Cullmann and Philippe Menoud, eds., *Aux sources de la tradition chrétienne* (Neuchâtel-Paris: Bibliothèque Théologique, 1950), 195-206.

33. Aquinas, *Summa theologiae*, II-II, q. 25, a. 12.

34. Cf. Egidio Forcellini, *Totius Latinitatis Lexicon*, vol. 2, Patavii (1771) 1940, pp. 215-16; Alfred Emout and Antoine Meillet, *Dictionnaire étymologique de la langue latine. Histoire des mots* (Paris: Klincksieck, 1932).

virtutis."[35] In fact, "in human acts there is a twofold measure," one immediate and homogeneous, constituted by reason working through the virtues, and another supreme and transcendent, God himself.[36] This second measure, which is supreme and transcendent, has become the rule for Christian action, as hope reaches God himself.

It is the Spirit who, like an inner impulse, incites human freedom, through love, to strive for ever greater excellence, but it does so before the concrete circumstances of existence. These circumstances are presented within the encounter with other persons, that is, within a relationship of love. As Romano Guardini asserts, "In the experience of a great love, the whole world is gathered up in the I-Thou relation, and everything that happens becomes an event within the ambit of this relation."[37] In the realm of charity — i.e., in the realm of the human person's friendship with God, just as in all affectionate bonds between persons — everything that happens becomes an event that provokes a new and original manifestation of love. Excellence is thus revealed to be the expression of the fruitfulness of the relationship and of the newness of the encounter with the person of the other provoked by events and things they experience.

The great Christian tradition has grasped a tension in the actions of the disciple of Jesus, one that is endlessly straining toward an ever greater reality. This tradition stretches from St. Paul, who, far from thinking he has won the prize or reached perfection, strives to "press on to make it my own, because Christ Jesus has made me his own" (Phil 3:12) to St. Gregory of Nyssa, for whom stopping at the rock who is Christ is always also drinking at a fountain that never lets one stop running, such that "the same thing is both a standing still and a moving" because "the firmer and more immovable one remains in the Good, the more he progresses in the course of virtue."[38] It continues from St. Bernard, according to whom "the measure of love is to be without measure,"[39] to St. Ignatius of Loyola, for whom God, *semper prior et semper*

35. Cf. Eberhard Schockenhoff, *Bonum hominis. Die anthropologischen und theologischen Grundlagen der Tugendethik des Thomas von Aquin* (Mainz: Matthias-Grünewald Verlag, 1987).

36. Aquinas, *Summa theologiae,* II-II, q. 17, a. 1.

37. Romano Guardini, *L'essenza del cristianesimo* (Brescia: Morcelliana, 1993), p. 12.

38. Gregory of Nyssa, *The Life of Moses,* trans. Abraham J. Malherbe and Everett Ferguson (New York: Paulist Press, 1978), p. 117.

39. Bernard of Clairvaux, *On the Love of God,* trans. Terence L. Connolly (Westminster: Newman Press, 1951), p. 27.

maior, urges to action in the perspective of the *semper maius.*[40] For this reason, Balthasar can say that the Christian's movement "is conditioned by the 'ever greater' that gave him his start," such that the existence of one who has been touched by Christ becomes a pursuit of what has happened to him, thereby giving him a future.[41]

The excellence of the Christian's actions becomes still clearer if it is put in more explicit association with charity, as in the *Summa* of St. Thomas Aquinas. Precisely in the treatise dedicated to this subject, and particularly in *quaestio* 24 of the *secunda secundae* on the growth of charity, we once again come upon the terminology of excellence and exceedance. Charity, which is not given to us by our natural faculties but by the infusion of the Holy Spirit, "excedit regulam rationis humanae," surpasses the rule of human reason (art. 1) and even "superexcedit proportionem naturae humanae" (art. 3), exceeds beyond every measure the proportion with human nature itself.

It is not a question of contradicting the rule of reason or the measure of the virtues. Reason and virtue belong to the essential criteria of human acting, laid down by the Creator in defense of basic human identity. They establish the minimum threshold below which action becomes a sin contradicting the very path leading to God.[42] Charity, however, is not a way that one may travel just by avoiding evil, but above all by walking with all one's strength toward the good, along a path of growth without a maximum limit in this life.[43] Charity always goes beyond every measure and can increase *ad infinitum,* not by extrinsic addition of parts but by intensification: *"per solam intensionem."*[44] There is, therefore, an intensification of action, implying not just an ever greater involvement of the subject in the act he or she performs, making the act increasingly one's own personal act through one's intelligence, will, and affections, but also a new direction, inasmuch as the person who acts is ever more intimately united to the Beloved and acts along with him.

The gift of wisdom, correlative to charity, permits us to have by connaturality a new light on the good beyond the natural light of rea-

---

40. Ignatius of Loyola, *Ejercicios spirituales,* n. 104, in *Obras* (Madrid: Bac, 1991), p. 248.

41. Hans Urs von Balthasar, *La semplicità del cristiano* (Milan: Jaca Book, 1987), p. 82.

42. Aquinas, *Summa theologiae,* II-II, q. 24, a. 12.

43. Aquinas, *Summa theologiae,* II-II, q. 24, a. 4.

44. Aquinas, *Summa theologiae,* II-II, q. 24, a. 5.

son.[45] In this way, charity acquires an original epistemological value that does not render the resources of prudence superfluous but goes beyond them by ordering its acts to a higher end and by shedding its light on a new form of excellence.[46] It is consequently right to speak of a new agapic rationality within charity, which has its reasons for acting that reason alone does not know but can come to know in communion with the Beloved when it opens up to the gift of the Spirit, through whom one senses and tastes the new horizons of the good. Therefore, instead of Pascal's opposition between reason and heart,[47] we should think in terms of an integration of reason in the context of *agapē* including both the interpersonal and affective dimension, which will enable us to grasp the modality of grace's influence on the dynamics of practical knowledge.

There is a singular continuity between the charity that Christians live through the beatitudes in this earthly life and the charity they will experience perfectly in eternal life. In excellent actions, performed in synergy between the action of the Spirit and human freedom, they have a real participation in the eternal beatitude of communion with God.

Christian joy is not only that which derives from the attainment of a human good according to reason, as Aristotle would have understood it by showing both the excellence of spiritual pleasure *(delectatio)* compared to purely animal pleasure and the possibility of integrating the latter in the former.[48] Since human action is strengthened by a gift of grace, within the joy *(gaudium)* over the human good attained by this action there is now an unexpected superabundance: being able to enjoy God himself *(fruitio)*. If the perfection of the vision of the divine essence is not possible in earthly life, it is nonetheless anticipated in a beatitude that certainly remains imperfect, but is in continuity with that of eternal life, because precisely in action one already participates and foretastes an intimate communion with the Beloved.[49]

---

45. Cf. Noriega, *Guiados por el Espiritu,* pp. 536-45.

46. Cf. Conrad van Ouwerkerk, *Caritas et ratio. Étude sur le double principe de la vie morale chrétienne d'après S. Thomas d'Aquin* (Nijmegen: Janssen, 1956); Livio Melina, "La prudenza secondo Tommaso d'Aquino," *Aquinas* 49 (2006): 381-93.

47. Cf. Blaise Pascal, *Pensées et opuscules,* ed. Leon Brunschvicg (Paris: Hachette, 1957), n. 146.

48. *Summa theologiae,* I-II, q. 31, a. 3.

49. *Summa theologiae,* I-II, q. 5, aa. 5 e 7. On this subject see: Denis J. Bradley, *Aquinas on the Twofold Human Good: Reason and Human Happiness in Aquinas' Moral Science* (Washington, DC: Catholic University of America Press, 1977).

This allows us to see something of a Christian resolution of the dichotomy between the "active life" and the "contemplative life" inherited from Platonistic and even Aristotelian approaches in which moral acts only have value prior to happiness, which remains substantially extraneous to action and is reached only in speculation. On this understanding, action can only prepare for the fullness that stands beyond it. On the contrary, in the Thomistic perspective outlined here, charity, standing at the outset of excellent action by a gift of grace and growing more and more through the human person's free cooperation, enables us to participate in a real yet preliminary manner in the beatitude of communion with God. This participation takes place precisely in the excellent actions of the beatitudes.

Conclusion

In the course of our reflection, the mutual connection between charity and hope as principles of Christian action has been made clear. "Hope sees and loves what will be," wrote Charles Péguy.[50] Hope is the dynamic element of the moral life, promoting both the light of faith and the energy of love through continuous growth. Action can be an expression of charity only if it is always in the tension of hope, which orients it to something more. On the other hand, only in this way does action manifest the proper dynamism of faith, "which works through charity" (Gal 5:6).[51]

Tension toward something more is not projection toward an unknown future that scorches past the present in its longing for a fullness always yearned for and never attained. One who runs toward Christ has already in fact been touched by him. Christians' action can reveal the glory of God, not so much because it strains with burning desire to reach a goal that is still unknown and foreign to them, but because they have taken within themselves a new divine principle that anticipates the ultimate good of eternal communion with God through the personal

---

50. Cf. Charles Péguy, *Portal of the Mystery of Hope,* trans. David L. Schindler, Jr. (New York: Continuum, 2005), p. 9.

51. On the connection between faith and charity in St. Thomas, which was the motive for harsh polemics during the period of the Protestant Reformation, see the recent study by Miriam Rose, *Fide caritate formata. Das Verhältnis von Glaube und Liebe in der Summa theologiae des Thomas von Aquin* (Göttingen: Vandenhoeck & Ruprecht, 2007).

friendship of charity. The superabundance of this love, able to give itself freely without fear of losing itself, constantly overcoming limitations, is the mark of the divine Gift that abides in the dynamism of action. The water for which we thirsted has now become a spring lavishly welling up to eternal life.

Bibliography

Abbà, Giuseppe. *Lex et virtus: Studi sull'evoluzione della dottrina morale di San Tommaso d'Aquino.* Rome: LAS, 1983.

———. *Felicità, vita buona e virtù: Saggio di filosofia morale.* Rome: LAS, 1989.

———. *Quale impostazione per la filosofia morale? Ricerche di filosofia morale,* vol. 1. Rome: LAS, 1996.

Alexander of Hales. *Summa Theologica.*

Altobelli, Romano. "Dall'etica delle virtù all'etica delle beatitudini," *Rivista di Teologia Morale* 115 (1997): 389-94.

Ambrose. *Expositiones in evangelium secundum Lucam.*

Angelini, Giuseppe. "Il senso orientato al sapere: L'etica come questione teologica." In *L'evidenza e la fede,* edited by G. Colombo, pp. 387-443. Milan: Glossa, 1988.

———. *Le virtù e la fede.* Milan: Glossa, 1994.

———. *Teologia morale fondamentale: Tradizione, Scrittura e teoria.* Milan: Glossa, 1999.

Anscombe, Gertrude E. M. *Intention.* Oxford: Blackwell, 1957.

Arendt, Hannah. *Der Liebesbegriff bei Augustin.* Berlin: Springer, 1929.

Aristotle. *Ethica Nicomachea.*

———. *Ethica Eudemia.*

———. *Rhetorica.*

Auer, Alfons. *Autonome Moral und christlicher Glaube.* Düsseldorf: Patmos, 1971.

Augustine. *De civitate Dei.*

———. *De Genesi ad litteram.*

———. *De moribus Ecclesiae catholicae.*

———. *De sermone Domini in monte.*

———. *Enarrationes in Psalmos.*

———. *Sermones.*

Babini, Ellero. *L'antropologia teologica di Hans Urs von Balthasar.* Milan: Jaca Book, 1988.

Bibliography

Bachelard, Gaston. *The Poetics of Space*. Boston: Beacon Press, 1994.

von Balthasar. Hans Urs. *The Theology of Karl Barth*. Translated by J. Drury. New York: Reinhart & Winston, 1971.

—————. *The Christian State of Life*. San Francisco: Ignatius Press, 1983.

—————. "Il grande respiro della *Lumen gentium*." In *La Chiesa del Concilio: Studi e contributi*, pp. 25-38. Milan: Istra-Edit, 1985.

—————. "Nine Propositions on Christian Ethics." In Heinz Schürmann, Joseph Ratzinger, and Hans Urs von Balthasar, *Principles of Christian Morality*, pp. 75-104. Translated by G. Harrison. San Francisco: Ignatius Press, 1986.

—————. *The Office of Peter and the Structure of the Church*. San Francisco: Ignatius Press, 1986.

—————. *La semplicità del cristiano*. Milan: Jaca Book, 1987.

—————. *The Glory of the Lord: A Theological Aesthetics*, vol. 7: *The New Covenant*. San Francisco: Ignatius Press, 1990.

—————. *Theo-Drama: Theological Dramatic Theory*, vol. 2: *The Dramatis Personae: Man in God*. Translated by G. Harrison. San Francisco: Ignatius Press, 1990.

—————. *La mia opera ed Epilogo*. Translated by G. Sommavilla. Milan: Jaca Book, 1993.

—————. *Theo-Drama: Theological Dramatic Theory*, vol. 3: *Dramatis Personae: The Person in Christ*. Translated by G. Harrison. San Francisco: Ignatius Press, 1993.

—————. *Theo-Drama: Theological Dramatic Theory*, vol. 4: *The Action*. Translated by G. Harrison. San Francisco: Ignatius Press, 1994.

Barth, Karl. *Die kirchliche Dogmatik*, vol. 3. Zurich: Theologischer Verlag Zürich, 1942.

—————. *Church Dogmatics: A Selection*. New York: Harper Torchbooks, 1961.

Bastianel, Sergio. *Autonomia morale del credente: Senso e motivazioni di un'attuale tendenza teologica*. Brescia: Morcelliana, 1980.

Beauchamp, Paul. *La legge di Dio*. Casale Monferrato: Piemme, 2000.

Benedict XVI. *Deus Caritas Est*. 25 December 2005.

—————. *Jesus of Nazareth*. New York: Doubleday, 2007.

Bernard, Charles-André. *Théologie de l'espérance selon saint Thomas d'Aquin*. Paris: Vrin, 1961.

—————. *Vie morale*. Rome: PUG, 1973.

Bernard of Clairvaux. *De diligendo Deo*.

—————. *On the Love of God*. Westminster: Newman Press, 1951.

Berti, Enrico. *Aristotele nel Novecento*. Rome: Laterza, 1992.

Bertrand, Louis. *Christ and Moral Theology*. New York: Alba House, 1967.

Best, Thomas F., and Martin Robra, eds. *Ecclesiology and Ethics: Ecumenical Ethical Engagement, Moral Formation and the Nature of the Church*. Geneva: WCC Publications, 1997.

Biffi, Giacomo. *Approccio al cristocentrismo: Note storiche per un tema eterno*. Milan: Jaca Book, 1994.

—————. *La Sposa chiacchierata: Invito all'ecclesiocentrismo*. Milan: Jaca Book, 1998.

Biffi, Inos. "Integralità cristiana e fondazione morale," *Scuola Cattolica* 115 (1987): 570-90.

———. *I misteri di Cristo in Tommaso d'Aquino,* vol. 1: *La costruzione della teologia.* Milan: Jaca Book, 1994.

Blondel, Maurice. *Action (1893): Essay on a Critique of Life and a Science of Practice.* Translated by Oliva Blanchette. Notre Dame: University of Notre Dame Press, 1984.

Böckle, Franz. *Fundamentalmoral.* Munich: Kösel, 1977.

———. "*Humanae vitae* als Prüfstein des wahren Glaubens? Zur kirchenpolitischen Dimension moraltheologischer Fragen," *Stimmen der Zeit* 115 (1990): 3-16.

Bonandi, Alberto. *Sistema ed esistenza: Il pensiero morale di Theodor Steinbüchel.* Brescia: Morcelliana, 1987.

———. "Veritatis Splendor": Trent'anni di teologia morale. Milan: Glossa, 1996.

———. "Modelli di teologia morale nel ventesimo secolo," *Teologia* 24 (1999): 89-138, 206-43.

Bonaventure. *Collationes in Hexaëmeron.*

Bonnewijn, Olivier. *La béatitude et les béatitudes: Une approche thomiste de l'éthique.* Rome: PUL-Mursia, 2001.

Borchardt, Rudolf. "Mit den Schuhen." In *Gesammelte Werke: Gedichte.* Stuttgart: Klett-Cotta, 2003.

Botturi, Francesco. *Desiderio e verità: Per un'antropologia cristiana nell'età secolarizzata.* Milan: Massimo, 1985.

Bradley, Denis J. *Aquinas on the Twofold Human Good: Reason and Human Happiness in Aquinas' Moral Science.* Washington, DC: Catholic University of America Press, 1977.

Brown, Raymond E. *The Gospel and Epistles of John: A Concise Commentary.* Collegeville, MN: Liturgical Press, 1988.

Caffarra, Carlo. *Living in Christ: Fundamental Principles of Catholic Moral Teaching.* San Francisco: Ignatius Press, 1987.

———. "'Primum quod cadit in apprehensione practicae rationis' (I-II, q. 94, a. 2): Variazioni su un tema tomista." In *Attualità della Teologia Morale: Punti fermi — problemi aperti, Studies in Honor of Rev. P. J. Visser, CSSR,* pp. 143-64. Studia Urbaniana 31. Rome: Urbaniana University Press, 1987.

———. "L'autonomia della coscienza e la sottomissione alla verità." In *La coscienza,* edited by G. Borgonovo, pp. 142-62. Vatican City: Libreria Editrice Vaticana, 1996.

Caldera, Rafael. *Le jugement par inclination chez saint Thomas d'Aquin.* Paris: Vrin, 1980.

Camisasca, Massimo. *Riflessioni de medio corso.* Forlì: Nuova Compagnia, 1994.

Cañizares Llovera, Antonio. "L'orizzonte teologico della morale cristiana." In *Camminare nella Luce: Prospettive della teologia morale a partire da Veritatis Splendor,* edited by Livio Melina and José Noriega, pp. 47-61. Rome: Lateran University Press, 2004.

Capaldi, Nichols. *Hume's Place in Moral Philosophy.* New York: Peter Lang, 1990.

Bibliography

Casciaro Ramírez, José María. *Estudios sobre cristología del Nuevo Testamento.* Pamplona: Eunsa, 1982.

Catechism of the Catholic Church.

Causse, Jean-Daniel. *L'instant d'un geste. Le sujet, l'éthique et le don.* Geneva: Labor et fides, 2004.

Ceccarini, Luigi. *La morale come Chiesa: Ricerca di una fondazione ontologica.* Naples: D'Auria, 1980.

Cessario, Romanus. "Casuistry and Revisionism: Structural Similarities in Method and Content." In *"Humanae vitae": 20 anni dopo, Atti del II Congresso Internazionale di Teologia Morale,* pp. 385-409. Milan: Ares, 1989.

————. *The Moral Virtues and Theological Ethics.* Notre Dame: University of Notre Dame Press, 1991.

Chapelle, Albert. *Les Fondements de l'Éthique. La symbolique de l'action.* Brussels: IET, 1988.

Chiodi, Maurizio. "La coscienza, l'agire, la fede: Oltre il dibattito sull'autonomia della morale." In *Invito alla teologia II — Teologia morale e spirituale,* edited by G. Angelini and M. Vergottini, pp. 51-78. Milan: Glossa, 1999.

Cicero, Marcus Tullius. *De inventione.*

Colombo, Giuseppe. *Del soprannaturale.* Milan: Glossa, 1996.

Compagnoni, Francesco, and Salvatore Privitera, eds. *Vita morale e beatitudini. Sacra Scrittura, storia, teoretica, esperienza.* Cinisello Balsamo: Edizioni San Paolo, 2000.

Congar, Yves M. J. "L'ecclésiologie de la révolution française au Concile du Vatican sous le signe de l'affirmation de l'autorité," *Revue de Sciences Religieuses* 4 (1960): 77-114.

————. *Sainte Église: Études et approches ecclésiologiques.* Paris: Cerf, 1963.

Cottier, Georges. "Racines philosophiques de la crise contemporaine," *Seminarium* 39 (1988): 331-33.

Council of Trent. *De iustificatione.*

Curran, Charles C. *The Catholic Moral Tradition Today: A Synthesis.* Washington, DC: Georgetown University Press, 1999.

Cyprian. *De unitate Ecclesiae.*

Cyril of Jerusalem, *Catechesis XVI on the Holy Spirit.*

Da Re, Antonio. "Il ruolo delle virtù nella filosofia morale." In *Virtù dell'uomo e responsabilità storica: Originalità, nodi critici e prospettive attuali della ricerca etica della virtù,* edited by F. Compagnoni and L. Lorenzetti, pp. 55-79. Cinisello Balsamo: Edizioni San Paolo, 1998.

Dante Alighieri. *The Divine Comedy.* Translated by John D. Sinclair. New York: Oxford University Press, 1961.

D'Avenia, Marco. *La conoscenza per connaturalità in S. Tommaso d'Aquino.* Bologna: Ed. Studio Domenicano, 1992.

Delhaye, Philippe. "Les points forts de la théologie morale à Vatican II," *Studia Moralia* 24 (1986): 5-40.

Demmer, Klaus. "Erwägungen über den Segen der Kasuistik," *Gregorianum* 63 (1982): 133-40.

Dinan, Stephen A. "The Particularity of Moral Knowledge," *The Thomist* 50 (1986): 66-84.

Dodd, Charles H. *The Parables of the Kingdom.* Glasgow: Collins, 1980.

Domingo de Soto. *De iustitia et iure.*

Dulles, Avery R. *Models of the Church.* New York: Doubleday, 2002.

Édart, Jean-Baptiste. "De la nécessité d'un sauveur: Rhétorique et théologie de Rm 7:7-25," *Revue Biblique* 105 (1998): 359-96.

Ernout, Alfred, and Antoine Meillet. *Dictionnaire étymologique de la langue latine: Histoire des mots.* Paris: C. Klincksieck, 1932.

Fabro, Cornelio. *Riflessioni sulla libertà.* Rimini: Maggioli, 1983.

Ferrara, Alessandro, ed. *Comunitarismo e liberalismo.* Rome: Editori Riuniti, 1992.

Fessard, Gaston. *La Dialectique des Exercices Spirituels de Saint Ignace de Loyola.* Tome II: *Fondement — Péché — Orthodoxie.* Paris: Montaigne, 1966.

de Finance, Joseph. *L'ouverture et la norme: Questions sur l'agir humain.* Vatican City: Libreria Editrice Vaticana, 1989.

———. *Saggio sull'agire umano.* Vatican City: Libreria Editrice Vaticana, 1992.

———. "La legge naturale." In *Veritatis Splendor: Testo integrale e commento filosofico-teologico,* edited by R. Lucas Lucas, pp. 287-98. Cinisello Balsamo: Edizioni San Paolo, 1994.

Finnis, John. *Moral Absolutes: Tradition, Revision, and Truth.* Washington, DC: Catholic University of America Press, 1991.

Flannery, Kevin. "Un aristotelico può considerarsi amico di Dio?" In *Domanda sul bene e domanda su Dio,* edited by Livio Melina and José Noriega, pp. 131-37. Rome: PUL-Mursia, 1999.

Flick, Maurizio, and Zoltán Alszeghy. *Il peccato originale,* 2nd ed. Brescia: Queriniana, 1974.

dalle Fratte, Gino, ed. *Concezioni del bene e teoria della giustizia: Il dibattito tra liberali e comunitari in prospettiva pedagogica.* Rome: Armando, 1995.

Fuchs, Josef. *Responsabilità personale e norma morale.* Bologna: Dehoniane, 1978.

———. "Esiste una morale propriamente cristiana?" In Joseph Fuchs, *Sussidi 1980 per lo studio della Teologia Morale fondamentale,* pp. 203-24. Rome: PUG, 1980.

———. "*Intrinsece malum:* Überlegungen zu einem umstritten Begriff." In *Sittliche Normen: Zum Problem ihrer allgemeinen und unwandelbaren Geltung,* edited by W. Kerber, pp. 74-91. Düsseldorf: Patmos, 1981.

———. "Verità morali — Verità di salvezza." In Joseph Fuchs, *Etica cristiana in una società secolarizzata,* pp. 59-78. Casale Monferrato: Piemme, 1984.

———. "Christian Morality: Biblical Orientation and Human Evaluation," *Gregorianum* 67 (1986): 745-63.

Gadamer, Hans-Georg. *Il problema della conoscenza storica.* Naples: Guida, 1974.

Garrigou-Lagrange, Reginald. "The Fecundity of Goodness," *The Thomist* 2 (1940): 226-36.

Bibliography

Gauthier, René-Antoine. *Magnanimité. L'idéal de la grandeur dans la philosophie païenne et dans la théologie chrétienne.* Paris: Vrin, 1951.

————. "Saint Maxime le Confesseur et la psychologie de l'acte humain," *Recherches de Théologie Ancienne et Médiévale* 21 (1954): 51-100.

Gerardi, Renzo. *Alla sequela di Gesù: Etica delle beatitudini, doni dello Spirito, virtù.* Bologna: Edizioni Dehoniane, 1998.

Gigante, Marcello. "Thelesis e Boulesis in S. Tommaso," *Asprenas* 26 (1979): 265-73.

Gillon, Louis-Bertrand. "La théologie morale et l'éthique de l'exemplarité personnelle," *Angelicum* 34 (1957): 241-59, 361-78.

Giussani, Luigi. *Morality: Memory and Desire.* Translated by K. D. Whitehead. San Francisco: Ignatius Press, 1986.

————. *The Religious Sense.* Translated by J. Zucchi. San Francisco: Ignatius Press, 1990.

————. *Si può vivere così? Uno strano approccio all'esistenza cristiana.* Milan: Rizzoli, 1994.

Gnilka, Joachim. *Das Matthäusevangelium.* Freiburg im Breisgau: Herder, 1988.

Goethe, Johann Wolfgang. "Comfort in Tears." In *The Poems of Goethe,* translated by E. A. Bowring. New York: Hurst & Company, 1881.

Gregory of Nyssa. *De vita Moysis.*

Grisez, Germain. *The Way of the Lord Jesus,* vol. 1: *Christian Moral Principles.* Chicago: Franciscan Herald Press, 1983.

————. "Legalism, Moral Truth, and Pastoral Practice." In *The Catholic Priest as Moral Teacher and Guide,* edited by T. J. Herron, pp. 107-30. San Francisco: Ignatius Press, 1990.

Guardini, Romano. *The End of the Modern World: A Search for Orientation.* Translated by J. Theman and H. Burke, and edited with an introduction by F. Wilhelmsen. London: Sheed & Ward, 1957.

————. *L'essenza del cristianesimo.* Brescia: Morcelliana, 1993.

Guindon, Roger. *Béatitude et théologie morale chez St. Thomas d'Aquin.* Ottawa: Éditions de l'Université d'Ottawa, 1956.

Guroian, Vigen. *Ethics after Christendom: Toward an Ecclesial Christian Ethics.* Grand Rapids: Eerdmans, 1994.

Häring, Bernhard. *Das Heilige und das Gute.* Krailling: Wewel, 1950.

————. "Il mistero della Chiesa e i suoi riflessi nella morale Cristiana." In *Orizzonti attuali della teologia,* vol. 2, edited by J. B. Metz, pp. 215-43. Rome: Paoline, 1967.

Hauerwas, Stanley. *A Community of Character: Toward a Constructive Christian Social Ethics.* Notre Dame: University of Notre Dame Press, 1981.

Hedwig, Klaus. "Circa particularia: Kontingenz, Klugheit und Notwendigkeit im Aufbau des ethischen Aktes bei Thomas von Aquin." In *The Ethics of St. Thomas Aquinas,* pp. 161-87. Vatican City: Libreria Editrice Vaticana, 1984.

Hengel, Martin. *The Charismatic Leader and His Followers.* Translated by J. C. G. Greig. Edinburgh: T. & T. Clark, 1981.

von Hildebrand, Dietrich. *Ethics.* Chicago: Franciscan Herald Press, 1953.

Bibliography

chapitre de l'Encyclique 'Veritatis Splendor.'" In *Gesù Cristo, legge vivente e personale della santa Chiesa: Atti del IX Colloquio Internazionale di Teologia di Lugano (15-17 June 1995),* edited by Graziano Borgonovo, pp. 211-23. Casale Monferrato: Piemme, 1996.

Laffitte, Jean, and Livio Melina. *Amor conyugal y vocación a la santidad.* Santiago de Chile: Ed. Universidad Católica de Chile, 1996.

Lafont, Ghislain. *Structures et méthode dans la Somme Théologique de saint Thomas d'Aquin.* Bruges: Desclée de Brouwer, 1961.

Ledrus, Michel. *I frutti dello Spirito: Saggi di "etica evangelica."* Edited by A. Tulumello. Cinisello Balsamo: Edizioni San Paolo, 1998.

Lemeer, B. "De relatione inter Regnum Dei et Ecclesia in doctrina S. Thomae," *Studi Tomistici* 13 (Vatican City: Libreria Editrice Vaticana, 1981): 339-49.

Leo the Great. *Tractatus.*

Léonard, André. *Le fondement de la morale: Essai d'éthique philosophique générale.* Paris: Cerf, 1991.

Lessing, Gotthold Ephraim. "Sopra la prova dello Spirito e della forza." In *Grande antologia filosofica,* vol. 15, edited by M. F. Sciacca and M. Schiavone, pp. 1557-59. Milan: Marzoati, 1968.

Lohfink, Norbert. *Höre, Israel! Auslegung von Texten aus dem Buch Deuteronomium.* Düsseldorf: Patmos Verlag, 1965.

Lombard, Peter. *Sententiae.*

de Lubac, Henri. "Credo sanctorum communionem," *Communio* 1 (1972): 22-31.

———. "La rivelazione divina e il senso dell'uomo: Commento alle Costituzioni conciliari *Dei Verbum* e *Gaudium et Spes.*" In *Opera Omnia* 14, edited by Elio Guerriero. Milan: Jaca Book, 1985.

Luther, Martin. *On Christian Liberty.* Minneapolis: Augsburg Fortress, 2003.

Lyotard, Jean-François. *The Postmodern Condition: A Report on Knowledge.* Manchester: Manchester University Press, 1984.

MacIntyre, Alasdair. *After Virtue: A Study in Moral Theory.* London: Duckworth, 1985.

———. *Whose Justice? Which Rationality?* Notre Dame: Notre Dame University Press, 1988.

———. *Three Rival Versions of Moral Enquiry: Encyclopaedia, Genealogy, and Tradition.* London: Duckworth, 1990.

Marion, Jean-Luc. *L'intentionnalité de l'amour: En hommage à E. Lévinas.* Paris: Vrin, 1986.

Maritain, Jacques. "The Immanent Dialectic of the First Act of Freedom." In Jacques Maritain, *The Range of Reason.* New York: Scribner, 1952.

———. "De la connaissance par connaturalité," *Nova et vetera* 55 (1980): 181-87.

Martinelli, Paolo. *Vocazione e stati di vita del cristiano: Riflessioni sistematiche in dialogo con H. U. von Balthasar.* Rome: Edizioni Collegio S. Lorenzo da Brindisi, 2001.

Marzotto, Damiano. *L'unità degli uomini nel vangelo di Giovanni.* Brescia: Paideia, 1977.

Bibliography

Maximus the Confessor. *Disputatio cum Pyrrho.*

May, William E. *Moral Absolutes: Catholic Tradition, Current Trends, and the Truth.* Milwaukee: Marquette University Press, 1989.

McNamara, K. "La vita in Cristo e la vita nella Chiesa." In *Il rinnovamento della teologia morale,* edited by E. McDonagh, pp. 110-32. Brescia: Queriniana, 1967.

Meilaender, Gilbert. *Friendship: A Study in Theological Ethics.* Notre Dame: University of Notre Dame Press, 1985.

Melina, Livio. *La conoscenza morale: Linee di riflessione sul Commento di san Tommaso all'Etica Nicomachea.* Rome: Città Nuova, 1987.

———. "Ecclesialità e teologia morale: Spunti per un 'ridimensionamento' teologico della morale," *Anthropotes* 5 (1989): 7-27.

———. "'Verità sul bene.' Razionalità practica, etica filosofica e teologia morale: Da *Veritatis Splendor* a *Fides et Ratio,*" *Anthropotes* 15 (1999): 125-43.

———. *Cristo e il dinamismo dell'agire: Linee di rinnovamento della teologia morale fondamentale.* Rome: PUL-Mursia, 2001.

———. *Sharing in Christ's Virtues: For a Renewal of Moral Theology in Light of Veritatis Splendor.* Translated by William E. May. Washington, DC: Catholic University of America Press, 2001.

———. "La prudenza secondo Tommaso d'Aquino," *Aquinas* 49 (2006): 381-93.

Melina, Livio, and Olivier Bonnewijn, eds. *La Sequela Christi. Dimensione morale e spirituale dell'esperienza cristiana.* Rome: Lateran University Press, 2003.

Melina, Livio, and Juan de Dios Larrú, eds. *Verità e libertà nella teologica morale.* Rome: Lateran University Press, 2001.

Melina, Livio, and José Noriega, eds. *Domanda sul bene e domanda su Dio.* Rome: PUL-Mursia, 1999.

———, eds. *Camminare nella Luce: Prospettive della teologia morale a partire da Veritatis Splendor.* Rome: Lateran University Press, 2004.

Melina, Livio, and Pablo Zanor, eds. *Quale dimora per l'agire? Dimensioni ecclesiologiche della morale.* Rome: PUL-Mursia, 2000.

Melina, Livio, José Noriega, and Juan José Pérez-Soba. *La plenitud del obrar cristiano: Dinámica de la acción y perspectiva teológica de la moral.* Madrid: Palabra, 2001.

———. *Camminare alla luce dell'amore. Fondamenti della morale cristiana.* Siena: Cantagalli, 2008.

Merklein, Helmut. *Die Gottesherrschaft als Handlungsprinzip: Untersuchung zur Ethik Jesu.* Würzburg: Echter Verlag, 1984.

———. *La signoria di Dio nell'annuncio di Gesù.* Brescia: Paideia, 1994.

Mersch, Emile. *The Theology of the Mystical Body.* St. Louis: Herder, 1955.

Mimeault, Jules. "Il riferimento a Cristo-verità nella Chiesa." In *Verità e libertà nella teologica morale,* edited by Livio Melina and Juan de Dios Larrú, pp. 155-73. Rome: Lateran University Press, 2001.

Moore, G. E. *Principia Ethica.* Cambridge: Cambridge University Press, 1993.

Mounier, Emmanuel. "Manifeste au service du personnalisme." In *Œuvres,* vol. 1. Paris: Éditions du Seuil, 1961.

Bibliography

Murdoch, Iris. *The Sovereignty of Good.* London: Routledge, 1980.

Nadeau-Lacour, Thérèse. "Il martirio, splendore dell'agire per la vita del mondo." In *Quale dimora per l'agire? Dimensioni ecclesiologiche della morale,* edited by Livio Melina and Pablo Zanor, pp. 161-72. Rome: PUL-Mursia, 2000.

Nault, Jean-Charles. *Le saveur de Dieu. L'acédie dans le dynamisme de l'agir.* Rome: Lateran University Press, 2002.

Nédoncelle, Maurice. *La réciprocité des consciences: Essai sur la nature de la personne.* Paris: Aubier-Montaigne, 1942.

————. *Vers une philosophie de l'amour et de la personne.* Paris: Montaigne, 1957.

Nelson, Daniel. *The Priority of Prudence: Virtue and Natural Law in Thomas Aquinas and the Implications for Modern Ethics.* University Park: Pennsylvania State University Press, 1992.

Nguyen Van Si, Ambrogio. *Seguire e imitare: Cristo secondo san Bonaventura.* Milan: Ed. Bibl. Francescana, 1995.

Noriega, José. *"Guidados por el Espíritu": El Espíritu Santo y el conocimiento moral en Tomás de Aquino.* Rome: PUL-Mursia, 2000.

————. "El camino al Padre." In Livio Melina, José Noriega, and Juan José Pérez-Soba, *La plenitud del obrar cristiano: Dinámica de la acción y perspectiva teológica de la moral,* pp. 157-68. Madrid: Palabra, 2001.

————. "Las virtudes y la comunión." In Livio Melina, José Noriega, and Juan José Pérez-Soba, *La plenitud del obrar cristiano: Dinámica de la acción y perspectiva teológica de la moral,* pp. 403-11. Madrid: Palabra, 2001.

————. "Movidos por el Espíritu." In Livio Melina, José Noriega, and Juan José Pérez-Soba, *La plenitud del obrar cristiano: Dinámica de la acción y perspectiva teológica de la moral,* pp. 183-200. Madrid: Palabra, 2001.

————. "'Sentite de Domino in bonitate': Prospettive sulla relazione tra moralità e spiritualità." In *La Sequela Christi. Dimensione morale e spirituale dell'esperienza cristiana,* edited by Livio Melina and Olivier Bonnewijn, pp. 199-213. Rome: Lateran University Press, 2003.

Nussbaum, Martha. *Poetic Justice: The Literary Imagination and Public Life.* Boston: Beacon Press, 1995.

Nygren, Anders. *Agape and Eros.* Philadelphia: Westminster Press, 1953.

Ognibeni, Bruno. *Il matrimonio alla luce del Nuovo Testamento.* Rome: Lateran University Press, 2007.

Origen. *In Exodum homiliae.*

————. *In Matthaeum commentarius.*

Ouellet, Marc. "Domanda sul bene, risposta di Cristo." In *Domanda sul bene e domanda su Dio,* edited by Livio Melina and José Noriega, pp. 143-46. Rome: PUL-Mursia, 1999.

van Ouwerkerk, Conrad A. J. *Caritas et ratio: Étude sur le double principe de la vie morale chrétienne d'après S. Thomas d'Aquin.* Nijmegen: Janssen, 1956.

Pannenberg, Wolfhart. *Ethik und Ekklesiologie: Gesammelte Aufsätze.* Göttingen: Vandenhoeck & Ruprecht, 1977.

Bibliography

————. *Grundlagen der Ethik: Philosophisch-theologische Perspektiven.* Göttingen: Vandenhoeck & Ruprecht, 1996.

————. "Eine Antwort," *Anthropotes* 13 (1997): 485-92.

Pascal, Blaise. *Pensées et opuscules.* Paris: Hachette, 1957.

Peghaire, Julien. "L'axiome *'bonum diffusivum sui'* dans le néoplatonisme et le thomisme," *Revue de l'Université d'Ottawa* 2 (1932): 5-30.

Péguy, Charles. *Portal of the Mystery of Hope.* Translated by David L. Schindler, Jr. New York: Continuum, 2005.

Pérez-Soba, Juan José. "La irreductibilidad de la relación interpersonal: Su estudio en Santo Tomás," *Anthropotes* 13 (1997): 175-200.

————. "Dall'incontro alla comunione: Amore del prossimo e amore di Dio." In *Domanda sul bene e domanda su Dio,* edited by Livio Melina and José Noriega, pp. 109-30. Rome: PUL-Mursia, 1999.

————. *Amor es nombre de persona: Estudio de la interpersonalidad en el amor en Santo Tomás de Aquino.* Rome: PUL-Mursia, 2001.

————. "Il bene e la persona: Chiavi per un colloquio morale," *La Scuola Cattolica* 129 (2001): 801-20.

————. "La fe como 'elección fundamental.'" In Livio Melina, José Noriega, and Juan José Pérez-Soba, *La plenitud del obrar cristiano: Dinámica de la acción y perspectiva teológica de la moral,* pp. 65-83. Madrid: Palabra, 2001.

————. "La persona y el bien." In Livio Melina, José Noriega, and Juan José Pérez-Soba, *La plenitud del obrar cristiano: Dinámica de la acción y perspectiva teológica de la moral,* pp. 293-318. Madrid: Palabra, 2001.

————. "Operari sequitur esse?" In Livio Melina, José Noriega, and Juan José Pérez-Soba, *La plenitud del obrar cristiano: Dinámica de la acción y perspectiva teológica de la moral,* pp. 65-83. Madrid: Palabra, 2001.

————. *La experiencia moral.* Madrid: Publicaciones de la Facultad de "Teología San Dámaso," 2002.

————. "'La fe que obra por la caridad' (Gal 5, 6): Un anuncio de vida cristiana." In *"Dar razón de la esperanza": Homenaje al Prof. Dr. José Luis Illanes,* edited by T. Trigo, pp. 677-706. Pamplona: Publicaciones de la Universidad de Navarra, 2003.

Peter Lombard. *Libri Sententiarum.*

Petrà, Basilio. "Communio ecclesiale e genesi del soggetto morale." In *Quale dimora per l'agire? Dimensioni ecclesiologiche della morale,* edited by Livio Melina and Pablo Zanor, pp. 73-97. Rome: PUL-Mursia, 2000.

Philippe, Marie-Dominique. "Personne et interpersonnalité: Être et esprit." In *L'anthropologie de saint Thomas,* edited by Norbert M. Luyten, pp. 124-60. Fribourg: Editions Universitaires Fribourg, 1974.

Philips, Gérard. *La Chiesa e il suo mistero nel Concilio Vaticano II: Storia, testo e commento della costituzione* Lumen gentium. Milan: Jaca Book, 1982.

Pieper, Josef. *Die Wirklichkeit und das Gute: Eine Untersuchung zur Anthropologie des Hochmittelalters.* Munich: Kösel, 1963.

————. *Über die Hoffnung.* In *Schriften zur Philosophischen Anthropologie und Ethik:*

Bibliography

Das Menschenbild der Tugendlehre, Werke — Vol. 4. Hamburg: Felix Meiner Verlag, 1996.

Pinckaers, Servais. *Le renouveau de la morale: Études pour une morale fidèle à ses sources et à sa mission présente.* Paris: Téqui, 1979.

————. *Ce qu'on ne peut jamais faire: La question des actes intrinsèquement mauvais, Histoire et discussion.* Fribourg-Paris: Editions Universitaires Fribourg/Du Cerf, 1986.

————. "Qu'est-ce que la spiritualité?" *Nova et vetera* 1 (1990): 7-19.

————. *L'Évangile et la morale.* Fribourg: Editions Universitaires Fribourg, 1990.

————. *The Sources of Christian Ethics.* Translated by M. T. Noble. Washington, DC: Catholic University of America Press, 1995.

————. "Rediscovering Virtue," *The Thomist* 60 (1996): 361-78.

————. *Morality: The Catholic View.* Notre Dame: St. Augustine's Press, 2001.

Pizzorni, Reginaldo. "Comandamenti e legge naturale," *Euntes Docete* 53 (2000): 127-37.

Prieto Lucena, Antonio. *De la experiencia de la amistad al misterio de la caridad. Estudio sobre la evolución historico-teológica desde Elredo de Rieval hasta Santo Tomás de Aquino.* Madrid: Facultad de Teología S. Dámaso, 2007.

Prümmer, Dominicus. *Manuale Theologiae Moralis secundum principia S. Thomae Aquinatis.* Freiburg im Breisgau: Herder, 1935.

Pseudo-Dionysius. *De divinis nominibus.*

Rahner, Karl. *Foundations of Christian Faith: An Introduction to the Idea of Christianity.* New York: Crossroad, 1989.

Ratzinger, Joseph. *The Open Circle: The Meaning of Christian Brotherhood.* Lanham, MD: Sheed & Ward, 1966.

————. "L'ecclesiologia del Vaticano II." In *La Chiesa del Concilio: Studi e contributi,* pp. 9-24. Milan: Istra-Edit, 1985.

————. *Principles of Catholic Theology: Building Stones for a Fundamental Theology.* San Francisco: Ignatius Press, 1987.

————. *To Look on Christ: Exercises in Faith, Hope, and Love.* Middlegreen, UK: St. Paul Publications; New York: Crossroad, 1991.

————. "Christian Faith as 'the Way': An Introduction to *Veritatis Splendor,*" *Communio* 21 (1994): 199-207.

————. *La via della fede: Le ragioni dell'etica nell'epoca presente.* Milan: Ares, 1996.

————. "Il rinnovamento della teologia morale: prospettive del Vaticano II e di *Veritatis splendor.*" In *Camminare nella Luce: Prospettive della teologia morale a partire da Veritatis Splendor,* edited by Livio Melina and José Noriega, pp. 35-45. Rome: Lateran University Press, 2004.

Ravasi, Gianfranco. "L'attesa di Abramo e la speranza del popolo ebraico: Il Cristo sperato," *Communio* (Italian edition) 148 (1996): 13-23.

Reicke, B. "The New Testament Conception of Reward." In *Aux sources de la tradition chrétienne,* edited by Oscar Cullmann and Philippe Menoud, pp. 195-206. Neuchâtel-Paris: Bibliothèque Théologique, 1950.

Reiter, Johannes. *Modelle christozentrischer Ethik: Eine historische Untersuchung in systematischer Absicht.* Düsseldorf: Patmos, 1984.

Reynier, Chantal. "La bénédiction en Éphésiens 1:3-14: Élection, filiation, redemption," *Nouvelle Revue Théologique* 118 (1996): 182-99.

Rhonheimer, Martin. "Die Konstituierung des Naturgesetzes und sittlichnormativer Objektivität durch die praktische Vernunft." In *Persona, verità e morale: Atti del Congresso Internazionale di Teologia Morale (Roma 7-12 aprile, 1986),* pp. 859-84. Rome: Città Nuova, 1987.

———. *Natur als Grundlage der Moral: Die personale Struktur des Naturgesetzes bei Thomas von Aquin.* Innsbruck-Wien: Tyrolia-Verlag, 1987.

———. *La prospettiva della morale: Fondamenti dell'etica filosofica.* Rome: Armando, 1994.

———. *Praktische Vernunft und Vernünftigkeit der Praxis: Handlungstheorie bei Thomas von Aquin in ihrer Entstehung aus dem Problemkontext der aristotelischen Ethik.* Berlin: Akademie Verlag, 1994.

———. "Ethik als Aufklärung über die Frage nach dem Gutem und die aristotelische 'Perversion des ethischen Themas': Anmerkungen zu W. Pannenbergs Aristoteleskritik," *Anthropotes* 13 (1997): 211-23.

———. *Natural Law and Practical Reason: A Thomistic View of Moral Autonomy.* Trans. G. Malsbary. New York: Fordham University Press, 2000.

Ricoeur, Paul. "Sympathie et respect: Phénoménologie et éthique de la seconde personne," *Revue de métaphysique et de morale* 59 (1954): 380-97.

———. *Amour et justice.* Tübingen: Mohr, 1990.

Rose, Miriam. *Fide caritate formata. Das Verhältnis von Glaube und Liebe in der* Summa Theologiae *des Thomas von Aquin.* Göttingen: Vandenhoeck & Ruprecht, 2007.

Ruggieri, Giuseppe. "Ecclesiologia ed etica," *Cristianesimo nella storia* 9 (1988): 1-22.

Sacred Congregation for Catholic Education. *The Theological Formation of Future Priests.* 22 February 1976.

Salmann, Elmar. "Felicità o salvezza? Riflessioni su un binomio difficile." In *Desiderio di felicità e dono della salvezza,* edited by R. Battocchio and A. Toniolo. Padua: Messaggero, 1998.

Sanchez Navarro, Luis. *"Venid a mí" (Mt 11, 28-30). El discipulado, fundamento de la ética en Mateo.* Madrid: Facultad de Teología San Dámaso, 2004.

———. *La Enseñanza de la Montaña. Commentario contextual a Mateo 5-7.* Estella: Verbo Divino, 2005.

———. "El Padre en la 'enseñanza de la Montagna' (Mt 5-7): Estructura y teología," *Revista española de teología* 65 (2005): 197-210.

Scarpelli, Uberto. *Etica senza verità.* Bologna: Il Mulino, 1982.

Scheler, Max. *Formalism in Ethics and Non-Formal Ethics of Values: A New Attempt Toward the Foundation of an Ethical Personalism.* Evanston, IL: Northwestern University Press, 1973.

Bibliography

Schleiermacher, Friedrich. *Introduction to Christian Ethics.* Translated by J. C. Shelley. Nashville: Abingdon Press, 1989.

Schlier, Heinrich. *Lettera ai Galati.* Brescia: Paideia, 1966. For the original German version see: *Der Brief an die Galater: Übersetzt und erklärt von H. Schlier.* Meyers Kommentar VII. Göttingen: Vandenhoeck & Ruprecht, 1962.

———. *Linee fondamentali di una teologia paolina.* Brescia: Queriniana, 1995.

Schlögel, Herbert. *Kirche und sittliches Handeln: Zur Ekklesiologie in der Grundlagendiskussion der deutschsprachigen katholischen Moraltheologie seit der Jahrhundertwende.* Mainz: Grünewald, 1981.

Schmitz, Philipp. "Ein Glaube — Kontroverse Gewissenentscheidungen." In *Gewissen: Aspekte eines vieldiskutierten Sachverhaltes,* edited by J. Horstmann, pp. 60-76. Schwerte: Katholische Akademie, 1983.

Schockenhoff, Eberhard. *Bonum hominis: Die anthropologischen und theologischen Grundlagen der Tugendethik des Thomas von Aquin.* Mainz: Matthias-Grünewald-Verlag, 1987.

Scola, Angelo. *La fondazione teologica della legge naturale nello "Scriptum super Sententiis" di san Tommaso d'Aquino.* Fribourg: Editions Universitaires Fribourg, 1982.

———. "L'essenza della Chiesa nella *Lumen gentium.*" In *La Chiesa del Concilio: Studi e contributi,* pp. 39-74. Milan: Istra-Edit, 1985.

———. "Christologie et morale," *Nouvelle Revue Théologique* 109 (1987): 382-410.

———. *Identidad y diferencia: La relación hombre y mujer.* Madrid: Encuentro, 1989.

———. *Hans Urs von Balthasar: A Theological Style.* Grand Rapids: Eerdmans, 1995.

———. *Questioni di antropologia teologica,* 2nd ed. Roma: PUL-Mursia, 1997.

———. "Differenza sessuale e procreazione." In *Quale vita? La bioetica in questione,* edited by Angelo Scola, pp. 143-68. Milan: Mondadori, 1998.

———, ed. *Quale vita? La bioetica in questione.* Milan: Mondadori, 1998.

———. *Gesù destino dell'uomo: Cammino di vita cristiana.* Cinisello Balsamo: Edizioni San Paolo, 1999.

———. *The Nuptial Mystery.* Translated by Michelle Borras et al. Grand Rapids: Eerdmans, 2005.

Scola, Angelo, Javier Prades, and Gilfredo Marengo. *La persona umana: Antropologia teologica.* Milan: Jaca Book, 2000.

Segalla, Giuseppe. *Introduzione all'etica biblica.* Brescia: Queriniana, 1989.

———. *Un'etica per tre comunità: L'etica di Gesù in Matteo, Marco e Luca.* Brescia: Paideia, 2000.

Sherwin, Michael. *Charity and Knowledge in the Moral Theology of St. Thomas Aquinas.* Washington, DC: Catholic University of America Press, 2005.

Sicari, Antonio. *Chiamati per nome: La vocazione nella Scrittura.* Milan: Jaca Book, 1979.

Spaemann, Robert. *Happiness and Benevolence.* Translated by J. Alberg. Notre Dame: Notre Dame University Press, 2000.

———. *Grenzen: Zur ethischen Dimension des Handelns.* Stuttgart: Klett-Cotta, 2001.

Spedalieri, Nicola. *Dei diritti dell'uomo.* Assisi, 1791.

Spicq, Ceslas. *Théologie morale du Nouveau Testament,* vol. 2. Paris: Gabalda, 1970.

————. *Connaissance et moral dans la Bible.* Fribourg-Paris: Editions Universitaires Fribourg/Du Cerf, 1985.

Spinelli, Mario, ed. *Le beatitudini nei Padri latini.* Rome: Paoline, 1982.

Steinbüchel, Theodor. *Religion und Moral im Lichte christlicher personaler Existenz.* Frankfurt: Knecht, 1951.

Taylor, Charles. *The Ethics of Authenticity.* Cambridge, MA: Harvard University Press, 1992.

Tertullian. *Adversus Marcionem.*

Theiner, Johann. *Die Entwicklung der Moraltheologie zur eigenständigen Disziplin.* Regensburg: Pustet, 1970.

Thomas Aquinas. *Compendium theologiae.*

————. *De malo.*

————. *De potentia.*

————. *De unitate intellectus contra Averroistas.*

————. *De veritate.*

————. *In De divinis nominibus.*

————. *Quaestio disputata de caritate.*

————. *Scriptum super Sententiis.*

————. *Sententia libri Ethicorum.*

————. *Summa contra gentiles.*

————. *Summa theologiae.*

————. *Super Epistolam ad Galatas lectura.*

————. *Super Epistolam ad Romanos lectura.*

————. *Super Evangelium Sancti Joannis lectura.*

Tillmann, Fritz. *Die Idee der Nachfolge Christi.* Düsseldorf: Schwann, 1934.

Tomas Caldera, Rafael. *Le jugement par inclination chez Saint Thomas d'Aquin.* Paris: Vrin, 1980.

Tremblay, Réal. *L'élévation du Fils: Axe de la vie morale.* St. Laurent, Québec: Fides, 2001.

Vatican Council II. *Dei Verbum.* 18 November 1965.

————. *Gaudium et Spes.* 7 December 1965.

————. *Optatam Totius.* 28 October 1965.

Venerable Bede. *In Lucae evangelium expositio.*

Vereecke, Louis. *Saggi di storia della teologia morale moderna da Guglielmo d'Ockham a sant'Alfonso de Liguori.* Cinisello Balsamo: San Paolo Edizioni, 1990.

Vigen, Guroian. *Incarnate Love: Essays in Orthodox Ethics.* Notre Dame: University of Notre Dame Press, 2002.

Wadell, Paul J. *Friendship and the Moral Life.* Notre Dame: University of Notre Dame Press, 1989.

————. *The Primacy of Love: An Introduction to the Ethics of Thomas Aquinas.* Mahwah, NJ: Paulist Press, 1992.

Bibliography

Wald, Berthold. *Genitrix virtutum: Zum Wandel des aristotelischen Begriffs praktischer Vernunft.* Münster: LIT, 1986.

Wawrykow, Joseph P. *God's Grace and Human Action: "Merit" in the Theology of Thomas Aquinas.* Notre Dame: University of Notre Dame Press, 1995.

Westberg, Daniel. *Right Practical Reason: Aristotle, Action, and Prudence in Aquinas.* Oxford: Clarendon Press, 1994.

Wojtyla, Karol. *Sources of Renewal: The Implementation of the Second Vatican Council.* San Francisco: HarperCollins, 1980.

———. *Love and Responsibility.* Translated by H. T. Willetts. San Francisco: Ignatius Press, 1981.

———. *The Acting Person.* Translated by A. Potocki. New York: Springer, 2000.

Yannaras, Christos. *The Freedom of Morality.* Crestwood, NY: St. Vladimir's Seminary Press, 1984.

Ziegler, Josef Georg. "Ekklesiologie und Moraltheologie: Ihre Beziehung im 20. Jahrhundert," *Theologie und Glaube* 87 (1997): 321-45, 527-40.

Ziviani, Giampietro. *La Chiesa madre nel Concilio Vaticano II.* Rome: PUG, 2001.

Zizioulas, John D. *Being as Communion: Studies in Personhood and the Church.* Crestwood, NY: St. Vladimir's Seminary Press, 1997.

Index of Subjects and Names

Index of Subjects and Names

Choice, 30-31, 41-42, 46; gnomic act of, 91

Christ: being "in," 61; body of, 134; contemporary to persons, 16, 42, 108; encounter with, 15, 16, 19, 34, 61, 81, 94, 107, 108, 116, 121; faith in, 72, 78; friendship with, xvii, 16, 17, 18, 19, 21, 22, 75, 119, 130, 141, 157; fullness of human action and morality, 81-84; imitation of, 88, 89, 100; the light of, xviii, xx, 42; as the origin of human action, 18; as the principal cause of merit, 21, 140, 121; as wisest and greatest friend, 17, 42;

Christocentrism, 68; incomplete, 86; moral, 82

Christusförmig, 84

Christuswidrig, 84

Church: as dwelling place, 36, 138, 125, 145; as event and witness, 105, 109; as moral community and *koinonia,* 104; as *morum regula,* 37, 144; as mother and teacher, 118-19, 122; as the sacrament of mystery, 109; as sustenance of hope, 142-44; and the theological virtues, 120

Communicatio Christi, 93

Communication: of eternal beatitudes, 53, 157; of good to the beloved, xix, 54; interpersonal 93, 98

Communion: as act, 28; acting for 25; as fulfillment of love, 27; with God, 31-33; the intentionality of action and, 30-31; as promise of fulfillment, 33-34; as the truth and the rule of action, 37-42

Communitarians, 111-12

Congar, Yves, 118

Connaturality, xvii, 39, 117; affective, 153-54; by knowledge, 153

Conscience, xiii, 46, 60, 68, 110; and law, 72, 111; subjective, xv, 43, 47, 80

Consequentialism, 48

Conversion, 96-97, 126, 130-31, 133

Cyril of Jerusalem, 150-51

Damascene, John, 90-91

Dante Alighieri, 7

Decisionism, 40

Desiderium naturale, 128

Desire: blind, 10, 24; and encounter with Christ, 15-18, 20-23, 27, 32, 43, 56, 62, 78, 108, 114, 127-28, 135, 141, 155, 161; in general, 5-10; and love, 10-15, 18-19, 114; natural, 21, 128, 141; and promise, 19, 145

Dichotomy, 56, 68, 161

Discipleship: practice of, 55, 77, 94, 127

Divine call. *See* Vocation

The Divine Comedy, 7

Ecclesial being, 112; and new ontology, 112-13

Ecclesiology: and ethics, 104, 110; and filial anthropology, 115-18; and morality, 109-14, 121-23

Einmaligkeit, 97

Emotionalism, 40, 53

Encounter: with Jesus Christ, 15-16, 19, 34, 61, 81, 94, 107-8, 116, 121; and love, 15-16; and moral experience, 75

End: of action, 31-32, 60-61, 75, 97, 142; final, 8, 14, 22; relative, 31

Enlightenment, 47, 85, 106, 111

Epistemology, 49

Eschaton, 126

Ethical: pluralism, xiv, xvi, 103; science, 57-58, 63

Ethics: first person and second person, 49, 75, 114; "situation," 85n.16

Ethos, 57-58, 111, 113

Eucharist, xix; the original gift of, 35-37, 114, 120, 133-35

Excellence of action, xvii, 21, 141, 157, 159

Existentiality, 121

Experience: of love, 72, 91, 98, 153, 158; moral, xv, xvii, 34, 48, 53, 54, 57, 60, 68, 75, 107, 114, 121

Extrinsicism, xvi, 56, 67; and its roots, 68-72

Index of Scripture References